Beginning Programming with Java™ For Dummies, 2nd Edition

Cheat Sheet

P9-AOX-918

Java Keywords

Keyword	What It Does
abstract	Indicates that the details of a class, a method, or an interface are given elsewhere in the code.
assert	Tests the truth of a condition that the programmer believes is true.
boolean	Indicates that a value is either true or false.
break	Jumps out of a loop or switch.
byte	Indicates that a value is an 8-bit whole number.
case	Introduces one of several possible paths of execution in a switch statement.
catch	Introduces statements that are executed when something interrupts the flow of execution in a try clause.
char	Indicates that a value is a character (a single letter, digit, punctuation symbol, and so on) stored in 16 bits of memory.
class	Introduces a class — a blueprint for an object.
const	You can't use this word in a Java program. The word has no meaning. Because it's a keyword, you can't create a const variable.
continue	Forces the abrupt end of the current loop iteration and begins another iteration.
default	Introduces a path of execution to take when no case is a match in a switch statement.
do	Causes the computer to repeat some statements over and over again (for example, as long as the computer keeps getting unacceptable results).
double	Indicates that a value is a 64-bit number with one or more digits after the decimal point.
else	Introduces statements that are executed when the condition in an if statement isn't true.
enum	Creates a newly defined *type* — a group of values that a variable can have.
extends	Creates a *subclass* — a class that reuses functionality from a previously defined class.
final	Indicates that a variable's value cannot be changed, that a class's functionality cannot be extended, or that a method cannot be overridden.
finally	Introduces the last will and testament of the statements in a try clause.
float	Indicates that a value is a 32-bit number with one or more digits after the decimal point.
for	Gets the computer to repeat some statements over and over again (for instance, a certain number of times).
goto	You can't use this word in a Java program. The word has no meaning. Because it's a keyword, you can't create a goto variable.
if	Tests to see whether a condition is true. If it's true, the computer executes certain statements; otherwise, the computer executes other statements.
implements	Reuses the functionality from a previously defined interface.
import	Enables the programmer to abbreviate the names of classes defined in a package.

(continued)

Beginning Programming with Java™ For Dummies, 2nd Edition

Cheat Sheet

Java Keywords (continued)

Keyword	What It Does
instanceof	Tests to see whether a certain object comes from a certain class.
int	Indicates that a value is a 32-bit whole number.
interface	Introduces an interface, which is like a class, but less specific. (Interfaces are used in place of the confusing multiple-inheritance feature that's in C++.)
long	Indicates that a value is a 64-bit whole number.
native	Enables the programmer to use code that was written in another language (one of those awful languages other than Java).
new	Creates an object from an existing class.
package	Puts the code into a *package* — a collection of logically related definitions.
private	Indicates that a variable or method can be used only within a certain class.
protected	Indicates that a variable or method can be used in subclasses from another package.
public	Indicates that a variable, class, or method can be used by any other Java code.
return	Ends execution of a method and possibly returns a value to the calling code.
short	Indicates that a value is a 16-bit whole number.
static	Indicates that a variable or method belongs to a class, rather than to any object created from the class.
strictfp	Limits the computer's ability to represent extra large or extra small numbers when the computer does intermediate calculations on float and double values.
super	Refers to the superclass of the code in which the word *super* appears.
switch	Tells the computer to follow one of many possible paths of execution (one of many possible cases), depending on the value of an expression.
synchronized	Keeps two threads from interfering with one another.
this	A self-reference — refers to the object in which the word *this* appears.
throw	Creates a new exception object and indicates that an exceptional situation (usually something unwanted) has occurred.
throws	Indicates that a method or constructor may pass the buck when an exception is thrown.
transient	Indicates that, if and when an object is serialized, a variable's value doesn't need to be stored.
try	Introduces statements that are watched (during runtime) for things that can go wrong.
void	Indicates that a method doesn't return a value.
volatile	Imposes strict rules on the use of a variable by more than one thread at a time.
while	Repeats some statements over and over again (as long as a condition is still true).

For Dummies: Bestselling Book Series for Beginners

Beginning Programming with Java™

FOR DUMMIES®

2ND EDITION

by **Barry Burd**

Wiley Publishing, Inc.

Beginning Programming with Java™ For Dummies®, 2nd Edition

Published by
Wiley Publishing, Inc.
111 River Street
Hoboken, NJ 07030-5774

www.wiley.com

Copyright © 2005 by Wiley Publishing, Inc., Indianapolis, Indiana

Published by Wiley Publishing, Inc., Indianapolis, Indiana

Published simultaneously in Canada

For general information on our other products and services, please contact our Customer Care Department within the U.S. at 800-762-2974, outside the U.S. at 317-572-3993, or fax 317-572-4002.

For technical support, please visit www.wiley.com/techsupport.

Wiley also publishes its books in a variety of electronic formats. Some content that appears in print may not be available in electronic books.

Library of Congress Control Number: 2005923219

ISBN-13: 978-0-7645-8874-7

ISBN-10: 0-7645-8874-5

Manufactured in the United States of America

10 9 8 7 6 5

2B/QU/QU/QV/IN

WILEY

About the Author

Dr. Barry Burd has an M.S. in Computer Science from Rutgers University, and a Ph.D. in Mathematics from the University of Illinois. As a teaching assistant in Champaign-Urbana, Illinois, he was elected five times to the university-wide List of Teachers Ranked as Excellent by their Students.

Since 1980, Dr. Burd has been a professor in the Department of Mathematics and Computer Science at Drew University in Madison, New Jersey. When he's not lecturing at Drew University, Dr. Burd leads training courses for professional programmers in business and industry. He has lectured at conferences in the United States, Europe, Australia, and Asia. He is the author of several articles and books, including *Java 2 For Dummies* and *Eclipse For Dummies,* both published by Wiley Publishing, Inc.

Dr. Burd lives in Madison, New Jersey, with his wife and two children. For hobbies he enjoys anything that wastes his and everyone else's time.

Dedication

For Harriet, Sam and Jennie, Sam and Ruth, Abram and Katie, Benjamin and Jennie

Author's Acknowledgments

Author's To-Do List, February 13, 2005:

Item: Send chocolate to Christine Berman — the book's project editor and copy editor. As anyone who reads Chapter 4 learns, chocolate is one of the most precious commodities on earth. So when I give chocolate, I give it thoughtfully and intentionally.

The only thing that rivals chocolate's goodness is the benefit of a good night's sleep. But with a 19-month-old child in the house, Christine probably isn't getting enough sleep. Even so, she has the time and patience to work on my manuscript. Yes, Christine deserves special thanks.

Item: Have a plaque erected in honor of Steven Hayes, your acquisitions editor at Wiley. While you dragged your heels, Steve kept on insisting that you write this book. (Sure, you wanted a long vacation instead of a big book project, but who cares? He was right; you were wrong.)

Item: Send a thank-you note to tech editor Jim Kelly who helped polish your original work and, miraculously, didn't make a lot of extra work for you.

Item: Recommend your agent Laura Lewin to other computer book authors. If it weren't for Laura, you'd still be roaming the book exhibits and looking needy at the technology conferences.

Item: Visit Frank Thornton, Bonnie Averbach, and Herbert Putz at Temple University. Thank them for steering you to a career as a professor. In any other career, you'd have no time left to write. (And by the way, while you're in Philly, don't forget to stop for a cheesesteak.)

Item: Send e-mail to Gaisi Takeuti at the University of Illinois, and to William Wisdom and Hughes LeBlanc at Temple University. Thank them for teaching you about Symbolic Logic. It's made your life as a computer scientist and mathematician much richer.

Item: Spend more time with your family. (Remind them that you're the guy who wandered around the house before this book project got started.) Renew your pledge to clean up after yourself. Don't be so highstrung, and finish each sentence that you start. Remember that you can never fully return the love they've given you, but you should always keep trying.

Publisher's Acknowledgments

We're proud of this book; please send us your comments through our online registration form located at www.dummies.com/register/.

Some of the people who helped bring this book to market include the following:

Acquisitions, Editorial, and Media Development

Project Editor: Christine Berman

Acquisitions Editor: Steve Hayes

Copy Editor: Christine Berman

Technical Editor: Jim Kelly

Editorial Manager: Carol Sheehan

Media Development Manager: Laura VanWinkle

Media Development Supervisor: Richard Graves

Editorial Assistant: Amanda Foxworth

Cartoons: Rich Tennant (www.the5thwave.com)

Composition Services

Project Coordinator: Maridee Ennis

Layout and Graphics: Andrea Dahl, Joyce Haughey, Lynsey Osborn, Melanee Prendergast, Heather Ryan

Proofreaders: Leeann Harney, Jessica Kramer, Carl William Pierce, Dwight Ramsey, TECHBOOKS Production Services

Indexer: TECHBOOKS Production Services

Publishing and Editorial for Technology Dummies

Richard Swadley, Vice President and Executive Group Publisher

Andy Cummings, Vice President and Publisher

Mary Bednarek, Executive Acquisitions Director

Mary C. Corder, Editorial Director

Publishing for Consumer Dummies

Diane Graves Steele, Vice President and Publisher

Joyce Pepple, Acquisitions Director

Composition Services

Gerry Fahey, Vice President of Production Services

Debbie Stailey, Director of Composition Services

Contents at a Glance

Table of Contents

Introduction

* *

*W*hat's your story?

- ✔ Are you a working stiff, interested in knowing more about the way your company's computers work?

- ✔ Are you a student who needs some extra reading in order to survive a beginning computer course?

- ✔ Are you a typical computer user — you've done lots of word processing, and you want to do something more interesting with your computer?

- ✔ Are you a job seeker with an interest in entering the fast-paced, glamorous, high-profile world of computer programming (or at least, the decent-paying world of computer programming)?

Well, if you want to write computer programs, this book is for you. This book avoids the snobby "of-course-you-already-know" assumptions, and describes computer programming from scratch.

The book uses Java — an exciting, relatively new computer programming language. But Java's subtleties and eccentricities aren't the book's main focus. Instead, this book emphasizes a process — the process of creating instructions for a computer to follow. Many highfalutin' books describe the mechanics of this process — the rules, the conventions, and the formalisms. But those other books aren't written for real people. Those books don't take you from where you are to where you want to be.

In this book, I assume very little about your experience with computers. As you read each section, you get to see inside my head. You see the problems that I face, the things that I think, and the solutions that I find. Some problems are the kind that I remember facing when I was a novice; other problems are the kind that I face as an expert. I help you understand, I help you visualize, and I help you create solutions on your own. I even get to tell a few funny stories.

How to Use This Book

I wish I could say, "Open to a random page of this book and start writing Java code. Just fill in the blanks and don't look back." In a sense, this is true. You can't break anything by writing Java code, so you're always free to experiment.

But I have to be honest. If you don't understand the bigger picture, writing a program is difficult. That's true with any computer programming language — not just Java. If you're typing code without knowing what it's about, and the code doesn't do exactly what you want it to do, then you're just plain stuck.

So in this book, I divide programming into manageable chunks. Each chunk is (more or less) a chapter. You can jump in anywhere you want — Chapter 5, Chapter 10, or wherever. You can even start by poking around in the middle of a chapter. I've tried to make the examples interesting without making one chapter depend on another. When I use an important idea from another chapter, I include a note to help you find your way around.

In general, my advice is as follows:

- ✔ If you already know something, don't bother reading about it.

- ✔ If you're curious, don't be afraid to skip ahead. You can always sneak a peek at an earlier chapter if you really need to do so.

Conventions Used in This Book

Almost every technical book starts with a little typeface legend, and *Beginning Programming with Java For Dummies,* 2nd Edition is no exception. What follows is a brief explanation of the typefaces used in this book:

- ✔ New terms are set in *italics*.

- ✔ When I want you to type something short or perform a step, I use **bold.**

- ✔ You'll also see this `computerese` font. I use the computerese font for Java code, filenames, Web page addresses (URLs), on-screen messages, and other such things. Also, if something you need to type is really long, it appears in computerese font on its own line (or lines).

- ✔ You need to change certain things when you type them on your own computer keyboard. For example, I may ask you to type

```
class Anyname
```

which means you should type **class** and then some name that you make up on you own. Words that you need to replace with your own words are set in *`italicized computerese`*.

What You Don't Have to Read

Pick the first chapter or section that has material you don't already know and start reading there. Of course, you may hate making decisions as much as I do. If so, here are some guidelines you can follow:

✔ If you already know what computer programming is all about, then skip the first half of Chapter 1. Believe me, I won't mind.

✔ If your computer has a Java compiler, and you're required to use a development environment other than JCreator, then you can skip Chapter 2. This applies if you plan to use Eclipse, JBuilder, NetBeans, BlueJ, or a number of other development environments.

Just make sure that your system uses Java 5.0 or later. This book's examples don't work on earlier versions of Java, including versions numbered 1.4.2 and below. So if you're not sure about your computer's Java version, or if you have leeway in choosing a development environment, your safest move is to read Chapter 3.

And by the way, if Eclipse is your thing, check my *Eclipse For Dummies* book, published by Wiley.

✔ If you've already done a little computer programming, be prepared to skim Chapters 6 through 8. Dive fully into Chapter 9, and see if it feels comfortable. (If so, then read on. If not, re-skim Chapters 6, 7, and 8.)

✔ If you feel comfortable writing programs in a language other than Java, then this book isn't for you. Keep this book as a memento, and buy my *Java 2 For Dummies* book, also published by Wiley Publishing, Inc.

If you want to skip the sidebars and the Technical Stuff icons, then please do. In fact, if you want to skip anything at all, feel free.

Foolish Assumptions

In this book, I make a few assumptions about you, the reader. If one of these assumptions is incorrect, then you're probably okay. If all these assumptions are incorrect . . . well, buy the book anyway.

✔ **I assume that you have access to a computer.** Here's good news. You can run the code in this book on almost any computer. The only computers you can't use to run this code are ancient things that are more than eight years old (give or take a few years).

Occasionally, I'm lazy and lapse into Microsoft Windows terminology, but that's only because so many people run Windows. You can run the latest version of Java on Windows computers, UNIX/Linux computers, and (by some time in 2005) the Macintosh.

✔ **I assume that you can navigate through your computer's common menus and dialog boxes.** You don't have to be a Windows, Unix, or Macintosh power user, but you should be able to start a program, find a file, put a file into a certain directory . . . that sort of thing. Most of the time, when you practice the stuff in this book, you're typing code on your keyboard, not pointing and clicking your mouse.

On those rare occasions when you need to drag and drop, cut and paste, or plug and play, I guide you carefully through the steps. But your computer may be configured in any of several billion ways, and my instructions may not quite fit your special situation. So when you reach one of these platform-specific tasks, try following the steps in this book. If the steps don't quite fit, send me an e-mail message, or consult a book with instructions tailored to your system.

✔ **I assume that you can think logically.** That's all there is to computer programming — thinking logically. If you can think logically, you've got it made. If you don't believe that you can think logically, read on. You may be pleasantly surprised.

✔ **I assume that you know little or nothing about computer programming.** This isn't one of those "all things to all people" books. I don't please the novice while I tease the expert. I aim this book specifically toward the novice — the person who has never programmed a computer, or has never felt comfortable programming a computer. If you're one of these people, you're reading the right book.

How This Book Is Organized

This book is divided into subsections, which are grouped into sections, which come together to make chapters, which are lumped finally into five parts. (When you write a book, you get to know your book's structure pretty well. After months of writing, you find yourself dreaming in sections and chapters when you go to bed at night.) The parts of the book are listed here.

Part I: Revving Up

The chapters in Part I prepare you for the overall programming experience. In these chapters, you find out what programming is all about and get your computer ready for writing and testing programs.

Part II: Writing Your Own Java Programs

This part covers the basic building blocks — the elements in any Java program, and in any program written using a Java-like language. In this part, you discover how to represent data, and how to get new values from existing values. The program examples are short, but cute.

Part III: Controlling the Flow

Part III has some of my favorite chapters. In these chapters, you make the computer navigate from one part of your program to another. Think of your program as a big mansion, with the computer moving from room to room. Sometimes the computer chooses between two or more hallways, and sometimes the computer revisits rooms. As a programmer, your job is to plan the computer's rounds through the mansion. It's great fun.

Part IV: Using Program Units

Have you ever solved a big problem by breaking it into smaller, more manageable pieces? That's exactly what you do in Part IV of this book. You discover the best ways to break programming problems into pieces and to create solutions for the newly found pieces. You also find out how to use other people's solutions. It feels like stealing, but it's not.

This part also contains a chapter about programming with windows, buttons, and other graphical items. If your mouse feels ignored by the examples in this book, read Chapter 20.

Part V: The Part of Tens

The Part of Tens is a little beginning programmer's candy store. In the Part of Tens, you can find lists — lists of tips, resources, and all kinds of interesting goodies.

I added an Appendix on this book's web site to help you feel comfortable with Java's documentation. I can't write programs without my Java programming documentation. In fact, no Java programmer can write programs without those all-important docs. These docs are in Web page format, so they're easy to find and easy to navigate. But if you're not used to all the terminology, the documentation can be overwhelming.

Icons Used in This Book

If you could watch me write this book, you'd see me sitting at my computer, talking to myself. I say each sentence several times in my head. When I have an extra thought, a side comment, something that doesn't belong in the regular stream, I twist my head a little bit. That way, whoever's listening to me (usually nobody) knows that I'm off on a momentary tangent.

Of course, in print, you can't see me twisting my head. I need some other way of setting a side thought in a corner by itself. I do it with icons. When you see a Tip icon or a Remember icon, you know that I'm taking a quick detour.

Here's a list of icons that I use in this book:

A tip is an extra piece of information — something helpful that the other books may forget to tell you.

Everyone makes mistakes. Heaven knows that I've made a few in my time. Anyway, when I think of a mistake that people are especially prone to make, I write about the mistake in a Warning icon.

Sometimes I want to hire a skywriting airplane crew. "Barry," says the white smoky cloud, "if you want to compare two numbers, use the double equal sign. Please don't forget to do this." Because I can't afford skywriting, I have to settle for something more modest. I create a Remember icon.

Occasionally, I run across a technical tidbit. The tidbit may help you understand what the people behind the scenes (the people who developed Java) were thinking. You don't have to read it, but you may find it useful. You may also find the tidbit helpful if you plan to read other (more geeky) books about Java.

This icon calls attention to useful material that you can find online. (You don't have to wait long to see one of these icons. I use one at the end of this introduction!)

Where to Go from Here

If you've gotten this far, then you're ready to start reading about computer programming. Think of me (the author) as your guide, your host, your personal assistant. I do everything I can to keep things interesting and, most importantly, help you understand.

If you like what you read, send me a note. My e-mail address, which I created just for comments and questions about this book, is BeginProg@BurdBrain.com. And don't forget — to get the latest information, visit one of this book's support Web sites. Mine is at www.BurdBrain.com. The Wiley site is at http://www.dummies.com/go/bpjavafd.

Part I
Revving Up

In this part . . .

You have to eat before you can cook. You have to wear before you can sew. You have to ride before you can drive. And you have to run computer programs before you can write computer programs.

In this part of the book, you run computer programs.

Chapter 1

Getting Started

C omputer programming? What's that? Is it technical? Does it hurt? Is it politically correct? Does Bill Gates control it? Why would anyone want to do it? And what about me? Can I learn to do it?

What's It All About?

You've probably used a computer to do word processing. Type a letter, print it out, and then send the printout to someone you love. If you have easy access to a computer, then you've probably surfed the Web. Visit a page, click a link, and see another page. It's easy, right?

Well, it's easy only because someone told the computer exactly what to do. If you take a computer right from the factory and give no instructions to this computer, the computer can't do word processing, the computer can't surf the Web, it can't do anything. All a computer can do is follow the instructions that people give to it.

Now imagine that you're using Microsoft Word to write the great American novel, and you come to the end of a line. (You're not at the end of a sentence, just the end of a line.) As you type the next word, the computer's cursor jumps automatically to the next line of type. What's going on here?

Well, someone wrote a *computer program* — a set of instructions telling the computer what to do. Another name for a program (or part of a program) is *code*. Listing 1-1 shows you what some of Microsoft Word's code may look like.

Listing 1-1:   A Few Lines in a Computer Program

```
if (columnNumber > 60) {
    wrapToNextLine();
}
else {
    continueSameLine();
}
```

If you translate Listing 1-1 into plain English, you get something like this:

```
If the column number is greater than 60,
    then go to the next line.
Otherwise (if the column number isn't greater than 60),
    then stay on the same line.
```

Somebody has to write code of the kind shown in Listing 1-1. This code, along with millions of other lines of code, makes up the program called Microsoft Word.

And what about Web surfing? You click a link that's supposed to take you directly to Yahoo.com. Behind the scenes, someone has written code of the following kind:

```
Go to <a href=http://www.yahoo.com>Yahoo</a>.
```

One way or another, someone has to write a program. That someone is called a *programmer*.

Telling a computer what to do

Everything you do with a computer involves gobs and gobs of code. Take a CD-ROM with a computer game on it. It's really a CD-ROM full of code. At some point, someone had to write the game program:

```
if (person.touches(goldenRing)) {
    person.getPoints(10);
}
```

Without a doubt, the people who write programs have valuable skills. These people have two important qualities:

> ✔ They know how to break big problems into smaller step-by-step procedures.
>
> ✔ They can express these steps in a very precise language.

A language for writing steps is called a *programming language,* and Java is just one of several thousand useful programming languages. The stuff in Listing 1-1 is written in the Java programming language.

Pick your poison

This book isn't about the differences among programming languages, but you should see code in some other languages so you understand the bigger picture. For example, there's another language, Visual Basic, whose code looks a bit different from code written in Java. An excerpt from a Visual Basic program may look like this:

```
If columnNumber > 60 Then
    Call wrapToNextLine
Else
    Call continueSameLine
End If
```

The Visual Basic code looks more like ordinary English than the Java code in Listing 1-1. But, if you think that Visual Basic is like English, then just look at some code written in COBOL:

```
IF COLUMN-NUMBER IS GREATER THAN 60 THEN
    PERFORM WRAP-TO-NEXT-LINE
ELSE
    PERFORM CONTINUE-SAME-LINE
END-IF.
```

At the other end of the spectrum, you find languages like ISETL. Here's a short ISETL program, along with the program's output:

```
{x | x in {0..100} | (exists y in {0..10} | y**2=x)};
{81, 64, 100, 16, 25, 36, 49, 4, 9, 0, 1};
```

Computer languages can be very different from one another but, in some ways, they're all the same. When you get used to writing IF COLUMN-NUMBER IS GREATER THAN 60, then you can also become comfortable writing if (columnNumber > 60). It's just a mental substitution of one set of symbols for another.

From Your Mind to the Computer's Processor

When you create a new computer program, you go through a multistep process. The process involves three important tools:

- ✔ **Compiler:** A compiler translates your code into computer-friendly (human-unfriendly) instructions.

- ✔ **Virtual machine:** A virtual machine steps through the computer-friendly instructions.

- ✔ **Application programming interface:** An application programming interface contains useful prewritten code.

The next three sections describe each of the three tools.

Translating your code

You may have heard that computers deal with zeros and ones. That's certainly true, but what does it mean? Well, for starters, computer circuits don't deal directly with letters of the alphabet. When you see the word *Start* on your computer screen, the computer stores the word internally as 01010011 01110100 01100001 01110010 01110100. That feeling you get of seeing a friendly looking five-letter word is your interpretation of the computer screen's pixels, and nothing more. Computers break everything down into very low-level, unfriendly sequences of zeros and ones, and then put things back together so that humans can deal with the results.

So what happens when you write a computer program? Well, the program has to get translated into zeros and ones. The official name for the translation process is *compilation.* Without compilation, the computer can't run your program.

I compiled the code in Listing 1-1. Then I did some harmless hacking to help me see the resulting zeros and ones. What I saw was the mishmash in Figure 1-1.

The compiled mumbo jumbo in Figure 1-1 goes by many different names:

- ✔ Most Java programmers call it *bytecode.*

- ✔ I often call it a *.class file.* That's because, in Java, the bytecode gets stored in files named *SomethingOrOther*.class.

- ✔ To emphasize the difference, Java programmers call Listing 1-1 the *source code,* and refer to the zeros and ones in Figure 1-1 as *object code.*

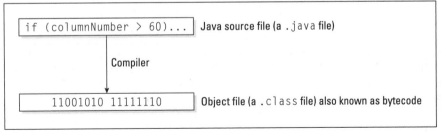

Figure 1-1:
My
computer
understands
these zeros
and ones,
but I don't.

To visualize the relationship between source code and object code, see Figure 1-2. You can write source code, and then get the computer to create object code from your source code. To create object code, the computer uses a special software tool called a *compiler*.

Figure 1-2:
The
computer
compiles
source code
to create
object code.

```
if (columnNumber > 60)...
```
Java source file (a .java file)

Compiler

```
11001010 11111110
```
Object file (a .class file) also known as bytecode

Your computer's hard drive may have a file named javac or javac.exe. This file contains that special software tool — the compiler. (Hey, how about that? The word javac stands for "Java compiler!") As a Java programmer, you often tell your computer to build some new object code. Your computer fulfills this wish by going behind the scenes and running the instructions in the javac file.

Running code

Several years ago, I spent a week in Copenhagen. I hung out with a friend who spoke both Danish and English fluently. As we chatted in the public park, I vaguely noticed some kids orbiting around us. I don't speak a word of Danish, so I assumed that the kids were talking about ordinary kid stuff.

Then my friend told me that the kids weren't speaking Danish. "What language are they speaking?" I asked.

"They're talking gibberish," she said. "It's just nonsense syllables. They don't understand English, so they're imitating you."

Now to return to present day matters. I look at the stuff in Figure 1-1, and I'm tempted to make fun of the way my computer talks. But then I'd be just like the kids in Copenhagen. What's meaningless to me can make perfect sense to my computer. When the zeros and ones in Figure 1-1 percolate through my computer's circuits, the computer "thinks" the thoughts in Figure 1-3.

Everyone knows that computers don't think, but a computer can carry out the instructions depicted in Figure 1-3. With many programming languages (languages like C++ and COBOL, for example), a computer does exactly what I'm describing. A computer gobbles up some object code, and does whatever the object code says to do.

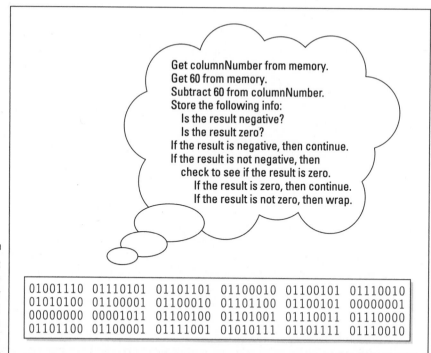

Figure 1-3:
What the computer gleans from a bytecode file.

What is bytecode, anyway?

Look at Listing 1-1, and at the listing's translation into bytecode in Figure 1-1. You may be tempted to think that a bytecode file is just a cryptogram — substituting zeros and ones for the letters in words like if and else. But it doesn't work that way at all. In fact, the most important part of a bytecode file is the encoding of a program's logic.

The zeros and ones in Figure 1-1 describe the flow of data from one part of your computer to another. I've illustrated this flow in the following figure. But remember, this figure is just an illustration. Your computer doesn't look at this particular figure, or at anything like it. Instead, your computer reads a bunch of zeros and ones to decide what to do next.

Don't bother to absorb the details in my attempt at graphical representation in the figure. It's not worth your time. The thing you should glean from my mix of text, boxes, and arrows is that bytecode (the stuff in a .class file) contains a complete description of the operations that the computer is to perform. When you write a computer program, your source code describes an overall strategy — a big picture. The compiled bytecode turns the overall strategy into hundreds of tiny, step-by-step details. When the computer "runs your program," the computer examines this bytecode and carries out each of the little step-by-step details.

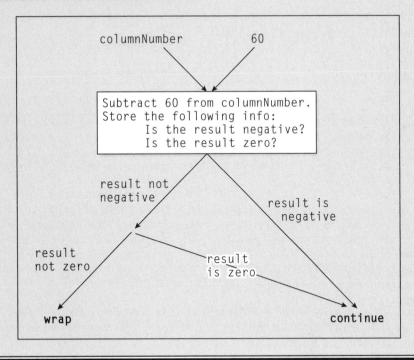

That's how it works in many programming languages, but that's not how it works in Java. With Java, the computer executes a different set of instructions. The computer executes instructions like the ones in Figure 1-4.

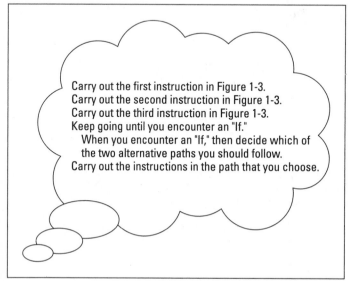

The instructions in Figure 1-4 tell the computer how to follow other instructions. Instead of starting with `Get columnNumber from memory`, the computer's first instruction is, "Do what it says to do in the bytecode file." (Of course, in the bytecode file, the first instruction happens to be `Get columnNumber from memory`.)

There's a special piece of software that carries out the instructions in Figure 1-4. That special piece of software is called the *Java virtual machine* (JVM). The JVM walks your computer through the execution of some bytecode instructions. When you run a Java program, your computer is really running the Java virtual machine. That JVM examines your bytecode, zero by zero, one by one, and carries out the instructions described in the bytecode.

Many good metaphors can describe the Java virtual machine. Think of the JVM as a proxy, an errand boy, a go-between. One way or another, you have the situation shown in Figure 1-5. On the (a) side is the story you get with most programming languages — the computer runs some object code. On the (b) side is the story with Java — the computer runs the JVM, and the JVM follows the bytecode's instructions.

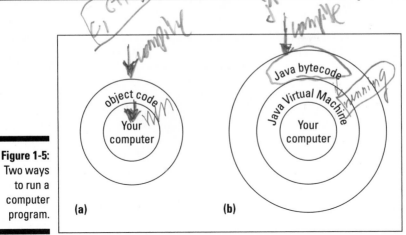

handwritten annotations: "C++ source code", "compile", "Java source code", "compile", "running"

Figure 1-5:
Two ways
to run a
computer
program.

Your computer's hard drive may have a file named `java` or `java.exe`. This file contains the instructions illustrated previously in Figure 1-4 — the instructions in the Java virtual machine. As a Java programmer, you often tell your computer to run a Java program. Your computer fulfills this wish by going behind the scenes and running the instructions in the `java` file.

Code you can use

During the early 1980s, my cousin-in-law Chris worked for a computer software firm. The firm wrote code for word processing machines. (At the time, if you wanted to compose documents without a typewriter, you bought a "computer" that did nothing but word processing.) Chris complained about being asked to write the same old code over and over again. "First, I write a search-and-replace program. Then I write a spell checker. Then I write another search-and-replace program. Then, a different kind of spell checker. And then, a better search-and-replace."

How did Chris manage to stay interested in his work? And how did Chris's employer manage to stay in business? Every few months, Chris had to reinvent the wheel. Toss out the old search-and-replace program, and write a new program from scratch. That's inefficient. What's worse, it's boring.

For years, computer professionals were seeking the Holy Grail — a way to write software so that it's easy to reuse. Don't write and rewrite your search-and-replace code. Just break the task into tiny pieces. One piece searches for a single character, another piece looks for blank spaces, a third piece substitutes one letter for another. When you have all the pieces, just assemble these pieces to form a search-and-replace program. Later on, when you think of a new feature for your word processing software, you reassemble the pieces in a slightly different way. It's sensible, it's cost efficient, and it's much more fun.

The late 1980s saw several advances in software development, and by the early 1990s, many large programming projects were being written from prefab components. Java came along in 1995, so it was natural for the language's founders to create a library of reusable code. The library included about 250 programs, including code for dealing with disk files, code for creating windows, and code for passing information over the Internet. Since 1995, this library has grown to include more than 3,000 programs. This library is called the *API* — the *Application Programming Interface*.

Every Java program, even the simplest one, calls on code in the Java API. This Java API is both useful and formidable. It's useful because of all the things you can do with the API's programs. It's formidable because the API is so extensive. No one memorizes all the features made available by the Java API. Programmers remember the features that they use often, and look up the features that they need in a pinch. They look up these features in an online document called the *API Specification* (known affectionately to most Java programmers as the *API documentation*, or the *Javadocs*).

The API documentation describes the thousands of features in the Java API. As a Java programmer, you consult this API documentation on a daily basis. You can bookmark the documentation at the Sun Microsystems Web site and revisit the site whenever you need to look up something. But in the long run (and in the not-so-long run), you can save time by downloading your own copy of the API docs. (For details, see Chapter 2.)

Write Once, Run Anywhere™

When Java first hit the tech scene in 1995, the language became popular almost immediately. This happened in part because of the Java virtual machine. The JVM is like a foreign language interpreter, turning Java bytecode into whatever native language a particular computer understands. So if you hand my Windows computer a Java bytecode file, then the computer's JVM interprets the file for the Windows environment. If you hand the same Java bytecode file to my colleague's Macintosh, then the Macintosh JVM interprets that same bytecode for the Mac environment.

Look again at Figure 1-5. Without a virtual machine, you need a different kind of object code for each operating system. But with the JVM, just one piece of bytecode works on Windows machines, Unix boxes, Macs, or whatever. This is called *portability*, and in the computer programming world, portability is a very precious commodity. Think about all the people using computers to browse the Internet. These people don't all run Microsoft Windows, but each person's computer can have its own bytecode interpreter — its own Java virtual machine.

The marketing folks at Sun Microsystems call it the *Write Once, Run Anywhere™* model of computing. I call it a great way to create software.

Your Java Programming Toolset

To write Java programs, you need the tools described previously in this chapter:

- ✔ **You need a Java compiler.** (See the section entitled, "Translating your code.")
- ✔ **You need a Java virtual machine.** (See the section entitled, "Running code.")
- ✔ **You need the Java API.** (See the section entitled, "Code you can use.")
- ✔ **You need the Java API documentation.** (Again, see the "Code you can use" section.)

You also need some less exotic tools:

- ✔ **You need an editor to compose your Java programs.**

    Listing 1-1 contains part of a computer program. When you come right down to it, a computer program is a big bunch of text. So to write a computer program, you need an *editor* — a tool for creating text documents.

    An editor is a lot like Microsoft Word, or like any other word processing program. The big difference is that an editor adds no formatting to your text — no bold, no italic, no distinctions among fonts. Computer programs have no formatting whatsoever. They have nothing except plain old letters, numbers, and other familiar keyboard characters.

- ✔ **You need a way to issue commands.**

    You need a way to say things like "compile this program" and "run the Java virtual machine."

    Every computer provides ways of issuing commands. (You can double-click icons or type verbose commands in a Run dialog box.) But when you use your computer's facilities, you jump from one window to another. You open one window to read Java documentation, another window to edit a Java program, and a third window to start up the Java compiler. The process can be very tedious.

In the best of all possible worlds, you do all your program editing, documentation reading, and command issuing through one nice interface. This interface is called an *integrated development environment* (IDE).

A typical IDE divides your screen's work area into several panes — one pane for editing programs, another pane for listing the names of programs, a third pane for issuing commands, and other panes to help you compose and test programs. You can arrange the panes for quick access. Better yet, if you change the information in one pane, the IDE automatically updates the information in all the other panes.

Some fancy environments give you point-and-click, drag-and-drop, plug-and-play, hop-skip-and-jump access to your Java programs. If you want your program to display a text box, then you click a text box icon and drag it to the workspace on your screen.

Figure 1-6 illustrates the use of a drag-and-drop IDE. In Figure 1-6, I create a program that displays two images, two text fields, and two buttons. To help me create the program, I use the Eclipse IDE with the Jigloo graphical plug-in. (For a taste of Eclipse, visit `www.eclipse.org`. For more info on the neato Jigloo graphical user interface builder, check out `www.cloudgarden.com`.)

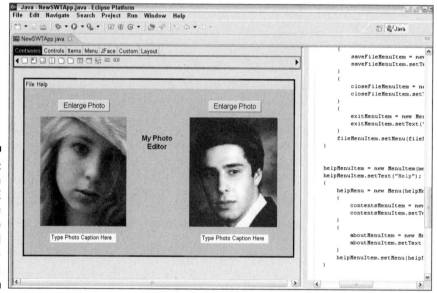

Figure 1-6:
Using the
Eclipse IDE
with the
Jigloo
graphical
user inter-
face builder.

An IDE helps you move seamlessly from one part of the programming endeavor to another. With an IDE, you don't have to worry about the mechanics of editing, compiling, and running a Java virtual machine. Instead, you can worry about the logic of writing programs. (Wouldn't you know it? One way or another, you always have something to worry about!)

What's already on your hard drive?

You may already have some of the tools you need for creating Java programs. Here are some examples:

- ✔ **Most versions of Windows come with a Java virtual machine.** Look for a file named `java.exe` in your `\windows\system32` directory.

- ✔ **Most computers running Mac OS X come with a Java compiler, a Java virtual machine, and a Java API.**

- ✔ **Some IDEs come with their own Java tools.** For example, when you buy the Borland JBuilder IDE you get a compiler, a Java virtual machine, and a copy of the Java API. When you download the free Eclipse IDE you get a Java compiler, but no Java virtual machine and no Java API.

You may already have some Java tools, but your tools may be obsolete. This book's examples use a relatively new version of Java — a version released in September 2004. Even computers and software sold in 2005 may not be up to date with the latest Java features. So if you use the tools that come with your computer, or if you use a commercial product's software tools, some of this book's examples may not run.

The safest bet is to download tools afresh from the Sun Microsystems Web site. To get detailed instructions on doing the download, see Chapter 2.

Many of this book's examples don't run on "older" versions of Java, and by "older" I mean versions created before the fall of 2004. If you have trouble running the programs in this book, check to make sure that your version of Java is numbered 5.0, 5.1, or something like that. Older versions (with version numbers like 1.4 or 1.4.2) just don't cut the muster.

JCreator

The programs in this book work with any IDE that can run Java 5.0. You can even run the programs without an IDE. But to illustrate the examples in this book, I use JCreator LE (Lite Edition). I chose JCreator LE over other IDEs for several reasons:

- ✔ JCreator LE is free.

- ✔ Among all the Java IDEs, JCreator represents a nice compromise between power and simplicity.

- ✔ Unlike some other Java IDEs, JCreator works with almost any version of Java, from the ancient version 1.0.2 to the new-and-revolutionary version 5.0.

- ✔ JCreator LE is free. (It's worth mentioning twice.)

This book's Web site has a special edition of JCreator LE — a version that's customized especially for *Beginning Programming with Java For Dummies,* 2nd Edition readers! For details on downloading and installing the special edition of JCreator, see Chapter 2.

JCreator runs only on Microsoft Windows. If you're a Unix, Linux, or Macintosh user, please don't be offended. All the material in this book applies to you, too. You just have to use a different IDE. My personal recommendations include Eclipse and Netbeans. For details, visit this book's Web site at `http://www.dummies.com/go/bpjavafd`.

Chapter 2

Setting Up Your Computer

*Y*ou've arrived home, fresh from your local computer store. You have a brightly colored box (a box with software in it). You tear open the box, take out a CD-ROM, and put the CD-ROM into your computer. In a few minutes (or maybe a few hours), you're off and running. The software is installed and you're typing your heart out. This scenario is typical for software that you buy at your neighborhood computer store.

But what about the software you need to begin writing your own computer programs? This book tells you how to write Java programs, but before you can write Java programs, you need several pieces of software. You need a Java compiler and a Java virtual machine (JVM, for short). You also need the Java API documentation and an integrated development environment (IDE).

You can get this software in a brightly colored box, but it's easier (and cheaper) to download the software from the Web. In fact, all the software you need is free. It comes as a few downloads — some from Sun Microsystems, and another from this book's Web site. Who needs another brightly colored box anyway?

This book's examples work on any system that supports Java 5.0 or later. If your computer already has a Java 5.0 compiler, you can skip the next section's steps. But if your computer doesn't have a Java compiler, or if you use an older version of Java (a version numbered 1.3, 1.4.2, or something like that) then many of this book's examples won't work with your current software configuration. In that case, you must download and install the latest Java compiler. (Even if your computer already has a Java compiler, it never hurts to download and install the latest version.) Just follow the steps in the next section.

Downloading and Installing the Software You Need

If you've paid for this book, and you already have a working computer, you've already spent all the money you need to spend. All the software you need for learning Java is free for the downloading.

Downloading and installing a Java compiler

When I want the weather to be sunny, I bring an umbrella to work. Bringing an umbrella tells the weather gods to do the opposite of whatever Barry anticipates. The same kind of thing happens with the Java Web site. If I want someone to redesign the Web site, I just write an article describing exactly how to navigate the site. Sometime between the time of my writing and the date of the article's publication, the people at Sun Microsystems reorganize the entire Web site. It's as dependable as the tides.

Anyway, the Java Web site is in a constant state of flux. That's why I don't put detailed instructions for navigating the Java Web site in this book. Instead, I offer some timeless tips.

If this section's "timeless tips" aren't specific enough for you, visit this book's Web site at `http://www.dummies.com/go/bpjavafd`. At the Web site, you can find up-to-date instructions on getting the software you need.

What number comes after 1.4.2_06?

The numbering of Java's versions is really confusing. First comes Java 1.0, then Java 1.1, then Java 2 Standard Edition 1.2 (J2SE 1.2). Yes, the "Java 2" numbering overlaps partially with the "1.x" numbering.

Next come versions 1.3 and 1.4. After version 1.4.1 comes version 1.4.2 (with intermediate stops at versions like 1.4.1_02). After 1.4.2_06, the next version is version 5.0. (That's no misprint. Version 5.0 comes immediately after the 1.4 versions, although some people use the term "Java 1.5" when they mean "Java 5.0.")

The formal name for version 5.0 is "Java 2 Platform, Standard Edition 5.0." And to make matters even worse, the people at Sun Microsystems are thinking about removing the extra "2." So after "Java 2, 5.1" you may see plain old "Java, 5.2." That's what happens when a company lets marketing people call the shots.

With all these disclaimers in mind, you can get a Java compiler by following these steps:

1. **Visit** `java.sun.com/j2se`.

2. **Look for a <u>Download J2SE</u> link (or something like that).**

   The page may have several J2SE version numbers for you to choose from. You may see links to J2SE 1.4.2, J2SE 5.0, and beyond. If you're not sure which version you want, choosing the highest version number is probably safe, even if that version number is labeled "Beta." (The Java beta releases are fairly sturdy.)

   While you wander around, you may notice links labeled *J2EE* or *J2ME*. If you know what these are, and you know you need them, then by all means, download these goodies. But if you're not sure, then bypass both the J2EE and the J2ME. Instead, follow the *J2SE* (Java 2 *Standard* Edition) links.

   The abbreviation J2EE stands for Java 2 Enterprise Edition and J2ME stands for Java 2 Micro Edition. You don't need the J2EE or the J2ME to run any of the examples in this book.

3. **On the J2SE download page, look for an appropriate download link.**

   A download link is "appropriate" as long as the link refers to J2SE (Java 2 Platform, Standard Edition), to JDK (Java Development Kit), and to your particular operating system (such as Windows, Linux, or Solaris). From all possible links, you may have to choose between links labeled for 32-bit systems and links labeled for 64-bit systems. If you don't know which to choose, and you're running Windows, then you probably have a 32-bit system.

   The Sun Microsystems download page offers you a choice between the JDK (Java Development Kit) and the JRE (Java Runtime Environment). The JDK download contains more than the JRE download, and you need more than that feeble JRE download. You need to download the entire JDK.

   Sun's regular J2SE page has links for Windows, Linux, and Solaris users. If your favorite operating system isn't Windows, Linux, or Solaris, don't despair. You can probably find an appropriate Java compiler by searching on the Web. If you use Macintosh OS X, go straight to `developer.apple.com/java`. Java 5.0 comes with OS 10.4.

   Another choice you may have to make is between an offline and online installation:

   - With the offline installation, you begin by downloading a 50MB setup file. The file takes up space on your hard drive, but if you ever need to install the JDK again, you have the file on your own computer. Until you update your version of the JDK, you don't need to download the JDK again.

• With the online installation, you don't download a big setup file. Instead, you download a teeny little setup file. Then you download (and discard) pieces of the big 50MB file as you need them. Using online installation saves you 50MB of hard drive space. But, if you want to install the same version of the JDK a second time, you have to redo the whole surf/click/download process.

Why would anyone want to install the same version of the JDK a second time? Typically, I have two reasons. Either I want to install the software on a second computer, or I mess something up and have to uninstall (and then reinstall) the software.

4. **Download whichever file you chose in Step 3.**

5. **Execute the file that you've downloaded.**

    With offline or online installation you download an executable file onto your computer's hard drive. Execute this file to begin the JDK installation.

6. **During the JDK installation, read the dialog boxes and wizards. Watch for the name of the directory in which the JDK is being installed.**

    On my computer, that directory's name is `c:\Program Files\Java\jdk1.5.0_01`, but on your computer, the name may be slightly different. This directory is called your *Java home* directory. (Depending on whom you ask, this may also be called the *JDK home* directory.) Write down the directory's name, because you'll need that name for stuff that comes later in this chapter.

If you don't catch the Java home directory's name during the JDK installation, then search your computer's hard drive for something named `jdksomething-or-other`. Write down the directory's name and keep the name in your back pocket.

That's how you put the Java compiler on your computer. But wait! Don't walk away from your Web browser yet. At the same java.sun.com Web site, you can find the precious Java API documentation.

Downloading and installing the Java API documentation

I introduced Java's API documentation in Chapter 1. Without access to the API documentation, you're a little lost puppy. With access to the documentation, you're a powerful Java programmer.

So follow this section's steps to get the API documentation (your very own copy on a computer near you).

1. **As in the previous section, visit** `java.sun.com/j2se` **and look for a Download J2SE link.**

2. **Find a link to the API documentation for the version of Java that you just downloaded.**

   The way the Sun Microsystems Web site is currently set up, it's not too hard to find the API documentation. In fact, the download links for the JDK and the Java API documentation are on the same page. This may not be true by the time you read *Beginning Programming with Java For Dummies*, but it's certainly true while I'm writing this book.

   The download page has a big table with the words Download Java 2 on it. Scroll down in the table, and you find a J2SE Documentation heading with an option to download the docs.

   A language like Java comes with many sets of docs. The documentation that you want is called the "API documentation," or the "J2SE documentation." If you see links to the "Java Language Specification" or the "Java Virtual Machine Specification," just ignore these links for now.

3. **Download the API documentation.**

   When the download is finished, you have a big ZIP file on your computer's hard drive. If you use Windows XP or some other ZIP-friendly operating system, you can just double-click the ZIP file's icon. Your operating system opens the file as if it's an ordinary directory.

   If you have Windows 98, Windows 2000, or some other system that doesn't recognize ZIP files, you need an additional archive handling program. You can find a bunch of these programs by searching on the Web.

4. **Extract the API documentation to your Java home directory.**

   The downloaded ZIP file is like a directory on your hard drive. The file contains another directory named `docs`. Just copy that `docs` directory (and all of its contents) to your Java home directory. By the time you're done, you have a Java home directory (with a name like `jdk1.5.0_01`) and a `docs` directory immediately inside the Java home directory. (See Figure 2-1.)

   I give this `docs` directory a special name. I call it your *JavaDoc directory*.

Figure 2-1:
The docs
subdirectory
of your Java
home
directory.

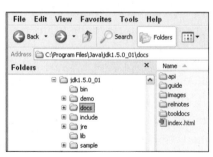

Two bags of goodies

Sun's Web site bundles the basic Java tools in two different ways:

- ✔ **The Java Runtime Environment (JRE):** This bundle includes a Java virtual machine and the Application Programming Interface. (See Chapter 1.) With the JRE, you can run existing Java programs. That's all. You can't create new Java programs, because you don't have a Java compiler.

- ✔ **The Java Development Kit (JDK):** This bundle includes three tools — a Java compiler, a Java virtual machine, and the Application Programming Interface. With the JDK, you can create and run your own Java programs.

Another name for the JDK is the *Java SDK* — the *Java Software Development Kit.* Some people still use the SDK acronym, even though the folks at Sun Microsystems don't use it anymore. (Actually, the original name was the JDK. Later Sun changed it to the SDK. A few years after that, Sun changed back to the name JDK. As an author, this constant naming and renaming drives me crazy.)

Downloading and installing the JCreator integrated development environment

In the previous sections, you get all the tools your *computer* needs for processing Java programs. This section is different. In this section you get the tool that *you* need for composing and testing your Java programs. You get JCreator — an integrated development environment for Java.

JCreator runs only on Microsoft Windows systems. If you use Linux, Unix, Macintosh, or some other non-Windows system, visit this book's Web site for further instructions.

If you have experience installing software, then downloading and installing JCreator is a routine procedure. Here's what you do:

1. **Look for the JCreator download link on this book's Web site.**

2. **Click the download link, and save the file to your computer's hard drive.**

   Like the Java API documentation, the JCreator installation comes to you as a compressed ZIP file. (See Step 3 in the section entitled "Downloading and installing the Java API documentation.")

3. **Unzip the JCreator installation file.**

   You can extract the file's contents to any directory on your hard drive. (Just make sure you remember the directory's name.)

4. **Open My Computer on your Windows desktop.**

5. **From My Computer navigate to whatever directory contains extracted contents of JCreator's installation file.**

   The directory contains a file named `Setup.exe` (or just plain `Setup`).

6. **Double-click the Setup file's icon.**

   In response, the computer fires up JCreator's installation wizard.

7. **Follow the instructions in JCreator's installation wizard.**

In the end, the installation wizard may offer to launch JCreator for you. (Alternatively, you can scan your Start menu for a new JCreator folder.) One way or another, you start running JCreator.

Running JCreator for the First Time

The first time you run JCreator, the program asks for some configuration information. Just follow these steps:

1. **If you haven't already done so, launch JCreator.**

   The JCreator Setup Wizard appears on your screen. The wizard's first page is for File Associations.

2. **Accept the File Associations defaults and click Next.**

   The wizard's next page (the JDK Home Directory page) appears.

3. **Look at the text field on the JDK Home Directory page. Make sure that this field displays the name of your Java home directory. (See Figure 2-2.)**

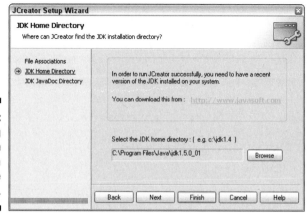

Figure 2-2: Confirming the location of your Java home directory.

If the wrong directory name appears in the text field, just click the Browse button and navigate to your computer's Java home directory.

For information on your computer's Java home directory, see Step 6 of this chapter's "Downloading and installing a Java compiler" section.

4. **When you're happy with the name in the home directory text field, click Next.**

   The wizard's last page (the JDK JavaDoc Directory page) appears.

5. **Look at the text field on the JDK JavaDoc Directory page. Make sure that this field displays the name of your JavaDoc directory. (See Figure 2-3.)**

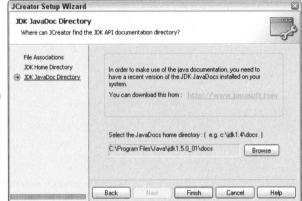

Figure 2-3: Confirming the location of your JavaDoc directory.

Normally, your JavaDoc directory's name is the name of your Java home directory, followed by \docs. For information on your computer's JavaDoc directory, see Step 4 of this chapter's "Downloading and installing the Java API documentation" section.

If the wrong directory name appears in the text field, just click the Browse button and navigate to your computer's JavaDoc directory.

If you do anything wrong in Steps 2 through 5, don't fret. You can correct your mistake later. See this book's Web site for details.

6. **Click Finish.**

   At this point, the JCreator work area opens. (See Figure 2-4.)

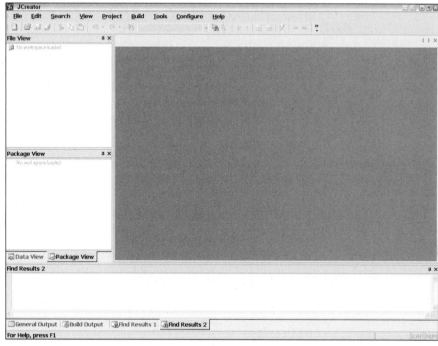

Figure 2-4:
JCreator's
work area.

In JCreator's help files, the stuff in Figure 2-4 is called the *workspace,* not the *work area.* But elsewhere in these help files, JCreator reuses the word *workspace* to mean something entirely different. To avoid any confusion, I use two different terms. I use *work area* for the stuff in Figure 2-4, and I use *workspace* for that other, entirely different thing. (I explain that entirely different thing in Chapter 3.)

Is That All There Is to It?

If you're reading this paragraph, you've probably followed some of the instructions in this chapter — instructions for installing a Java compiler, the Java API documentation, and the JCreator IDE on your computer. So the burning question is, have you done the installation correctly? The answer to that question lies in Chapter 3, because in that chapter, you use these tools to run a brand new computer program.

Chapter 3

Running Programs

*I*f you're a programming newbie, for you, running a program probably means clicking a mouse. You want to run Internet Explorer. So you double-click the Internet Explorer icon, or maybe you choose Internet Explorer from the Start menu. That's all there is to it.

When you create your own programs, the situation is a bit different. With a new program, the programmer (or someone from the programmer's company) creates the icons. Before that, a perfectly good program may not have an icon at all. So what do you do with a brand new Java program? How do you get the program to run? This chapter tells you what you need to know.

Running a Canned Java Program

The best way to get to know Java is to do Java. When you're doing Java, you're writing, testing, and running your own Java programs. This section prepares you by describing how you run and test a program. Instead of writing your own program, you run a program that I've already written for you. The program calculates your monthly payments on a home mortgage loan.

The mortgage-calculating program doesn't open its own window. Instead, the program runs in JCreator's General Output pane. (See Figure 3-1.) A program that operates completely in this General Output pane is called a *text-based program*.

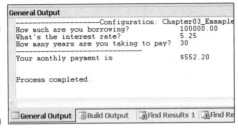

Figure 3-1:
A run of the
text-based
mortgage
program.

If you're using Linux, Unix, Mac, or some other non-Windows system, the instructions in this section don't apply to you. Visit this book's Web site at http://www.dummies.com/go/bpjavafd for an alternative set of instructions.

Actually, as you run the mortgage program, you see two things in the General Output pane:

✓ **Messages and results that the mortgage program sends to you.** Messages include things like How much are you borrowing? Results include lines like Your monthly payment is $552.20.

✓ **Responses that you give to the mortgage program while it runs.** If you type **100000.00** in response to the program's question about how much you're borrowing, you see that number echoed in the General Output pane.

Those pesky filename extensions

The filenames displayed in My Computer or in an Open dialog box can be misleading. You may visit the Chapter03_Example01 directory and see the name Mortgage. Instead of just Mortgage, the file's full name is Mortgage.java. You may even see two Mortgage files. What you don't see is that one file's real name is Mortgage.java, and the other file's real name is Mortgage.class.

The ugly truth is that Windows and its dialog boxes can hide parts of filenames. This awful feature tends to confuse Java programmers. So, if you don't want to be confused, modify the Windows Hide Extensions feature. To do this, you have to open the Folder Options dialog box. Here's how:

✓ **In Windows 95, 98, or NT:** In the Windows Explorer menu bar, choose View⇨Folder Options (or just View⇨Options).

✓ **In Windows Me or 2000:** Choose Start⇨ Settings⇨Control Panel⇨Folder Options.

✓ **In Windows XP with the control panel's default (category) view:** Choose Start⇨Control Panel⇨Performance and Maintenance⇨ File Types.

✓ **In Windows XP with the control panel's classic view:** Choose Start⇨Control Panel⇨ Folder Options.

In the Folder Options dialog box, click the View tab. Then look for the Hide File Extensions for Known File Types option. Make sure that this check box is *not* selected.

Running the mortgage program is easy. Here's how you do it:

1. **Make sure that you've followed the instructions in Chapter 2 — instructions for installing the JDK and configuring JCreator.**

   Thank goodness! You don't have to follow those instructions more than once.

2. **Launch JCreator.**

   The big JCreator work area stares at you from your computer screen. (See Figure 3-2.)

   If this is your first time running JCreator, you don't see JCreator's work area. Instead you see the JCreator Setup Wizard. To get past the Setup Wizard, see the instructions in Chapter 2.

3. **In JCreator's menu bar, choose File⇨Open Workspace from the main menu.**

   Don't choose File⇨*Open*. Instead, choose File⇨*Open Workspace*.

   A familiar-looking Open dialog box appears. This dialog box looks in your `MyProjects` directory. This `MyProjects` directory is a subdirectory of the directory in which JCreator is installed.

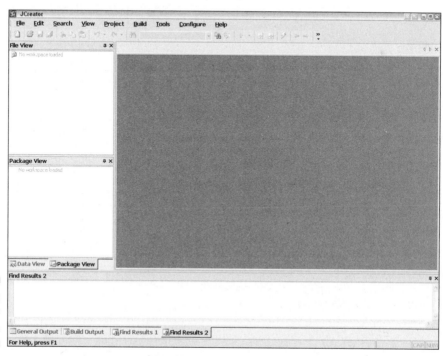

Figure 3-2:
An empty
work area.

In this book's special edition of JCreator the `MyProjects` directory has subdirectories named `Chapter03_Example01`, `Chapter04_Listing01` and so on. The `MyProjects` directory also has files with names like `Chapter03` and `Chapter04`. If you set your computer so that it doesn't hide file extensions, then the names of the files are `Chapter03.jcw`, `Chapter04.jcw`, and so on. (See the sidebar entitled "Those pesky file-name extensions.")

4. **Select the file named** `Chapter03` **(or** `Chapter03.jcw`**), and then click Open.**

Clicking Open may coax out a message box asking if you want to "Save the workspace modifications?" If so, click Yes. Clicking Open may coax out another box asking if you want to ". . . close all document Windows?" If so, click Yes.

JCreator divides things into *workspaces*. Each workspace is further subdivided into *projects*. To organize this book's examples, I made a workspace for each chapter, and then made a project for each complete Java program. When you open `Chapter03.jcw`, you get my Chapter03 workspace — a workspace that contains two projects. The project's names are `Chapter03_Example01` and `Chapter03_Listing01`. That's why, in JCreator's File View pane, you see a `Chapter03` tree with branches labeled `Chapter03_Example01` and `Chapter03_Listing01`. (See Figure 3-3.)

In `MyWorkspace.jcw`, the extension `.jcw` stands for "JCreator workspace."

Figure 3-3:
Two projects
in the File
View pane.

5. **In the File View's tree, right-click the** `Chapter03_Example01` **branch. In the resulting context menu, choose Sets as Active Project. (See Figure 3-3.)**

Choosing Sets as Active Project makes `Chapter03_Example01` the *active project*.

In JCreator, only one project at a time can be the active project. To run a particular program, the program's code has to be in whatever project is currently active. In JCreator's File View, you can tell which project is active by looking for the project whose name is boldface. (Refer to Figure 3-3.) On some systems, the active project's name is a hazy, light-gray boldface.

If a particular program isn't in the active project, you can't run that program, but you can do some other things with that program. For example, you can see the program in one of JCreator's panes, make changes to the program, save the program, and so on. For this reason, it's really easy to get confused and forget which project is active. So always keep the active project in the forefront of your mind. If your code doesn't do what you think it should do, check to make sure that the project you want to run is the active project.

6. **Choose Build⇨Compile Project from the main menu.**

   Choosing Compile Project does exactly what it says. It *compiles* the project's code. (To find out what *compile* means, see Chapter 1.)

   After some pleasant chirping sounds from your hard drive, JCreator's Build Output pane displays a `Process completed` message. (The Build Output pane appears in the lower portion of JCreator's work area. See Figure 3-4.)

Figure 3-4: The compiling process is completed.

```
Build Output
---------------------Configurati
Process completed.



General Output    Build Output
```

7. **Choose Build⇨Execute Project from the main menu.**

   When you choose Execute Project, the computer runs the project's code. (In this example, the computer runs a Java program that I wrote.) As part of the run, the message `How much are you borrowing?` appears in JCreator's General Output pane. (The General Output pane and the Build Output pane share the lower portion of JCreator's work area. Refer to Figure 3-1.)

8. **Click anywhere inside JCreator's General Output pane, and then type a number, like** 100000.00, **and press Enter.**

When you type a number in Step 8, don't include your country's currency symbol. (U.S. residents, don't type a dollar sign.) Things like $100000.00 cause the program to crash. You see a `NumberFormatException` message in the General Output pane.

After you press Enter, the Java program displays another message (`What's the interest rate?`) in JCreator's General Output pane.

9. **In response to the interest rate question, type a number, like** 5.25, **and press Enter.**

After you press Enter, the Java program displays another message (`How many years . . . ?`) in JCreator's General Output pane.

10. **Type a number, like** 30, **and press Enter.**

In response to the numbers that you've typed, the Java program displays a monthly payment amount. Again, refer to Figure 3-1.

Disclaimer: Your local mortgage company charges more than the amount that my Java program calculates. (A lot more.)

When you type a number in Step 10, don't include a decimal point. Things like 30.0 cause the program to crash. You see a `NumberFormatException` message in the General Output pane.

Occasionally you decide in the middle of a program's run that you've made a mistake of some kind. You want to stop the program's run dead in its tracks. To do this, choose Tools⇨Stop Tool from the main menu.

If you follow this section's instructions, and you don't get the results that I describe, there are three things you can try. I list them in order from best to worst:

- ✔ Check all the steps to make sure you did everything correctly.
- ✔ Send email to me at `BeginProg2@BurdBrain.com`. If you describe what happened, I can probably figure out what went wrong and tell you how to correct the problem.
- ✔ Panic.

Typing and Running Your Own Code

The first half of this chapter is about running someone else's Java code (code that you download from this book's Web site). But eventually, you'll write code on your own. This section shows you how to create code with the JCreator development environment.

Do I see formatting in my Java program?

When you use an editor to write a Java program, you may notice words in various colors. Certain words are always blue. Other words are always black. You may even see some bold and italic phrases. You may think you see formatting, but you don't. Instead, what you see is called *syntax coloring* or *syntax highlighting*.

No matter what you call it, the issue is as follows:

✔ With Microsoft Word, things like bold formatting are marked inside a document. When you save `MyPersonalDiary.doc`, the instructions to make the words "love" and "hate" bold are recorded inside the `MyPersonalDiary.doc` file.

✔ With a Java program editor, things like bold and coloring aren't marked inside the Java program file. Instead, the editor displays each word in a way that makes the Java program easy to read.

For example, in a Java program, certain words (words like `class`, `public`, and `void`) have their own special meanings. So JCreator's editor displays `class`, `public`, and `void` in blue letters. When I save my Java program file, the computer stores nothing about blue letters in my Java program file. But the editor uses its discretion to highlight special words with blue coloring.

Some other editor may display the same words in a bold, red font. Another editor (like Windows Notepad) displays all words in plain old black.

The version of JCreator that you download from this book's Web site has a specially customized `MyProjects` directory. The `MyProjects` directory contains several readymade workspaces. One of these workspaces (named *MyWorkspace*) has no projects in it. Here's how you create a project in MyWorkspace:

1. **Launch JCreator.**

2. **From JCreator's menu bar, choose File➪Open Workspace.**

   An Open dialog box appears.

3. **In the Open dialog box, select `MyWorkspace.jcw` (or simply `MyWorkspace`). Then click Open.**

   Clicking Open may coax out a message box asking whether you want to "Save the workspace modifications?" If so, click Yes. Clicking Open may coax out another box asking if you want to ". . . close all document Windows?" If so, click Yes.

   After clicking Open, you see MyWorkspace in JCreator's File View pane. The next step is to create a new project within MyWorkspace.

4. In the File View pane, right-click MyWorkspace. Then choose Add new Project from the context menu that appears, as shown in Figure 3-5.

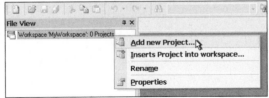

Figure 3-5:
Getting JCreator to add a new project.

JCreator's Project Wizard opens. (See Figure 3-6.)

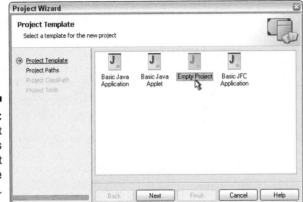

Figure 3-6:
The Project Wizard's Project Template page.

5. On the wizard's Project Template page, select the Empty Project icon, and then click Next.

After clicking Next, you see the wizard's Project Paths page, as shown in Figure 3-7.

6. In the Name field, type MyFirstProject.

You can add blank spaces, making the name My First Project, but I don't recommend it. In fact, having a blank space in any name (a workspace name, a project name, a filename, or whatever) is generally a bad idea.

7. Make sure that the Add to Current Workspace radio button is selected, and then click Finish.

If you click Next instead of Finish, you see some other options that you don't need right now. So to avoid any confusion, just click Finish.

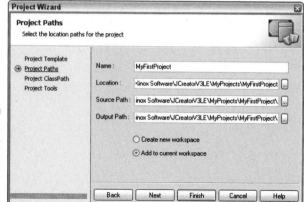

Figure 3-7:
The Project
Wizard's
Project
Paths page.

Clicking Finish brings you back to JCreator's work area, with MyFirst Project set in bold. The bold typeface means that MyFirstProject is the active project. The next step is to create a new Java source code file.

8. **In the File View pane, right-click** MyFirstProject. **Then choose Add➪ New Class from the context menu that appears, as shown in Figure 3-8.**

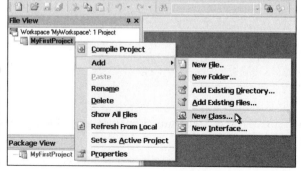

Figure 3-8:
Getting
JCreator
to add a
new class.

JCreator's Class Wizard opens. (See Figure 3-9.)

Like every other windowed environment, JCreator provides many ways to accomplish the same task. Instead of right-clicking MyFirstProject and choosing Add➪New Class, you can start at the menu bar and choose File➪New➪Class. But right-clicking a project has a small benefit. If you right-click the name of a project, the newly created class is without a doubt in that project. If you use the menu bar instead, the newly created class goes in whichever project happens to be the active project. So if your workspace contains many projects, you can accidentally put the new class into the wrong project.

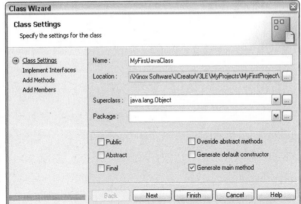

Figure 3-9:
The Class
Wizard's
Class
Settings
page.

9. **In the Class Wizard's Name field, type the name of your new class.**

   In this example, use the name **MyFirstJavaClass**, with no blank spaces between any of the words in the name. (Refer to Figure 3-9.)

   The name in the Class Wizard must not have blank spaces. And the only allowable punctuation symbol is the underscore character (_). You can name your class **MyFirstJavaClass** or **My_First_Java_Class**, but you can't name it **My First Java Class**, and you can't name it **JavaClass,MyFirst**.

10. **Put a checkmark in the Generate Main Method check box.**

    I created most of this book's examples without putting a checkmark in the Generate Main Method check box. But for this example, just this once, putting a checkmark in the Generate Main Method check box is very helpful.

11. **Skip everything in the Class Wizard except the Name field and the Generate Main Method check box. (In other words, click Finish.)**

    Clicking Finish brings you back to JCreator's work area. Now the Editor pane has a tab named *MyFirstJavaClass.java*. For your convenience, the MyFirstJavaClass.java tab already has some code in it. (See Figure 3-10.)

Figure 3-10:
JCreator
writes some
code in the
Editor pane.

```
MyFirstJavaClass.java

class MyFirstJavaClass {

    /**
     * Method main
     *
     *
     * @param args
     *
     */
    public static void main(String[] args) {
        // TODO: Add your code here
    }
}
```

12. **Replace an existing line of code in your new Java program.**

    Type a line of code in JCreator's Editor pane. Replace the line

    ```
    // TODO: Add your code here
    ```

    with the line

    ```
    System.out.println("Chocolate, royalties, sleep");
    ```

    Copy the new line of code exactly as you see it in Listing 3-1.

    • Spell each word exactly the way I spell it in Listing 3-1.

    • Capitalize each word exactly the way I do in Listing 3-1.

    • Include all the punctuation symbols — the dots, the quotation marks, the semicolon, everything.

Listing 3-1:   A Program to Display the Things I Like

```
class MyFirstJavaClass {

    /**
     * Method main
     *
     *
     * @param args
     *
     */
    public static void main(String[] args) {
        System.out.println("Chocolate, royalties, sleep");
    }
}
```

Java is *case-sensitive*, which means that `system.out.printLn` isn't the same as `System.out.println`. If you type `system.out.printLn`, you're program won't work. Be sure to capitalize your code eXactLy as it is in Listing 3-1.

13. **From the menu bar, choose Build⇨Compile Project.**

    If you typed everything correctly, you see the comforting `Process completed` message, with no error messages, at the bottom of JCreator's work area. The text appears in JCreator's Build Output pane in the lower portion of JCreator's work area. (Refer to Figure 3-4.)

When you choose Build⇨Compile Project, JCreator compiles whichever project is currently active. Only one project at a time is active. So if your workspace contains several projects, make sure that the project you want to compile is currently the active project.

14. Check for error messages at the bottom of JCreator's work area.

If, in Step 12, you don't type the code exactly as it's shown in Listing 3-1, then in this step you get error messages in JCreator's Task List pane. (Like so many other things, the Task List pane appears in the lower portion of JCreator's work area. See Figure 3-11.)

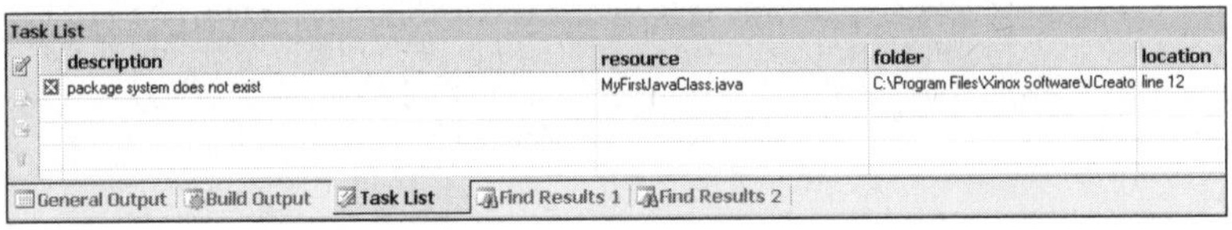

Figure 3-11:
An error message in the Task List pane.

Figure 3-11: An error message in the Task List pane.

Each error message refers to a specific place in your Java code. To jump the cursor to that place in the Editor pane, double-click the message in the Task List pane. Compare everything you see, character by character, with my code in Listing 3-1. Don't miss a single detail, including spelling, punctuation, and uppercase versus lowercase.

15. Make any changes or corrections to the code in the Editor pane. Then repeat Steps 13 and 14.

When at last you see the `Process completed` message with no error messages, you're ready to run the program.

16. From the menu bar choose Build➪Execute Project.

That does the trick. Your new Java program runs in JCreator's General Output pane. If you're running the code in Listing 3-1, you see the `Chocolate, royalties, sleep` message in Figure 3-12. It's like being in heaven!

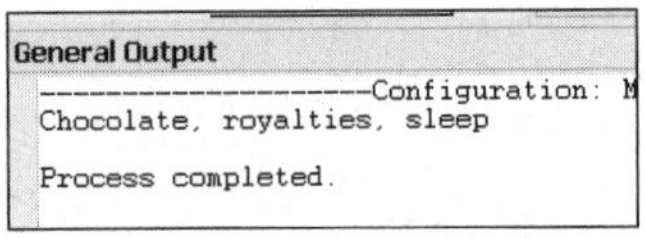

Figure 3-12:
Running the program in Listing 3-1.

Figure 3-12: Running the program in Listing 3-1.

Part II
Writing Your Own Java Programs

In this part . . .

This part features some of the world's simplest programs. And, as simple as they are, these programs illustrate the fundamental ideas behind all computer code. The ideas include things such as variables, values, types, statements, methods, and lots of other important stuff. This part of the book is your springboard, your launch pad, your virtual catapult.

Chapter 4

Exploring the Parts of a Program

. . . .

In This Chapter

▶ Identifying the words in a Java program

▶ Using punctuation and indentation

▶ Understanding Java statements and methods

. . . .

I work in the science building at a liberal arts college. When I walk past the biology lab, I always say a word of thanks under my breath. I'm thankful for not having to dissect small animals. In my line of work, I dissect computer programs instead. Computer programs smell much better than preserved dead animals. Besides, when I dissect a program, I'm not reminded of my own mortality.

In this chapter, I invite you to dissect a program with me. I have a small program, named ThingsILike. I cut apart the program, and carefully investigate the program's innards. Get your scalpel ready. Here we go!

Checking Out Java Code for the First Time

I have a confession to make. The first time I look at somebody else's computer program, I feel a bit queasy. The realization that I don't understand something (or many things) in the code makes me nervous. I've written hundreds (maybe thousands) of programs, but I still feel insecure when I start reading someone else's code.

The truth is, learning about a computer program is a bootstrapping experience. First I gawk in awe of the program. Then I run the program to see what it does. Then I stare at the program for a while, or read someone's explanation of the program and its parts. Then I gawk a little more and run the program again. Eventually, I come to terms with the program. Don't believe the wise guys who say they never go through these steps. Even the experienced programmers approach a new project slowly and carefully.

Behold! A program!

In Listing 4-1, you get a blast of Java code. Like all novice programmers, you're expected to gawk humbly at the code. But *don't be intimidated*. When you get the hang of it, programming is pretty easy. Yes, it's fun too.

Listing 4-1:   A Simple Java Program

```
/*
 * A program to list the good things in life
 * Author: Barry Burd, BeginProg2@BurdBrain.com
 * February 13, 2005
 */

class ThingsILike {

    public static void main(String args[]) {
        System.out.println("Chocolate, royalties, sleep");
    }
}
```

When I run the program in Listing 4-1, I get the result shown in Figure 4-1: The computer displays the words Chocolate, royalties, sleep on the screen. Now I admit that writing and running a Java program is a lot of work just to get the words Chocolate, royalties, sleep to appear on somebody's computer screen, but every endeavor has to start somewhere.

Figure 4-1:
Running the
program in
Listing 4-1.

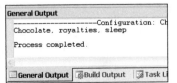

You can run the code in Listing 4-1 on your computer. Here's how:

1. **Follow the instructions in Chapter 2 for installing the special edition of JCreator (the edition that you find on this book's Web site).**

2. **Next follow the instructions in the first half of Chapter 3.**

    Those instructions tell you how to run the Chapter03_Example01 project, which is in the Chapter03 workspace. To run the code in Listing 4-1, select the Chapter04_Listing01 project in the Chapter04 workspace.

What the program's lines say

If the program in Listing 4-1 ever becomes famous, someone will write a Cliffs Notes book to summarize the program. The book will be really short, because you can summarize the action of Listing 4-1 in just one sentence. Here's the sentence:

```
Display Chocolate, royalties, sleep on the computer screen.
```

Now compare the sentence above with the bulk in Listing 4-1. Because Listing 4-1 has so many more lines, you may guess that Listing 4-1 has lots of boiler-plate code. Well, your guess is correct. You can't write a Java program without writing the boilerplate stuff but, fortunately, the boilerplate text doesn't change much from one Java program to another. Here's my best effort at summarizing all the Listing 4-1 text in 57 words or less:

```
This program lists the good things in life.
Barry Burd wrote this program on February 13, 2005.
Barry realizes that you may have questions about this
code, so you can reach him at BeginProg2@BurdBrain.com.

This code defines a Java class named ThingsILike.
     Here's the main starting point for the instructions:
          Display Chocolate, royalties, sleep on the screen.
```

The rest of this chapter (about 4,500 more words) explains the Listing 4-1 code in more detail.

The Elements in a Java Program

That both English and Java are called *languages* is no coincidence. You use a language to express ideas. English expresses ideas to people, and Java expresses ideas to computers. What's more, both English and Java have things like words, names, and punctuation. In fact, the biggest difference between the two languages is that Java is easier to learn than English. (If English were easy, then computers would understand English. Unfortunately, they can't.)

Take an ordinary English sentence and compare it with the code in Listing 4-1. Here's the sentence:

Suzanne says "eh" because, as you know, she lives in Canada.

In your high school grammar class, you worried about verbs, adjectives, and other such things. But in this book, you'll think in terms of keywords and identifiers, as summarized in Figure 4-2.

Suzanne's sentence has all kinds of things in it. They're the same kinds of things that you find in a computer program. So here's the plan: Compare the elements in Figure 4-1 with similar elements in Listing 4-1. You already understand English, so you use this understanding to figure out some new things about Java.

But first, here's a friendly reminder: In the next several paragraphs, I draw comparisons between English and Java. As you read these paragraphs, it's important to keep an open mind. For example, in comparing Java with English, I may write that "names of things aren't the same as dictionary words." Sure, you can argue that some dictionaries list proper nouns, and that some people have first names like Hope, Prudence, and Spike, but please don't. You'll get more out of the reading if you avoid nitpicking. Okay? Are we still friends? Then read on.

Keywords:
    Suzanne **says** "eh" **because**, **as** **you** **know**, **she** **lives** **in** Canada.

An identifier that you or I can define:
    Suzanne says "eh" because, as you know, she lives in Canada.

An identifier with a commonly agreed upon meaning:
    Suzanne says "eh" because, as you know, she lives in **Canada**.

A literal:
    Suzanne says **"eh"** because, as you know, she lives in Canada.

Punctuation:
    Suzanne says "eh" because**,** as you know**,** she lives in Canada**.**

A comment:
    Suzanne says "eh" because, as you know, she lives in Canada.

Figure 4-2: The things you find in a simple sentence.

Keywords

A *keyword* is a dictionary word — a word that's built right into a language.

In Figure 4-2, a word like "says" is a keyword, because "says" plays the same role whenever it's used in an English sentence. The other keywords in the Suzanne sentence are "because," "as," "you," "know," "she," "lives," and "in."

Computer programs have keywords, too. In fact, the program in Listing 4-1 uses four of Java's keywords (shown in bold):

```
class ThingsILike {

    public static void main(String args[]) {
```

Each Java keyword has a specific meaning — a meaning that remains unchanged from one program to another. For example, whenever I write a Java program, the word `public` always signals a part of the program that's accessible to any other piece of code.

The Java programming language is *case-sensitive*. This means that if you change a lowercase letter in a word to an uppercase letter, you change the word's meaning. Changing case can make the entire word go from being meaningful to being meaningless. In Listing 4-1, you can't replace *public* with *Public*. If you do, the whole program stops working.

This chapter has little or no detail about the meanings of the keywords `class`, `public`, `static`, and `void`. You can peek ahead at the material in other chapters, but you can also get along by cheating. When you write a program, just start with

```
class SomethingOrOther {
```

and then paste the text

```
public static void main(String args[]) {
```

into your code. In your first few programs, this strategy serves you well.

The Cheat Sheet in the front of this book has a complete list of Java keywords.

Here's one thing to remember about keywords: In Java, each keyword has an official, predetermined meaning. The people at Sun Microsystems, who have the final say on what constitutes a Java program, have created all of Java's keywords. You can't make up your own meaning for any of the Java keywords. For example, you can't use the word `public` in a calculation:

```
//This is BAD, BAD CODE:
public = 6;
```

If you try to use a keyword this way, then the compiler displays an error message and refuses to translate your source code. It works the same way in English. Have a baby, and name it "Because."

> "Let's have a special round of applause for tonight's master of ceremonies — Because O. Borel."

You can do it, but the kid will never lead a normal life.

Identifiers that you or I can define

I like the name Suzanne, but if you don't like traditional names, then make up a brand new name. You're having a new baby. Call her "Deneen" or "Chrisanta." Name him "Belton" or "Merk."

A *name* is a word that identifies something, so I'll stop calling these things names and start calling them *identifiers*. In computer programming, an *identifier* is a noun of some kind. An identifier refers to a value, a part of a program, a certain kind structure, or any number of things.

Listing 4-1 has two identifiers that you or I can define on our own. They're the made-up words `ThingsILike` and `args`.

```
class ThingsILike {

    public static void main(String args[]) {
```

Just as the names Suzanne and Chrisanta have no special meaning in English, so the names `ThingsILike` and `args` have no special meaning in Java. In Listing 4-1, I use `ThingsILike` for the name of my program, but I could also have used a name like `GooseGrease`, `Enzyme`, or `Kalamazoo`. I have to put (`String someName[]`) in my program, but I could use (`String args[]`), (`String commandLineArguments[]`), or (`String cheese[]`).

Do as I say, not as I do. Make up sensible, informative names for the things in your Java programs. Names like `GooseGrease` are cute, but they don't help you keep track of your program-writing strategy.

When I name my Java program, I can use `ThinksILike` or `GooseGrease`, but I can't use the word `public`. Words like `class`, `public`, `static`, and `void` are keywords in Java.

The `args` in (`String args[]`) holds anything extra that you type when you issue the command to run a Java program. For example, if you get the program to run by typing `java ThingsILike won too 3`, then `args` stores the extra values `won`, `too`, and `3`. As a beginning programmer, you don't need to think about this feature of Java. Just paste (`String args[]`) into each of your programs.

Identifiers with agreed upon meanings

Many people are named Suzanne, but only one country is named Canada. That's because there's a standard, well-known meaning for the word "Canada." It's the country with a red maple leaf on its flag. If you start your own country, you should avoid naming it Canada, because naming it Canada would just confuse everyone. (I know, a town in Kentucky is named Canada, but that doesn't count. Remember, you should ignore exceptions like this.)

Most programming languages have identifiers with agreed upon meanings. In Java, almost all of these identifiers are defined in the Java API. Listing 4-1 has five such identifiers. They're the words `main`, `String`, `System`, `out`, and `println`:

```
public static void main(String args[]) {
    System.out.println("Chocolate, royalties, sleep");
}
```

Here's a quick rundown on the meaning of each of these names (more detailed descriptions appear throughout this book):

- **main:** The main starting point for execution in every Java program.

- **String:** A bunch of text; a row of characters, one after another.

- **System:** A canned program in the Java API. (This program accesses some features of your computer that are outside the direct control of the Java virtual machine.)

- **out:** The place where a text-based program displays its text. (For a program running in JCreator, the word `out` represents the General Output pane. To read more about text-based programs, check the first several paragraphs of Chapter 3.)

- **println:** Display text on your computer screen.

Strictly speaking, the meanings of the identifiers in the Java API are not cast in stone. Although you can make up your own meanings for the words like `System` or `println`, this isn't a good idea. If you did, you would confuse the dickens out of other programmers, who are used to the standard API meanings for these familiar identifier names.

Literals

A *literal* is a chunk of text that looks like whatever value it represents. In Suzanne's sentence (refer to Figure 4-2), "eh" is a literal, because "eh" refers to the word "eh."

Programming languages have literals too. For example, in Listing 4-1, the stuff in quotes is a literal:

```
System.out.println("Chocolate, royalties, sleep");
```

When you run the `ThingsILike` program, you see the words `Chocolate,
royalties, sleep` on the screen. In Listing 4-1, the text `"Chocolate,
royalties, sleep"` refers to these words, exactly as they appear on the
screen (minus the quotation marks).

Most of the numbers that you use in computer programs are literals. If you
put the statement

```
mySalary = 1000000.00;
```

in a computer program, then `1000000.00` is a literal. It stands for the number
1000000.00 (one million).

Punctuation

A typical computer program has lots of punctuation. For example, consider
the program in Listing 4-1:

```
class ThingsILike {

    public static void main(String args[]) {
        System.out.println("Chocolate, royalties, sleep");
    }
}
```

Each bracket, each brace, each squiggle of any kind plays a role in making the
program meaningful.

In English, you write all the way across one line, and then you wrap your text
to the start of the next line. In programming, you seldom work this way. Instead,
the code's punctuation guides the indenting of certain lines. The indentation
shows which parts of the program are subordinate to which other parts. It's
as if, in English, you wrote Suzanne's sentence like this:

> Suzanne says "eh" because
>
> ,
>   as you know
>
> ,
> she lives in Canada.

The diagrams in Figures 4-3 and 4-4 show you how parts of the `ThingsILike`
program are contained inside other parts. Notice how a pair of curly braces
acts like a box. To make the program's structure be visible at a glance, you
indent all the stuff inside of each box.

```
class ThingsILike {

    public static void main(String args[]) {

        System.out.println("Chocolate, royalties, sleep");

    }

}
```

Figure 4-3:
A pair of
curly braces
acts like
a box.

Here's a Java class named ThingsILike:

Here's the main *starting point for the instructions:*

Display Chocolate, royalties, sleep *on the screen.*

Figure 4-4:
The ideas in
a computer
program
are nested
inside of
one another.

I can't emphasize this point enough. If you don't indent your code, or if you indent but you don't do it carefully, then your code still compiles and runs correctly. But this successful run gives you a false sense of confidence. The minute you try to update some poorly indented code, you become hopelessly confused. So take my advice: Keep your code carefully indented at every step in the process. Make your indentation precise, whether you're scratching out a quick test program, or writing code for a billionaire customer.

Comments

A *comment* is text that's outside the normal flow. In Figure 4-2, words "A comment:" aren't part of the Suzanne sentence. Instead, these words are *about* the Suzanne sentence.

The same is true of comments in computer programs. The first five lines in Listing 4-1 form one big comment. The computer doesn't act on this comment. There are no instructions for the computer to perform inside this comment. Instead, the comment tells other programmers something about your code.

Comments are for your own benefit, too. Imagine that you set aside your code for a while and work on something else. When you return later to work on the code again, the comments help you remember what you were doing.

The Java programming language has three different kinds of comments:

✔ **Traditional comments:** The comment in Listing 4-1 is a *traditional* comment. The comment begins with /* and ends with */. Everything between the opening /* and the closing */ is for human eyes only. Nothing between /* and */ gets translated by the compiler.

The second, third, and fourth lines in Listing 4-1 have extra asterisks. I call them "extra" because these asterisks aren't required when you create a comment. They just make the comment look pretty. I include them in Listing 4-1 because, for some reason that I don't entirely understand, most Java programmers add these extra asterisks.

✔ **End-of-line comments:** Here's some code with end-of-line comments:

```
class ThingsILike {                    //One thing is miss-
      ing

    public static void main(String args[]) {
        System.out.println("Royalties, sleep");
          //Chocolate
    }
}
```

An *end-of-line* comment starts with two slashes, and goes to the end of a line of type.

You may hear programmers talk about "commenting out" certain parts of their code. When you're writing a program, and something's not working correctly, it often helps to try removing some of the code. If nothing else, you find out what happens when that suspicious code is removed. Of course, you may not like what happens when the code is removed, so you don't want to delete the code completely. Instead, you turn your ordinary Java statements into comments. For example, turn System.out.println("Sleep"); into /* System.out.println("Sleep"); */.

This keeps the Java compiler from seeing the code while you try to figure out what's wrong with your program.

✔ **Javadoc comments:** A special *Javadoc* comment is any traditional comment that begins with an extra asterisk.

```
/**
 * Print a String and then terminate the line.
 */
```

This is a cool Java feature. The software that you can download from java.sun.com includes a little program called javadoc. The javadoc program looks for these special comments in your code. The program uses these comments to create a brand new Web page — a customized documentation page for your code. To find out more about turning Javadoc comments into Web pages, visit this book's Web site.

Understanding a Simple Java Program

The following sections present, explain, analyze, dissect, and otherwise demystify the Java program in Listing 4-1.

What is a method?

You're working as an auto mechanic in an upscale garage. Your boss, who's always in a hurry and has a habit of running words together, says, "FixThe Alternator on that junkyOldFord." Mentally, you run through a list of tasks. "Drive the car into the bay, lift the hood, get a wrench, loosen the alternator belt," and so on. Three things are going on here:

✔ **You have a name for the thing you're supposed to do.** The name is FixTheAlternator.

✔ **In your mind, you have a list of tasks associated with the name FixTheAlternator.** The list includes "Drive the car into the bay, lift the hood, get a wrench, loosen the alternator belt," and so on.

✔ **You have a grumpy boss who's telling you to do all this work.** Your boss gets you working by saying, "FixTheAlternator." In other words, your boss gets you working by saying the name of the thing you're supposed to do.

In this scenario, using the word *method* wouldn't be a big stretch. You have a method for doing something with an alternator. Your boss calls that method into action, and you respond by doing all the things in the list of instructions that you've associated with the method.

Java methods

If you believe all that stuff in the last several paragraphs, then you're ready to read about Java methods. In Java, a *method* is a list of things to do. Every method has a name, and you tell the computer to do the things in the list by using the method's name in your program.

I've never written a program to get a robot to fix an alternator. But, if I did, the program may include a method named `FixTheAlternator`. The list of instructions in my `FixTheAlternator` method would look something like the text in Listing 4-2.

Listing 4-2:   A Method Declaration

```
void FixTheAlternator() {
    DriveInto(car, bay);
    Lift(hood);
    Get(wrench);
    Loosen(alternatorBelt);
    ...
}
```

Somewhere else in my Java code (somewhere outside of Listing 4-2), I need an instruction to call my `FixTheAlternator` method into action. The instruction to call the `FixTheAlternator` method into action may look like the line in Listing 4-3.

Listing 4-3:   Calling a Method

```
FixTheAlternator(junkyOldFord);
```

Don't scrutinize Listings 4-2 and 4-3 too carefully. All the code in Listings 4-2 and 4-3 is fake! I made up this code so that it looks a lot like real Java code, but it's not real. What's more important, the code in Listings 4-2 and 4-3 isn't meant to illustrate all the rules about Java. So if you have a grain of salt handy, take it with Listings 4-2 and 4-3.

Almost every computer programming language has something akin to Java's methods. If you've worked with other languages, you may remember things like subprograms, procedures, functions, subroutines, `Sub` procedures, or `PERFORM` statements. Whatever you call it in your favorite programming language, a *method* is a bunch of instructions collected together and given a new name.

The declaration, the header, and the call

If you have a basic understanding of what a method is and how it works, you can dig a little deeper into some useful terminology:

✔ If I'm being lazy, I refer to the code in Listing 4-2 as a *method*. If I'm not being lazy, I refer to this code as a *method declaration*.

✔ The method declaration in Listing 4-2 has two parts. The first line (the part with the name `FixTheAlternator` in it, up to but not including the open curly brace) is called a *method header*. The rest of Listing 4-2 (the part surrounded by curly braces) is a *method body*.

✔ The term *method declaration* distinguishes the list of instructions in Listing 4-2 from the instruction in Listing 4-3, which is known as a *method call*.

For a handy illustration of all the method terminology, see Figure 4-5.

A method's header and declaration are like an entry in a dictionary. An entry doesn't really use the word that it defines. Instead, an entry tells you what happens if and when you use the word.

> **chocolate** (choc-o-late) *n.* **1.** The most habit-forming substance on earth. **2.** Something you pay for with money from royalties. **3.** The most important nutritional element in a person's diet.

> **FixTheAlternator**() Drive the car into the bay, lift the hood, get the wrench, loosen the alternator belt, and then eat some chocolate.

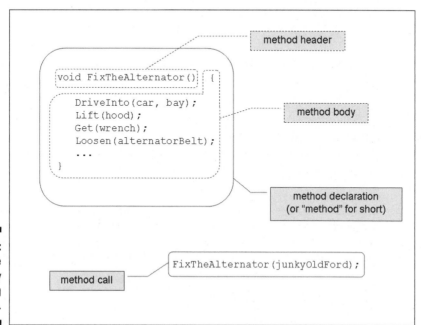

Figure 4-5: The terminology describing methods.

In contrast, a method call is like the use of a word in a sentence. A method call sets some code in motion.

"I want some chocolate, or I'll throw a fit."

"FixTheAlternator on that junkyOldFord."

A *method's declaration* tells the computer what will happen if you call the method into action. A *method call* (a separate piece of code) tells the computer to actually call the method into action. A method's declaration and the method's call tend to be in different parts of the Java program.

The main method in a program

In Listing 4-1, the bulk of the code is the declaration of a method named *main*. (Just look for the word main in the code's method header.) For now, don't worry about the other words in the method header — the words public, static, void, String, and args. I explain these words (on a need-to-know basis) in the next several chapters.

Like any Java method, the main method is a recipe:

```
How to make biscuits:
    Preheat the oven.
    Roll the dough.
    Bake the rolled dough.
```

or

```
How to follow the main instructions in the ThingsILike code:
    Display Chocolate, royalties, sleep on the screen.
```

The word main plays a special role in Java. In particular, you never write code that explicitly calls a main method into action. The word main is the name of the method that is called into action automatically when the program begins running.

When the ThingsILike program runs, the computer automatically finds the program's main method and executes any instructions inside the method's body. In the ThingsILike program, the main method's body has only one instruction. That instruction tells the computer to print Chocolate, royalties, sleep on the screen.

None of the instructions in a method are executed until the method is called into action. But if you give a method the name main, then that method is called into action automatically.

How you finally tell the computer to do something

Buried deep in the heart of Listing 4-1 is the single line that actually issues a direct instruction to the computer. The line

```
System.out.println("Chocolate, royalties, sleep");
```

tells the computer to display the words Chocolate, royalties, sleep. (If you use JCreator, the computer displays Chocolate, royalties, sleep in the General Output pane.) I can describe this line of code in at least two different ways:

- ✔ **It's a statement:** In Java, a direct instruction that tells the computer to do something is called a *statement*. The statement in Listing 4-1 tells the computer to display some text. The statements in other programs may tell the computer to put 7 in certain memory location, or make a window appear on the screen. The statements in computer programs do all kinds of things.

- ✔ **It's a method call:** In the "What is a method?" section, earlier in this chapter, I describe something named a "method call." The statement

  ```
  FixTheAlternator(junkyOldFord);
  ```

  is an example of a method call, and so is

  ```
  System.out.println("Chocolate, royalties, sleep");
  ```

  Java has many different kinds of statements. A method call is just one kind.

Ending a statement with a semicolon

In Java, each statement ends with a semicolon. The code in Listing 4-1 has only one statement in it, so only one line in Listing 4-1 ends with a semicolon.

Take any other line in Listing 4-1, like the method header, for example. The method header (the line with the word main in it) doesn't directly tell the computer to do anything. Instead, the method header describes some action for future reference. The header announces "Just in case someone ever calls the main method, the next few lines of code tell you what to do in response to that call."

Every complete Java statement ends with a semicolon. A method call is a statement, so it ends with a semicolon, but neither a method header nor a method declaration is a statement.

The method named System.out.println

The statement in the middle of Listing 4-1 calls a method named `System.out.println`. This method is defined in the Java API. Whenever you call the `System.out.println` method, the computer displays text on its screen.

Think about names. Believe it or not, I know two people named Pauline Ott. One of them is a nun; the other is physicist. Of course, there are plenty of Paulines in the English-speaking world, just as there are several things named `println` in the Java API. So to distinguish the physicist Pauline Ott from the film critic Pauline Kael, I write the full name "Pauline Ott." And, to distinguish the nun from the physicist, I write "Sister Pauline Ott." In the same way, I write either `System.out.println` or `DriverManager.println`. The first (which you use often) writes text on the computer's screen. The second (which you don't use at all in this book) writes to a database log file.

Just as Pauline and Ott are names in their own right, so `System`, `out`, and `println` are names in the Java API. But to use `println`, you must write the method's full name. You never write `println` alone. It's always `System.out.println` or some other combination of API names.

The Java programming language is case-sensitive. If you change a lowercase letter to an uppercase letter (or vice versa), you change a word's meaning. You can't replace `System.out.println` with `system.out.Println`. If you do, your program won't work.

Methods, methods everywhere

Two methods play roles in the `ThingsILike` program. Figure 4-6 illustrates the situation, and the next few bullets give you a guided tour:

- ✔ **There's a declaration for a main method.** I wrote the `main` method myself. This `main` method is called automatically whenever I start running the `ThingsILike` program.

- ✔ **There's a call to the `System.out.println` method.** The method call for the `System.out.println` method is the only statement in the body of the `main` method. In other words, calling the `System.out.println` method is the only thing on the `main` method's to-do list.

  The declaration for the `System.out.println` method is buried inside the official Java API. For a refresher on the Java API, see the Chapter 1.

When I say things like "`System.out.println` is buried inside the API," I'm not doing justice to the API. True, you can ignore all the nitty-gritty Java code inside the API. All you need to remember is that `System.out.println` is defined somewhere inside that code. But I'm not being fair when I make the API code sound like something magical. The API is just another bunch of Java code. The statements in the API that tell the computer what it means to carry out a call to `System.out.println` look a lot like the Java code in Listing 4-1.

```
101010000111000...
```

The Java Virtual Machine calls your
main method automatically, and then ...

```
class ThingsILike {

    public static void main(String args[]) {
        System.out.println("Chocolate, royalties, sleep");
    }
}
```

... a statement in your main method calls the
System.out.println method.

```
public void println(String s) {
    ensureOpen();
    textOut.write(s);
    textOut.flushBuffer();
    ...
}
```

Figure 4-6:
Calling the
System.out.
println
method.

Somewhere inside
the Java API....

The Java class

Have you heard the term *object-oriented programming* (also known as *OOP*)?
OOP is a way of thinking about computer programming problems — a way
that's supported by several different programming languages. OOP started in
the 1960s with a language called Simula. It was reinforced in the 1970s with
another language named Smalltalk. In the 1980s, OOP took off big time with
the language C++.

Some people want to change the acronym, and call it COP — class-oriented programming. That's because object-oriented programming begins with something
called a *class*. In Java, everything starts with classes, everything is enclosed
in classes, and everything is based on classes. You can't do anything in Java
until you've created a class of some kind. It's like being on *Jeopardy!,* hearing
Alex Trebek say, "Let's go to a commercial," and then interrupting him by
saying, "I'm sorry, Alex. You can't issue an instruction without putting your
instruction inside a class."

It's important for you to understand what a class really is, so I dare not give a
haphazard explanation in this chapter. Instead, I devote much of Chapter 17
to the question, "What is a class?" Anyway, in Java, your main method has to
be inside a class. I wrote the code in Listing 4-1, so I got to make up a name
for my new class. I chose the name ThingsILike, so the code in Listing 4-1
starts with the words class ThingsILike.

Take another look at Listing 4-1, and notice what happens after the line `class ThingsILike`. The rest of the code is enclosed in curly braces. These braces mark all the stuff inside the class. Without these braces, you'd know where the declaration of the `ThingsILike` class starts, but you wouldn't know where the declaration ends.

It's as if the stuff inside the `ThingsILike` class is in a box. (Refer to Figure 4-3.) To box off a chunk of code, you do two things:

- **You use curly braces:** These curly braces tell the compiler where a chunk of code begins and ends.

- **You indent code:** Indentation tells your human eye (and the eyes of other programmers) where a chunk of code begins and ends.

Don't forget. You have to do both.

Chapter 5

Composing a Program

. . . .

In This Chapter

▶ Reading input from the keyboard

▶ Editing a program

▶ Shooting at trouble

. . . .

*J*ust yesterday, I was chatting with my servant, RoboJeeves. (RoboJeeves is an upscale model in the RJ-3000 line of personal robotic life-forms.) Here's how the discussion went:

> *Me:* RoboJeeves, tell me the velocity of an object after it's been falling for three seconds in a vacuum.
>
> *RoboJeeves:* All right, I will. "The velocity of an object after it's been falling for three seconds in a vacuum." There, I told it to you.
>
> *Me:* RoboJeeves, don't give me that smart-alecky answer. I want a number. I want the actual velocity.
>
> *RoboJeeves:* Okay! "A number; the actual velocity."
>
> *Me:* RJ, these cheap jokes are beneath your dignity. Can you or can't you tell me the answer to my question?
>
> *RoboJeeves:* Yes.
>
> *Me:* "Yes," what?
>
> *RoboJeeves:* Yes, I either can or can't tell you the answer to your question.
>
> *Me:* Well, which is it? Can you?
>
> *RoboJeeves:* Yes, I can.
>
> *Me:* Then do it. Tell me the answer.
>
> *RoboJeeves:* The velocity is 153,984,792 miles per hour.

Me: (After pausing to think . . .) RJ, I know you never make a mistake, but that number, 153,984,792, is much too high.

RoboJeeves: Too high? That's impossible. Things fall very quickly on the giant planet Mangorrrrkthongo. Now, if you wanted to know about objects falling on Earth, you should have said so in the first place.

Sometimes that robot rubs me the wrong way. The truth is, RoboJeeves does whatever I tell him to do — nothing more and nothing less. If I say "Feed the cat," then RJ says, "Feed it to whom? Which of your guests will be having cat for dinner?"

Handy as they are, all computers do the same darn thing. They do *exactly* what you tell them to do, and that's sometimes very unfortunate. For example, in 1962, a Mariner spacecraft to Venus was destroyed just four minutes after its launch. Why? It was destroyed because of a missing keystroke in a FORTRAN program. Around the same time, NASA scientists caught an error that could have trashed the Mercury space flights. (Yup! These were flights with people on board!) The error was a line with a period instead of a comma. (A computer programmer wrote DO 10 I=1.10 instead of DO 10 I=1,10.)

With all due respect to my buddy RoboJeeves, he and his computer cousins are all incredibly stupid. Sometimes they look as if they're second-guessing us humans, but actually they're just doing what other humans told them to do. They can toss virtual coins and use elaborate schemes to mimic creative behavior, but they never really think on their own. If you say, "Jump," then they do what they're programmed to do in response to the letters J-u-m-p.

So when you write a computer program, you have to imagine that a genie has granted you three wishes. Don't ask for eternal love because, if you do, then the genie will give you a slobbering, adoring mate — someone that you don't like at all. And don't ask for a million dollars, unless you want the genie to turn you into a bank robber.

Everything you write in a computer program has to be very precise. Take a look at an example. . . .

A Program to Echo Keyboard Input

Listing 5-1 contains a small Java program. The program lets you type one line of characters on the keyboard. As soon as you press Enter, the program displays a second line that copies whatever you typed.

Listing 5-1:   A Java Program

```java
import java.util.Scanner;

class EchoLine {

    public static void main(String args[]) {
        Scanner myScanner = new Scanner(System.in);

        System.out.println(myScanner.nextLine());
    }
}
```

Figure 5-1 shows a run of the `EchoLine` code (the code in Listing 5-1). The text in the figure is a mixture of my own typing and the computer's responses.

Figure 5-1:
What part of
the word
"don't" do
you not
understand?

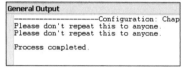

To illustrate the situation, I concocted Figure 5-2. In Figure 5-2, I added high-light to the text that I type. (Everything that I type is highlighted. Everything the computer displays on its own is in regular, un-highlighted style.)

Figure 5-2:
Whatever
you get
to type is
highlighted.

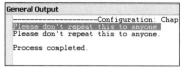

Here's what happens when you run the code in Listing 5-1:

1. At first, the computer does nothing. You see a cursor on the left edge of the General Output pane, as shown in Figure 5-3. The computer is wait-ing for you to type something.

Figure 5-3:
The
computer
waits for
you to type
something.

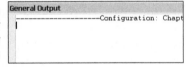

2. You type one line of text — any text at all. (See Figure 5-4.)

Figure 5-4:
You type a
sentence.

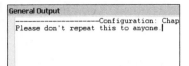

3. You press Enter, and the computer displays another copy of the line that you typed, as shown in Figure 5-5.

Figure 5-5:
The
computer
echoes
your input.

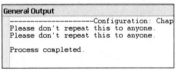

After displaying a copy of your input, the program's run comes to an end. JCreator adds Process completed to the text in the General Output pane.

Typing and running a program

This book's special edition of JCreator has a Chapter05 workspace. Within that workspace you can find a Chapter05_Listing01 project. To test the code in Listing 5-1, you can just open and run the readymade Chapter05_Listing01 project.

But instead of running the readymade code, I encourage you to start from scratch — to type Listing 5-1 yourself and then to test your newly-created code. Just follow these steps:

1. **Launch JCreator.**

2. **From JCreator's menu bar, choose File⇨Open Workspace.**

   An Open dialog box appears.

3. **In the Open dialog box, select** `MyWorkspace.jcw` **(or simply** `MyWorkspace`**). Then click Open.**

   After clicking Open, you see MyWorkspace in JCreator's File View pane. The next step is to create a new project within MyWorkspace.

4. **In the File View pane, right-click MyWorkspace. Then choose Add new Project from the context menu that appears.**

   JCreator's Project Wizard opens.

5. **In the wizard's Project Template tab, select the Empty Project icon, and then click Next.**

   After clicking Next, you see the wizard's Project Paths tab.

6. **In the Name field, type MyNewProject.**

7. **Click Finish.**

   Clicking Finish brings you back to JCreator's work area, with `MyNew Project` set in bold. The bold typeface means that `MyNewProject` is the active project. The next step is to create a new Java source code file.

8. **In the File View pane, right-click** `MyNextProject`**. Then choose Add⇨ New Class from the context menu that appears.**

   JCreator's Class Wizard opens.

9. **In the Class Wizard's Name field, type the name of your new class.**

   In this example, use the name **EchoLine**. Spell **EchoLine** exactly the way I spell it in Listing 5-1, with a capital **E**, a capital **L**, and no blank space.

   In Java, consistent spelling and capitalization are very important. If you're not consistent within a particular program, then you'll get error messages when you try to compile the program.

10. **Skip everything in the Class Wizard except the Name field. (In other words, click Finish.)**

    Clicking Finish brings you back to JCreator's work area. Now the Editor pane has a tab named *EchoLine.java*.

11. **Type the program of Listing 5-1 in the Editor pane's EchoLine.java tab.**

    Copy the code exactly as you see it in Listing 5-1.

    - Spell each word exactly the way I spell it in Listing 5-1.

    - Capitalize each word exactly the way I do in Listing 5-1.

    - Include all the punctuation symbols — the dots, the semicolons, everything.

12. **From the menu bar, choose Build⇨Compile Project.**

    If you typed everything correctly, you see the comforting `Process completed` message, with no error messages, in JCreator's Build Output pane.

    If you see error messages, then go back to Step 11, and compare everything you typed with the stuff in Listing 5-1. Compare every letter, every word, every squiggle, every smudge.

13. **Make any changes or corrections to the code in the Editor pane. Then repeat Step 12.**

    When at last you see the `Process completed` message with no error messages, you're ready to run the program.

14. **From the menu bar choose Build⇨Execute Project.**

    Your new Java program runs. A cursor sits on the left edge of JCreator's General Output pane. (Refer to Figure 5-3.) The computer is waiting for you to type something.

15. **Type a line of text, and then press Enter.**

    In response, the computer displays a second copy of your line of text. Then JCreator displays `Process completed`, and the program's run comes to an end. (Refer to Figure 5-5.)

If this list of steps seems a bit sketchy, you can find much more detail in Chapter 3. (Look first at the section in Chapter 3 about compiling and running a program.) For the most part, the steps here in Chapter 5 are a quick summary of the material in Chapter 3. The big difference is, in Chapter 3, I don't encourage you to type the program yourself.

This section tells you how to type the program with JCreator running on Microsoft Windows. If you don't use Windows, or if you use Windows but you don't use JCreator, then visit this book's Web site at `http://www.dummies.com/go/bpjavafd`. On that site, I've posted some handy tips for creating Java programs in other environments.

So what's the big deal when you type the program yourself? Well, lots of interesting things can happen when you apply fingers to keyboard. That's why the second half of this chapter is devoted to troubleshooting.

How the EchoLine program works

When you were a tiny newborn, resting comfortably in your mother's arms, she told you how to send characters to the computer screen:

```
System.out.println(whatever text you want displayed);
```

What she didn't tell you was how to fetch characters from the computer keyboard. There are lots of ways to do it, but the one I recommend in this chapter is:

```
myScanner.nextLine()
```

Now, here's the fun part. Calling the nextLine method doesn't just scoop characters from the keyboard. When the computer runs your program, the computer *substitutes whatever you type on the keyboard* in place of the text myScanner.nextLine().

To understand this, look at the statement in Listing 5-1:

```
System.out.println(myScanner.nextLine());
```

When you run the program, the computer sees your call to nextLine and stops dead in its tracks. (Refer to Figure 5-3.) The computer waits for you to type a line of text. So (refer to Figure 5-4) you type the line

```
Hey, there's an echo in here.
```

The computer substitutes this entire Hey line for the myScanner.nextLine() call in your program. The process is illustrated in Figure 5-6.

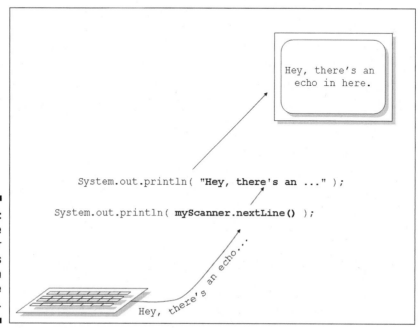

Figure 5-6: The computer substitutes text in place of the nextLine call.

The call to `myScanner.nextLine()` is nestled inside the `System.out.println` call. So when all is said and done, the computer behaves as if the statement in Listing 5-1 looks like this:

```
System.out.println("Hey, there's an echo in here.");
```

The computer displays another copy of the text `Hey, there's an echo in here.` on the screen. That's why you see two copies of the `Hey` line in Figure 5-5.

Getting numbers, words, and other things

In Listing 5-1, the words `myScanner.nextLine()` get an entire line of text from the computer keyboard. So if you type

```
Testing 1 2 3
```

the program in Listing 5-1 echoes back your entire `Testing 1 2 3` line of text.

Sometimes you don't want a program to get an entire line of text. Instead, you want the program to get a piece of a line. For example, when you type `1 2 3`, you may want the computer to get the number 1. (Maybe the number 1 stands for one customer or something like that.) In such situations, you don't put `myScanner.nextLine()` in your program. Instead, you use `myScanner.nextInt()`.

Table 5-1 shows you a few variations on the `myScanner.next` business. Unfortunately, the table's entries aren't very predictable. To read a line of input, you call `nextLine`. But to read a word of input, you don't call `nextWord`. (The Java API has no `nextWord` method.) Instead, to read a word, you call `next`.

Table 5-1	Some Scanner Methods
To Read This . . .	*. . . Make This Method Call*
A number with no decimal point in it	`nextInt()`
A number with a decimal point in it	`nextDouble()`
A word (ending in a blank space, for example)	`next()`
A line (or what remains of a line after you've already read some data from the line)	`nextLine()`
A single character (such as a letter, a digit, or a punctuation character)	`findInLine(".").charAt(0)`

Also, the table's story has a surprise ending. To read a single character, you don't call next*Something*. Instead, you can call the bizarre findInLine (".").charAt(0) combination of methods. (You'll have to excuse the folks who created the Scanner class. They approached the input problem from a specialized point of view.)

A quick look at the Scanner

In this chapter, I advise you to ignore any meanings behind the lines import java.util. Scanner and Scanner myScanner, *etc.* Just paste these two lines mindlessly in your code, and then move on.

Of course, you may not want to take my advice. You may not like ignoring things in your code. If you happen to be such a stubborn person, I have a few quick facts for you.

✔ **The word** Scanner **is defined in the Java API.**

A Scanner is something you can use for getting input.

This Scanner class is new in version 5.0 of the Java API. If you use version Java 1.4.2, then you don't have access to the Scanner class. (You get an error when you try to compile Listing 5-1.)

✔ **The words** System **and** in **are defined in the Java API.**

Taken together, the words System.in stand for the computer keyboard.

In later chapters you see things like new Scanner(new File("myData.txt")). In those chapters, I replace System.in with the words new File("myData.txt") because I'm not getting input from the keyboard. Instead, I'm getting input from a file on the computer's hard drive.

✔ **The word** myScanner **doesn't come from the Java API.**

The word myScanner is a Barry Burd creation. Instead of myScanner, you can use

readingThingie (or any other name you want to use) as long as you use the name consistently. So, if you want to be creative, you can write

```
Scanner readingThingie = new
    Scanner(System.in);

System.out.println(readingThing
    ie.nextLine());
```

The revised Listing 5-1 (with reading Thingie instead of myScanner) compiles and runs without a hitch.

✔ **The line** import java.util.Scanner **is an example of an** *import declaration.*

An optional import declaration allows you to abbreviate names in the rest of your program. You can remove the import declaration from Listing 5-1. But if you do, you must use the Scanner class's *fully qualified name* throughout your code. Here's how:

```
class EchoLine {

    public static void
    main(String args[]) {
        java.util.Scanner
    myScanner =
            new
    java.util.Scanner(System.in)
    ;

        System.out.println(myScanne
    r.nextLine());
    }
}
```

To see some of the table's methods in action, check other program listings in this book. Chapters 6, 7, and 8 have some particularly nice examples.

Type two lines of code, and don't look back

Buried innocently inside Listing 5-1 are two extra lines of code. These lines help the computer read input from the keyboard. The two lines are

```
import java.util.Scanner;

        Scanner myScanner = new Scanner(System.in);
```

Concerning these two lines, I have bad news and good news.

- ✔ **The bad news is, the reasoning behind these lines is difficult to understand.** That's especially true here in Chapter 5, where I introduce Java's most fundamental concepts.

- ✔ **The good news is, you don't have to understand the reasoning behind these two lines.** You can copy and paste these lines into any program that gets input from the keyboard. You don't have to change the lines in any way. These lines work without any modifications in all kinds of Java programs.

Just be sure to put these lines in the right places:

- ✔ Make the `import java.util.Scanner` line be the first line in your program.

- ✔ Put the `Scanner myScanner = new Scanner(System.in)` line inside your `main` method immediately after the `public static void main (String args[]) {` line.

At some point in the future, you may have to be more careful about the positioning of these two lines. But for now, the rules I give will serve you well.

Expecting the Unexpected

Not long ago, I met an instructor with an interesting policy. He said, "Sometimes when I'm lecturing, I compose a program from scratch on the computer. I do it right in front of my students. If the program compiles and runs correctly on the first try, I expect the students to give me a big round of applause."

At first you may think this guy has an enormous ego, but you have to put things in perspective. It's unusual for a program to compile and run correctly the first time. There's almost always a typo or another error of some kind.

So this section deals with the normal, expected errors that you see when you compile and run a program for the first time. Everyone makes these mistakes, even the most seasoned travelers. The key is keeping a cool head. Here's my general advice:

✔ **Don't expect a program that you type to compile the first time.**

Be prepared to return to your editor and fix some mistakes.

✔ **Don't expect a program that compiles flawlessly to run correctly.**

Getting a program to compile without errors is the easier of the two tasks.

✔ **Read what's in JCreator's Editor pane, not what you assume is in JCreator's Editor pane.**

Don't assume that you've typed words correctly, that you've capitalized words correctly, or that you've matched curly braces or parentheses correctly. Compare the code you typed with any sample code that you have. Make sure that every detail is in order.

✔ **Be patient.**

Every good programming effort takes a long time to get right. If you don't understand something right away, then be persistent. Stick with it (or put it away for a while and come back to it). There's nothing you can't understand if you put in enough time.

✔ **Don't become frustrated.**

Don't throw your pie crust. Frustration (not lack of knowledge) is your enemy. If you're frustrated, you can't accomplish anything.

✔ **Don't think you're the only person who's slow to understand.**

I'm slow, and I'm proud of it. (Christine, Chapter 6 will be a week late.)

✔ **Don't be timid.**

If your code isn't working, and you can't figure out why it's not working, then ask someone. Post a message on `groups.google.com`, or send me an e-mail message. (Send it to `BeginProg2@BurdBrain.com`.) And don't be afraid of anyone's snide or sarcastic answer. (For a list of gestures you can make in response to peoples' snotty answers, see Appendix Z.)

Diagnosing a problem

The "Typing and running a program" section, earlier in this chapter, tells you how to run the EchoLine program. If all goes well, your screen ends up looking like the one shown in Figure 5-1. But things don't always go well. Sometimes your finger slips, inserting a typo into your program. Sometimes you ignore one of the details in Listing 5-1, and you get a nasty error message.

Of course, some things in Listing 5-1 are okay to change. Not every word in Listing 5-1 is cast in stone. So here's a nasty wrinkle — I can't tell you that you must always retype Listing 5-1 exactly as it appears. Some changes are okay; others are not. Keep reading for some "f'rinstances."

Case sensitivity

Java is *case-sensitive*. Among other things, this means that, in a Java program, the letter P isn't the same as the letter p. If you send me some fan mail and start with "Dear barry" instead of "Dear Barry," then I still know what you mean. But Java doesn't work that way.

So change just one character in a Java program, and instead of an uneventful compilation you get a big headache! Change p to P like so:

```
//The following line is incorrect:
System.out.Println(myScanner.nextLine());
```

When you try to compile and run the program, you get the ugliness shown in Figure 5-7.

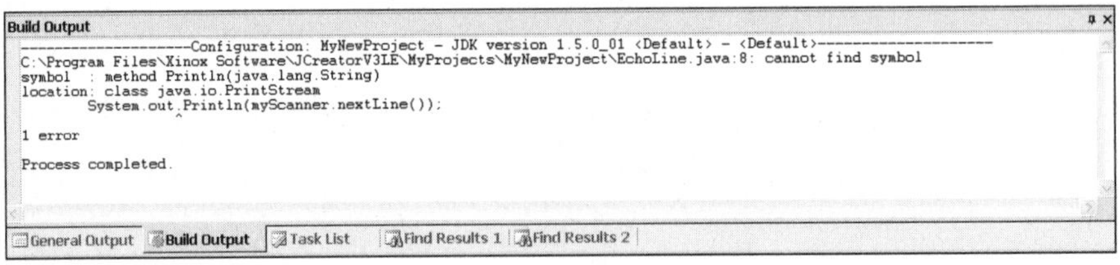

Figure 5-7:
The Java compiler understands println, but not Println.

```
Build Output                                                                    ⊕ ×
              ----------Configuration: MyNewProject - JDK version 1.5.0_01 <Default> - <Default>----------
C:\Program Files\Xinox Software\JCreatorV3LE\MyProjects\MyNewProject\EchoLine.java:8: cannot find symbol
symbol  : method Println(java.lang.String)
location: class java.io.PrintStream
        System.out.Println(myScanner.nextLine());
                   ^
1 error

Process completed.
```
General Output | **Build Output** | Task List | Find Results 1 | Find Results 2

When you get messages like the ones in Figure 5-7, your best bet is to stay calm and read the messages carefully. Sometimes, the messages contain useful hints. (Of course sometimes, they don't.) The messages in Figure 5-7 start with EchoLine.java:8: cannot find symbol. In plain English, this means "There's *something* that the Java compiler can't interpret on line 8 of your EchoLine.java file."

"And what may that *something* be?" you ask. The answer is also in Figure 5-7. The second line of the message says `symbol : method Println`, which means, "The Java compiler can't interpret the word `Println`." (The message stops short of saying, "It's the word `Println`, you dummy!" In any case, if the computer says you're one of us Dummies, you should take it as a compliment.)

Now, there are plenty of reasons why the compiler may not be able to understand a word like `Println`. But, for a beginning programmer, there are two important things that you should check right away:

- ✔ **Have you spelled the word correctly?**

  Did you type `prntlin` instead of `println`?

- ✔ **Have you capitalized all letters correctly?**

  Did you type `Println` or `PrintLn` instead of `println`?

Either of these errors can send the Java compiler into a tailspin. So compare your typing with the approved typing word for word (and letter for letter). When you find a discrepancy, go back to the editor and fix the problem. Then try compiling the program again.

When an error message says `EchoLine.java:67`, you don't need to count to the program's 67th line. Just double-click the phrase `EchoLine.java:67` in JCreator's Build Output pane. When you do, JCreator draws a little red arrow next to line 67 (and moves the cursor to line 67) in the Editor pane.

Omitting punctuation

In English and in, Java using the; proper! punctuation is important)

Take, for instance, the semicolons in Listing 5-1. What happens if you forget to type a semicolon?

```
//The following code is incorrect:

    System.out.println(myScanner.nextLine())
}
```

If you leave off the semicolon, you get the message shown in Figure 5-8.

```
Build Output
-----------------Configuration: MyNewProject - JDK version 1.5.0_01 <Default> - <Default>-----------
C:\Program Files\Xinox Software\JCreatorV3LE\MyProjects\MyNewProject\EchoLine.java:9: ';' expected
        }
1 error
```

A message like the one in Figure 5-8 makes your life much simpler. I don't have to explain the message, and you don't have to puzzle over the message's meaning. Just take the message `';'` `expected` on its face value. The message says, "I expect to see a semicolon at this point in your program." A caret (a ^ thingy) points to the place in the program where the computer expects to see a semicolon. The computer expects a semicolon after the `System.out.println` `(myScanner.nextLine())` statement and before the close curly brace.

So do what the message tells you to do. Go back to the editor and put a semicolon after the `System.out.println(myScanner.nextLine())` statement. That settles it.

Using too much punctuation

In junior high school, my English teacher said I should use a comma whenever I would normally pause for a breath. This advice doesn't work well during allergy season, when my sentences have more commas in them than words. Even as a paid author, I have trouble deciding where the commas should go, so I often add extra commas for good measure. This makes more work for my editor, Christine, who has a recycle bin full of commas by the desk in her office.

It's the same way in a Java program. You can get carried away with punctuation. Consider, for example, the `main` method header in Listing 5-1. This line is a dangerous curve for novice programmers.

For information on the terms *method header* and *method body,* see Chapter 4.

Normally, you shouldn't be ending a method header with a semicolon. But people add semicolons anyway. (Maybe, in some subtle way, a method header looks like it should end with a semicolon.)

```
//The following line is incorrect:
public static void main(String args[]); {
```

If you add this extraneous semicolon to the code in Listing 5-1, you get the message shown in Figure 5-9.

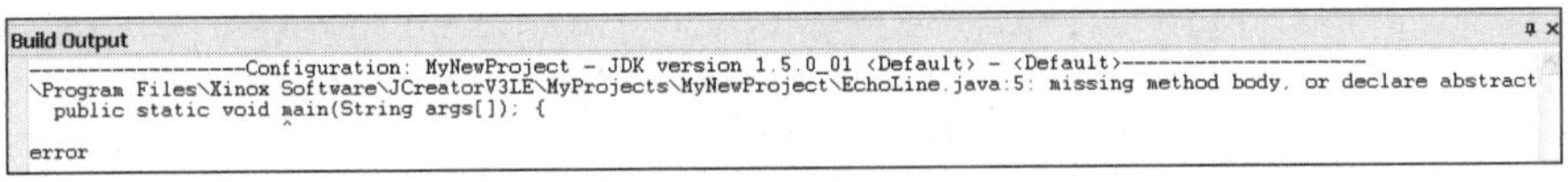

Figure 5-9:
A not-so-helpful error message.

The error message in Figure 5-9 is a bit misleading. Instead of saying `extra semicolon should be removed`, the message says `missing method body, or declare abstract`. What the heck does that mean?

Is there life after a failed compilation?

In the section entitled "Typing and running a program" you create a file named `EchoLine.java`. (See Step 10 of the instructions in that section.) When you successfully compile the project, the computer creates another file — a file named `EchoLine.class`. (You don't see EchoLine. class in JCreator's File View pane, but even so, the computer creates an `EchoLine.class` file.) Later, to run the program, the Java virtual machine follows the instructions in this `EchoLine.class` file. For details, see Chapter 1.

That's what happens when the computer successfully compiles your program. But what happens if your program contains errors? Whenever an attempted compilation isn't successful, the computer doesn't create a `.class` file. And without this `.class` file, an attempted run isn't successful either.

But sometimes, the story has a peculiar twist. Imagine this unfortunate sequence of events:

✔ **You type Listing 5-1 exactly as it appears in this book.**

✔ **On JCreator's menu bar, you choose Build⇨ Compile Project.** This creates an `Echo Line.class` file. Very nice!

✔ **On JCreator's menu bar, you choose Build⇨ Execute Project.** You see the program's output. Wonderful!

✔ **You make a harmful change to your** `Echo Line.java` **file.** For instance, you turn the p in `println` into a heinous, unwanted capital P.

✔ **You choose Build⇨Compile Project again.** This gives you your favorite `cannot find symbol` error message. The computer *doesn't* create a new `EchoLine.class` file.

✔ **You choose Build⇨Execute Project once again.**

And what happens when you choose Build⇨ Execute Project the second time? If you guessed that the old `EchoLine` program runs correctly, then you're right.

Even though your latest compiler effort was a failure, your earlier compilation created a good `EchoLine.class` file. That `EchoLine. class` file is still on your hard drive. The file wasn't replaced during the failed compilation. So when you choose Build⇨Execute Project the second time, the computer uses that old `EchoLine.class` file and correctly runs the code in Listing 5-1.

This can be really confusing. When you choose Build⇨Execute Project, your gut tells you that you're getting the results of your most recent compiling attempt. But your gut can be wrong, wrong, wrong. In the scenario that I just described, an unsuccessful compilation is followed by what appears to be a successful run. It's a mess, so you have to keep your wits about you. If a compilation fails, then don't march on and try to run the project. Instead, go back and figure out why the compilation failed.

Well, when the computer tries to compile the bad code (Listing 5-1 with one too many semicolons), it gets confused. I illustrate the confusion in Figure 5-10. Your eye sees an extra semicolon, but the computer's eye interprets this as a method without a body. So that's the first part of the error message — the computer says missing method body.

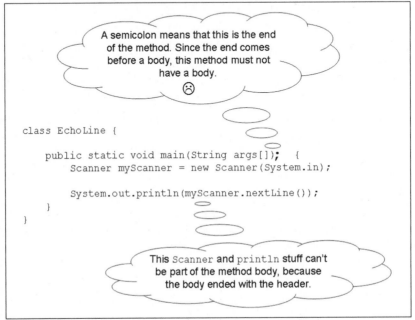

Figure 5-10:
What's
on this
computer's
mind?

We all know that a computer is a very patient, very sympathetic machine. That's why the computer looks at your code, and decides to give you one more chance. The computer remembers that Java has an advanced feature in which you write a method header without writing a method body. When you do this, you get what's called an *abstract method* — something that I don't use at all in this book. Anyway, in Figure 5-10, the computer sees a header with no body. So the computer says to itself, "I know! Maybe the programmer is trying to write an abstract method. The trouble is, an abstract method's header has to have the word abstract in it. I should remind the programmer about that." So the computer displays the declare abstract message in Figure 5-9.

One way or another, you can't interpret the message in Figure 5-9 without reading between the lines. So here are some tips to help you decipher murky messages:

✔ **Avoid the knee-jerk response.**

Some people see the `declare abstract` message in Figure 5-9 and wonder how they can declare a method to be abstract. Unfortunately, this isn't the right approach. If you don't know what it means to `declare abstract` then, chances are, you didn't mean to declare anything to be abstract in the first place.

✔ **Stare at the bad line of code for a long, long time.**

If you look carefully at the `public static . . .` line in Figure 5-9, then eventually you'll notice that it's different from the corresponding line in Listing 5-1. The line in Listing 5-1 has no semicolon, but the line in Figure 5-9 has a semicolon.

Of course, you won't always be starting with some prewritten code like the stuff in Listing 5-1. That's where practice makes perfect. The more code you write, the more sensitive your eyes will become to things like extraneous semicolons and other programming goofs.

Often the first message is the best

You're looking for the nearest gas station, so you ask one of the locals. "Go to the first traffic light and make a left," says the local. You go straight for a few streets, and see a blinking yellow signal. You turn left at the signal, and travel for a mile or so. What? No gas station? Maybe you mistook the blinking signal for a real traffic light.

Why can't the computer fix it?

How often do you get to finish someone else's sentence? "Please," says your supervisor, "go over there and connect the . . ."

"Wires," you say. "I'll connect the wires." If you know what someone means to say, why wait for them to say it?

This same question comes up in connection with computer error messages. Take a look at the message in Figure 5-8. The computer expects a semicolon before the curly brace on line 9. Well, Mr. Computer, if you know where you want a semicolon, then just add the semicolon, and be done with it. Why are you bothering me about it?

The answer is simple. The computer isn't interested in taking any chances. What if you *don't* really want a semicolon before the curly brace on line 9? What if the missing semicolon represents a more profound problem? If the computer added the extra semicolon, it could potentially do more harm than good.

Returning to you and your supervisor . . .

Boom! A big explosion. "Not the wires, you Dummy. The dots. I wanted you to connect the dots."

"Sorry," you say.

You come to a fork in the road. "The directions said nothing about a fork. Which way should I go?" You veer right, but a minute later you're forced onto a highway. You see a sign that says, "Next Exit 24 Miles." Now you're really lost, and the gas gauge points to "S." (The "S" stands for "Stranded.")

So here's what happened: You made an honest mistake. You shouldn't have turned left at the yellow blinking light. That mistake alone wasn't so terrible. But that first mistake lead to more confusion, and eventually, your choices made no sense at all. If you hadn't turned at the blinking light, you'd never have encountered that stinking fork in the road. Then, getting on the highway was sheer catastrophe.

Is there a point to this story? Of course there is. A computer can get itself into the same sort of mess. The computer notices an error in your program. Then, metaphorically speaking, the computer takes a fork in the road — a fork based on the original error — a fork for which none of the alternatives lead to good results.

Here's an example. You're retyping the code in Listing 5-1, and you forget to type a close parenthesis:

```
//The following line is incorrect:
public static void main(String args[] {
```

When you try to compile the code, you get the messages shown in Figure 5-11.

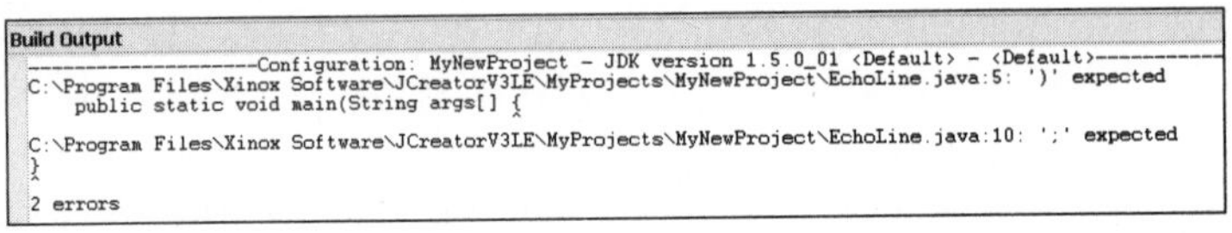

Figure 5-11:
Two error
messages.

```
Build Output
------------------------Configuration: MyNewProject - JDK version 1.5.0_01 <Default> - <Default>------------
C:\Program Files\Xinox Software\JCreatorV3LE\MyProjects\MyNewProject\EchoLine.java:5: ')' expected
    public static void main(String args[] {
C:\Program Files\Xinox Software\JCreatorV3LE\MyProjects\MyNewProject\EchoLine.java:10: ';' expected
}
2 errors
```

The computer reports two errors — one error on line 5, and another error on line 10. "Let's see," you say to yourself. "Line 10 is the last line of the main method. The message says ';' expected. Why would I want a semicolon at the end of my main method?"

Well, you better take a step backward. In Figure 5-11, the first error message says ')' expected. That's okay. But after that first message, the computer is really confused. In the second message, the computer suggests that you end the main method with a semicolon, as if that would fix anything. The computer is trying to make the best of a bad situation but, at this point, you shouldn't believe a word that the computer says.

One message and none very helpful

Look at the following sidebar figure and think about what happened. The computer got all upset because it didn't see one of the words that it expected. The computer expected to see either `class` or `interface`, and it scolded me for not using one of these two words.

Oddly enough, the computer was going out on a limb when it suggested the words `class` and `interface`. The fact is, not all programs begin with the word `class` or the word `interface`. For example, the code in Listing 5-1 begins with the word `import`.

Now, what happens if your pinky finger becomes heavy, and you type `Import` instead of `import`?

```
//The following line is incor-
    rect:
Import java.util.Scanner;
```

Then, much to your dismay, you get the message shown in the accompanying figure. The figure has yet another `'class' or 'interface'` expected message, but this time, the message is all wrong. Sure, you should have typed `import` instead of `Import`. But no, the computer's suggestion that the word `class` or `interface` will fix everything is incorrect.

Now unfortunately, in this particular figure, you don't get a message saying `cannot find symbol . . . Import`. And you certainly don't see a message like `'import' expected`. Either of those messages would be more helpful than `'class' or 'interface' expected`, but neither message is destined to appear. That's just the way the cookie crumbles. Computers aren't smart animals, and if someone programs the computer to say `'class' or 'interface' expected`, then that's exactly what the computer says.

Some people say that computers make them feel stupid. For me, it's the opposite. A computer reminds me how dumb a machine can be, and how smart a person can be. I like that.

```
Build Output
--------------------Configuration: MyNewProject - JDK version 1.5.0_01 <Default> - <Default>--------------------
C:\Program Files\Xinox Software\JCreatorV3LE\MyProjects\MyNewProject\EchoLine.java:1: 'class' or 'interface' expected
Import java.util.Scanner;

1 error
```

The moral of this story is simple. The first of the computer's error messages is often the most reliable. The rest of the messages may be nothing but confusing drivel.

If you get more than one error message, always look carefully at the first message in the bunch. That first error message is often the most informative of all the error messages.

Occasionally, the first error message isn't the most informative. Take time reading the messages and look for the most helpful among them.

Same kind of error; different kind of message

You've found an old family recipe for deviled eggs (one of my favorites). You follow every step as carefully as you can, but you leave out the salt because of your grandmother's high blood pressure. You hand your grandmother an egg (a finished masterpiece). "Not enough pepper," she says, and she walks away.

The next course is beef bourguignon. You take an unsalted slice to dear old Granny. "Not sweet enough," she groans, and she leaves the room. "But that's impossible," you think. "There's no sugar in beef bourguignon. I left out the salt." Even so, you go back to the kitchen and prepare mashed potatoes. You use unsalted butter, of course. "She'll love it this time," you think.

"Sour potatoes! Yuck!" Granny says, as she goes to the sink to spit it all out. Because you have a strong ego, you're not insulted by your grandmother's behavior. But you're somewhat confused. Why is she saying such different things about three unsalted recipes? Maybe there are some subtle differences that you don't know about.

Well, the same kind of thing happens when you're writing computer programs. You can make the same kind of mistake twice (or at least, make what you think is the same kind of mistake twice), and get different error messages each time. For example, if you read the earlier stuff in this chapter, you may come to believe that every unrecognized word leads to a `cannot find symbol` message. Well, I'm sorry. It just doesn't work that way.

Take, for example, the word `class` in Listing 5-1. Change the lowercase `c` to an uppercase `C`:

```
//The following line is incorrect:
Class EchoLine {
```

When it sees this line, the compiler doesn't even bother to tell you that it can't find a symbol. The compiler just thinks, "Most programs start with the word `class`, and some start with the word `interface`. This incorrect program starts with a word that I don't understand (because I don't think about the letters `C` and `c` having anything to do with one another). I'll suggest either `class` or `interface`. That should fix it." So the computer sends you the message that's shown in Figure 5-12.

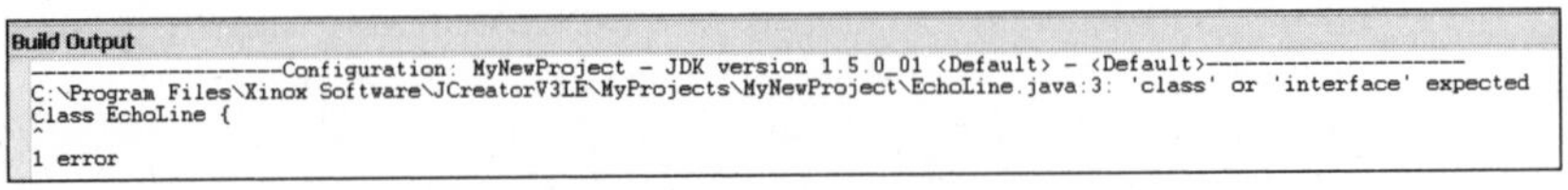

Figure 5-12:
Spelling
"Class"
incorrectly
(with a
capital "C").

```
Build Output
---------------Configuration: MyNewProject - JDK version 1.5.0_01 <Default> - <Default>-----------------
C:\Program Files\Xinox Software\JCreatorV3LE\MyProjects\MyNewProject\EchoLine.java:3: 'class' or 'interface' expected
Class EchoLine {
^
1 error
```

In fact, that fixes it, because a change from `Class` to `class` gets your code running again.

An *interface* is like a class. But unlike a class, an interface can't stand on its own. For instance, you can't put your `static void main` method in a Java interface. None of the programs in this book use interfaces, so don't worry about interfaces until you advance past the beginning programming stage.

Run-time error messages

Up to this point in the chapter, I describe errors that crop up when you compile a program. Another category of errors hides until you run the program. A case in point is the improper capitalization of the word `main`.

Assume that, in a moment of wild abandon, you incorrectly spell `main` with a capital `M`:

```
//The following line is incorrect:
public static void Main(String args[]) {
```

When you compile the code, everything is hunky-dory. You see a friendly `Process completed` message — nothing else.

But then you try to run your program. At this point, the bits hit the fan. The catastrophe is illustrated in Figure 5-13.

Figure 5-13:
Whadaya mean "NoSuch Method Error"?

Sure, your program has something named `Main`, but does it have anything named `main`? (Yes, I've heard of a famous poet named e. e. cummings, but who the heck is E. E. Cummings?) The computer doesn't presume that your word `Main` means the same thing as the expected word `main`. You need to change `Main` back to `main`. Then everything will be okay.

But in the meantime (or in the maintime), how does this improper capitalization make it past the compiler? Why don't you get any error messages when you compile the program? And if a capital `M` doesn't upset the compiler, why does this capital `M` mess everything up at run time?

The answer goes back to the different kinds of words in the Java programming language. As it says in Chapter 4, Java has identifiers and keywords.

The keywords in Java are cast in stone. If you change `class` to `Class`, or change `public` to `Public`, then you get something new — something that the computer probably can't understand. That's why the compiler chokes on improper keyword capitalizations. It's the compiler's job to make sure that all the keywords are used properly.

On the other hand, the identifiers can bounce all over the place. Sure, there's an identifier named `main`, but you can make up a new identifier named `Main`. (You shouldn't do it, though. It's too confusing to people who know Java's usual meaning for the word `main`.) When the compiler sees a mistyped line, like `public static void Main`, the compiler just assumes that you're making up a brand new name. So the compiler lets the line pass. You get no complaints from your old friend, the compiler.

But then, when you try to run the code, the computer goes ballistic. The Java virtual machine always looks for something spelled `main`, with a small `m`. If the JVM doesn't see anything named `main`, then the JVM gets upset. "NoSuch Method . . . main," says the JVM. So now the JVM, and not the compiler, gives you an error message.

What problem? I don't see a problem

I end this chapter on an upbeat note by showing you some of the things you can change in Listing 5-1 without rocking the boat.

The identifiers that you create

If you create an identifier, then that name is up for grabs. For instance, in Listing 5-1, you can change `EchoLine` to `RepeatAfterMe`.

```
class RepeatAfterMe {

    public static void main ... etc.
```

This presents no problem at all, as long as you're willing to be consistent. Just follow most of the steps in this chapter's "Typing and running a program" section.

- ✔ In Step 9, instead of typing **EchoLine**, type **RepeatAfterMe** in the Class Wizard's Name field.
- ✔ In Step 11, when you copy the code from Listing 5-1, don't type

```
class EchoLine {
```

near the top of the listing. Instead, type the words

```
class RepeatAfterMe {
```

Spaces and indentation

Java isn't fussy about the use of spaces and indentation. All you need to do is keep your program well-organized and readable. Here's an example:

```
import java.util.Scanner;

class EchoLine
{

        public static void main( String args[] )
        {
                Scanner myScanner = new Scanner( System.in );
                System.out.println
                        ( myScanner.nextLine() );
        }
}
```

How you choose to do things

A program is like a fingerprint. No two programs look very much alike. Say I discuss a programming problem with a colleague. Then we go our separate ways and write our own programs to solve the same problem. Sure, we're duplicating the effort. But will we create the exact same code? Absolutely not. Everyone has his or her own style, and everyone's style is unique.

I asked fellow Java programmer David Herst to write his own EchoLine program without showing him my code from Listing 5-1. Here's what he wrote:
0
```
import java.io.BufferedReader;
import java.io.InputStreamReader;
import java.io.IOException;

public class EchoLine {
    public static void main(String[] args)
        throws IOException {
        InputStreamReader isr =
          new InputStreamReader(System.in);
        BufferedReader br = new BufferedReader(isr);
        String input = br.readLine();
        System.out.println(input);
    }
}
```

Don't worry about BufferedReader, InputStreamReader, or things like that. Just notice that, like snowflakes, no two programs are written exactly alike, even if they accomplish the same task. That's nice. It means your code, however different, can be as good as the next person's. That's very encouraging.

Chapter 6

Using the Building Blocks: Variables, Values, and Types

*B*ack in 1946, John von Neumann wrote a groundbreaking paper about the newly emerging technology of computers and computing. Among other things, he established one fundamental fact: For all their complexity, the main business of computers is to move data from one place to another. Take a number — the balance in a person's bank account. Move this number from the computer's memory to the computer's processing unit. Add a few dollars to the balance, and then move it back to the computer's memory. The movement of data . . . that's all there is; there ain't no more.

Good enough! This chapter shows you how to move around your data.

Using Variables

Here's an excerpt from a software company's Web site:

SnitSoft recognizes its obligation to the information technology community. For that reason, SnitSoft is making its most popular applications available for a nominal charge. For just $5.95 plus shipping and handling, you receive a CD-ROM containing SnitSoft's premier products.

Go ahead. Click the <u>Order Now!</u> link. Just see what happens. You get an order form with two items on it. One item is labeled $5.95 (CD-ROM), and the other item reads $25.00 (shipping and handling). What a rip-off! Thanks to SnitSoft's generosity, you can pay $30.95 for ten cents worth of software.

Behind the scenes of the SnitSoft Web page, a computer program does some scoundrel's arithmetic. The program looks something like the code in Listing 6-1.

Listing 6-1: **SnitSoft's Grand Scam**

```
class SnitSoft {

    public static void main(String args[]) {
        double amount;

        amount = 5.95;
        amount = amount + 25.00;

        System.out.print("We will bill $");
        System.out.print(amount);
        System.out.println(" to your credit card.");
    }
}
```

When I run the Listing 6-1 code on my own computer (not the SnitSoft computer), I get the output shown in Figure 6-1.

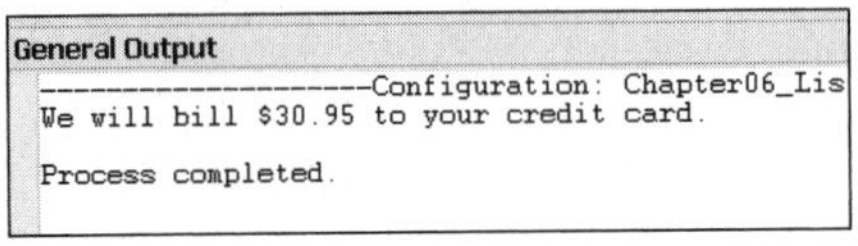

Figure 6-1:
Running the
code from
Listing 6-1.

```
General Output
-------------------Configuration: Chapter06_Lis
We will bill $30.95 to your credit card.

Process completed.
```

Using a variable

The code in Listing 6-1 makes use of a variable named amount. A *variable* is a placeholder. You can stick a number like 5.95 into a variable. After you've placed a number in the variable, you can change your mind and put a different number, like 30.95, into the variable. (That's what varies in a variable.) Of course, when you put a new number in a variable, the old number is no longer there. If you didn't save the old number somewhere else, the old number is gone.

Figure 6-2 gives a before-and-after picture of the code in Listing 6-1. When the computer executes `amount = 5.95`, the variable `amount` has the number 5.95 in it. Then, after the `amount = amount + 25.00` statement is executed, the variable `amount` suddenly has 30.95 in it. When you think about a variable, picture a place in the computer's memory where wires and transistors store 5.95, 30.95, or whatever. In Figure 6-2, imagine that each box is surrounded by millions of other such boxes.

Now you need some terminology. (You can follow along in Figure 6-3.) The thing stored in a variable is called a *value*. A variable's value can change during the run of a program (when SnitSoft adds the shipping and handling cost, for example). The value stored in a variable isn't necessarily a number. (You can, for example, create a variable that always stores a letter.) The kind of value stored in a variable is a variable's *type*. (You can read more about types in the rest of this chapter and in the next two chapters as well.)

There's a subtle, almost unnoticeable difference between a variable and a variable's *name*. Even in formal writing, I often use the word *variable* when I mean *variable name*. Strictly speaking, `amount` is the variable name, and all the memory storage associated with `amount` (including the value and type of `amount`) is the variable itself. If you think this distinction between *variable* and *variable name* is too subtle for you to worry about, join the club.

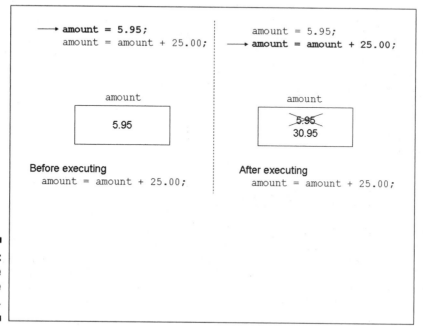

Figure 6-2:
A variable
(before
and after).

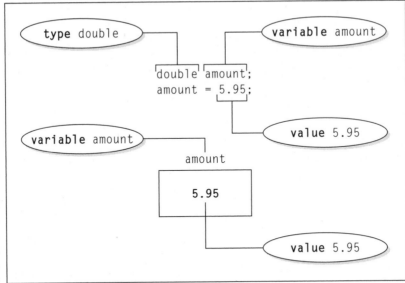

Figure 6-3:
A variable,
its value,
and its type.

Every variable name is an identifier — a name that you can make up in your own code (for more about this, see Chapter 4). In preparing Listing 6-1, I made up the name amount.

Understanding assignment statements

The statements with equal signs in Listing 6-1 are called *assignment statements*. In an assignment statement, you assign a value to something. In many cases, this something is a variable.

You should get into the habit of reading assignment statements from right to left. For example, the first assignment statement in Listing 6-1 says, "Assign 5.95 to the amount variable." The second assignment statement is just a bit more complicated. Reading the second assignment statement from right to left, you get "Add 25.00 to the value that's already in the amount variable and make that number (30.95) be the new value of the amount variable." For a graphic, hit-you-over-the-head illustration of this, see Figure 6-4.

In an assignment statement, the thing being assigned a value is always on the left side of the equal sign.

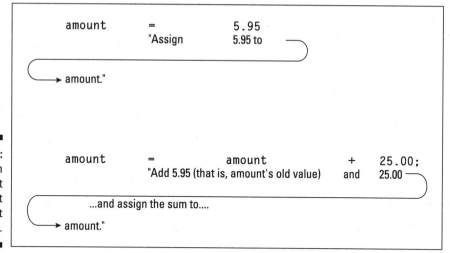

Figure 6-4:
Reading an
assignment
statement
from right
to left.

To wrap or not to wrap?

The last three statements in Listing 6-1 use a neat trick. You want the program to display just one line on the screen, but this line contains three different things:

- ✔ The line starts with We will bill $.
- ✔ The line continues with the amount variable's value.
- ✔ The line ends with to your credit card.

These are three separate things, so you put these things in three separate statements. The first two statements are calls to System.out.print. The last statement is a call to System.out.println.

Calls to System.out.print display text on part of a line and then leave the cursor at the end of the current line. After executing System.out.print, the cursor is still at the end of the same line, so the next System.out.*whatever* can continue printing on that same line. With several calls to print capped off by a single call to println, the result is just one nice-looking line of output, as Figure 6-5 illustrates.

A call to System.out.print writes some things and leaves the cursor sitting at the end of the line of output. A call to System.out.println writes things and then finishes the job by moving the cursor to the start of a brand new line of output.

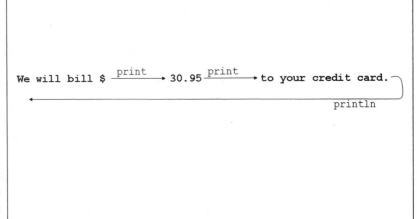

What Do All Those Zeros and Ones Mean?

Here's a word:

gift

The question for discussion is, what does that word mean? Well, it depends on who looks at the word. For example, an English-speaking reader would say that "gift" stands for something one person bestows upon another in a box covered in bright paper and ribbons.

Look! I'm giving you a **gift**!

But in German, the word "gift" means "poison."

Let me give you some **gift**, my dear.

And in Swedish, "gift" can mean either "married" or "poison."

As soon as they got **gift**, she slipped a **gift** into his drink.

Then there's French. In France, there's a candy bar named "Gift."

He came for the holidays, and all he gave me was a bar of **Gift**.

So what do the letters g-i-f-t really mean? Well, they don't mean anything until you decide on a way to interpret them. The same is true of the zeros and ones inside a computer's circuitry.

Take, for example, the sequence 01001010. This sequence can stand for the letter J, but it can also stand for the number 74. That same sequence of zeros and ones can stand for $1.0369608636003646 \times 10^{-43}$. And when interpreted as screen pixels, the same sequence can represent the dots shown in Figure 6-6. The meaning of 01001010 depends entirely on the way the software interprets this sequence.

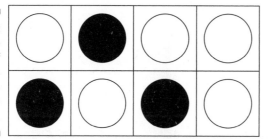

Figure 6-6:
An extreme close-up of eight black-and-white screen pixels.

Types and declarations

How do you tell the computer what 01001010 stands for? The answer is in the concept called *type*. The type of a variable describes the kinds of values that the variable is permitted to store.

In Listing 6-1, look at the first line in the body of the `main` method.

```
double amount;
```

This line is called a *variable declaration*. Putting this line in your program is like saying, "I'm declaring my intention to have a variable named `amount` in my program." This line reserves the name `amount` for your use in the program.

In this variable declaration, the word *double* is a Java keyword. This word `double` tells the computer what kinds of values you intend to store in `amount`. In particular, the word `double` stands for numbers between -1.8×10^{308} and

1.8×10^{308}. That's an enormous range of numbers. Without the fancy ×10 notation, the second of these numbers is

```
1800000000000000000000000000000000000000000000000000000000
0000000000000000000000000000000000000000000000000000000000
0000000000000000000000000000000000000000000000000000000000
0000000000000000000000000000000000000000000000000000000000
0000000000000000000000000000000000000000000000000000000000
0000.0
```

If the folks at SnitSoft ever charge that much for shipping and handling, they can represent the charge with a variable of type `double`.

What's the point?

More important than the humongous range of the `double` keyword's numbers is the fact that a `double` value can have digits to the right of the decimal point. After you declare `amount` to be of type `double`, you can store all sorts of numbers in `amount`. You can store 5.95, 0.02398479, or –3.0. In Listing 6-1, if I hadn't declared `amount` to be of type `double`, then I may not have been able to store 5.95. Instead, I would have had to store plain old 5 or dreary old 6, without any digits beyond the decimal point.

For more info on numbers without decimal points, see Chapter 7.

This paragraph deals with a really picky point, so skip it if you're not in the mood. People often use the phrase "decimal number" to describe a number with digits to the right of the decimal point. The problem is, the syllable "dec" stands for the number ten, so the word "decimal" implies a base-10 representation. Because computers store base-2 (not base-10) representations, the word "decimal" to describe such a number is a misnomer. But in this book, I just can't help myself. I'm calling them "decimal numbers" whether the techies like it or not.

Reading Decimal Numbers from the Keyboard

I don't believe it! SnitSoft is having a sale! For one week only, you can get the SnitSoft CD-ROM for the low price of just $5.75! Better hurry up and order one.

No, wait! Listing 6-1 has the price fixed at $5.95. I have to revise the program.

I know. I'll make the code more versatile. I'll input the amount from the keyboard. Listing 6-2 has the revised code, and Figure 6-7 shows a run of the new code.

Listing 6-2:   Getting a Double Value from the Keyboard

```
import java.util.Scanner;

class VersatileSnitSoft {

    public static void main(String args[]) {
        Scanner myScanner = new Scanner(System.in);
        double amount;

        System.out.print("What's the price of a CD-ROM? ");
        amount = myScanner.nextDouble();
        amount = amount + 25.00;

        System.out.print("We will bill $");
        System.out.print(amount);
        System.out.println(" to your credit card.");
    }
}
```

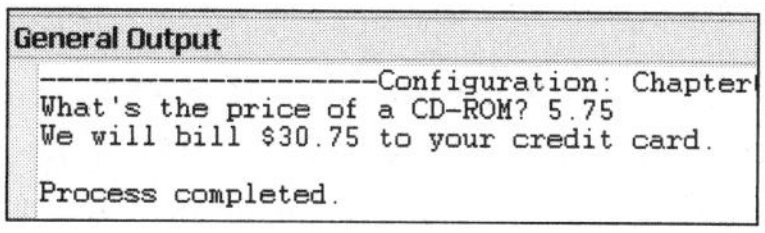

Figure 6-7:
Getting the
value of
a double
variable.

```
General Output
------------------Configuration: Chapter
What's the price of a CD-ROM? 5.75
We will bill $30.75 to your credit card.

Process completed.
```

Though these be methods, yet there is madness in 't

Notice the call to the nextDouble method in Listing 6-2. Back in Listing 5-1, I use nextLine, but here in Listing 6-2, I use nextDouble.

In Java, each type of input requires its own special method. If you're getting a line of text, then nextLine works just fine. But if you're reading stuff from the keyboard, and you want that stuff to be interpreted as a number, you need a method like nextDouble.

To go from Listing 6-1 to Listing 6-2, I added an `import` declaration and some stuff about `new Scanner(System.in)`. You can find out more about these things by reading the section on input and output in Chapter 5. (You can find out even more about input and output by visiting Chapter 13.) And more examples (more `myScanner.nextSomething` methods) are in Chapters 7 and 8.

Who does what, and how?

When you write a program, you're called a *programmer,* but when you run a program, you're called a *user.* So when you test your own code, you're being both the programmer and the user.

Suppose that your program contains a `myScanner.nextSomething()` call, like the calls in Listings 5-1 and 6-2. Then your program gets input from the user. But, when the program runs, how does the user know to type something on the keyboard? If the user and the programmer are the same person, and the program is fairly simple, then knowing what to type is no big deal. For example, when you start running the code in Listing 5-1, you have this book in front of you, and the book says "The computer is waiting for you to type something . . . You type one line of text . . ." So you type the text and press Enter. Everything is fine.

But very few programs come with their own books. In many instances, when a program starts running, the user has to stare at the screen to figure out what to do next. The code in Listing 6-2 works in this stare-at-the-screen scenario. In Listing 6-2, the first call to `print` puts an informative message (`What's the price of a CD-ROM?`) on the user's screen. A message of this kind is called a *prompt.*

When you start writing programs, you can easily confuse the roles of the prompt and the user's input. So remember, no preordained relationship exists between a prompt and the subsequent input. To create a prompt, you call `print` or `println`. Then, to read the user's input, you call `nextLine`, `nextDouble`, or one of the Scanner class's other `nextSomething` methods. These `print` and `next` calls belong in two separate statements. Java has no commonly used, single statement that does both the prompting and the "next-ing."

As the programmer, your job is to combine the prompting and the `next`-ing. You can combine prompting and `next`-ing in all kinds of ways. Some ways are helpful to the user, and some ways aren't.

- ✔ **If you don't have a call to `print` or `println`, then the user sees no prompt.** A blinking cursor sits quietly and waits for the user to type something. The user has to guess what kind of input to type. Occasionally that's okay, but usually it isn't.

- ✔ **If you call `print` or `println`, but you don't call a `myScanner.nextSomething` method, then the computer doesn't wait for the user to type anything.** The program races to execute whatever statement comes immediately after the `print` or `println`.

- ✔ **If your prompt displays a misleading message, then you mislead the user.** Java has no built-in feature that checks the appropriateness of a prompt. That's not surprising. Most computer languages have no prompt-checking feature.

So be careful with your prompts and gets. Be nice to your user. Remember, you were once a humble computer user too.

Methods and assignments

Note how I use `myScanner.nextDouble` in Listing 6-2. The method `myScanner.nextDouble` is called as part of assignment statement. If you look in Chapter 5 at the section on how the EchoLine program works, you see that the computer can substitute something in place of a method call. The computer does this in Listing 6-2. When you type `5.75` on the keyboard, the computer turns

```
amount = myScanner.nextDouble();
```

into

```
amount = 5.75;
```

(The computer doesn't really rewrite the code in Listing 6-2. This `amount = 5.75` line just illustrates the effect of the computer's action.) In the second assignment statement in Listing 6-2, the computer adds 25.00 to the 5.75 that's stored in `amount`.

Some method calls have this substitution effect, and others (like `System.out.println`) don't. To find out more about this, see Chapter 19.

Variations on a Theme

Look back at Listing 6-1. In that listing, it takes two lines to give the `amount` variable its first value:

```
double amount;
amount = 5.95;
```

You can do the same thing with just one line:

```
double amount=5.95;
```

When you do this, you don't say that that you're "assigning" a value to the `amount` variable. The line `double amount=5.95` isn't called an "assignment statement." Instead, this line is called a declaration with an *initialization*. You're *initializing* the `amount` variable. You can do all sorts of things with initializations, even arithmetic.

```
double gasBill  = 174.59;
double elecBill =  84.21;
double H20Bill  =  22.88;
double total    = gasBill + elecBill + H20Bill;
```

Moving variables from place to place

It helps to remember the difference between initializations and assignments. For one thing, you can drag a declaration with its initialization outside of a method.

```
//This is okay:
class SnitSoft {
    static double amount = 5.95;

    public static void main(String args[]) {
        amount = amount + 25.00;

        System.out.print("We will bill $");
        System.out.print(amount);
        System.out.println(" to your credit card.");
    }
}
```

You can't do the same thing with assignment statements. (See the following code and Figure 6-8.)

```
//This does not compile:
class BadSnitSoftCode {
    static double amount;

    amount = 5.95;              //Misplaced statement

    public static void main(String args[]) {
        amount = amount + 25.00;

        System.out.print("We will bill $");
        System.out.print(amount);
        System.out.println(" to your credit card.");
    }
}
```

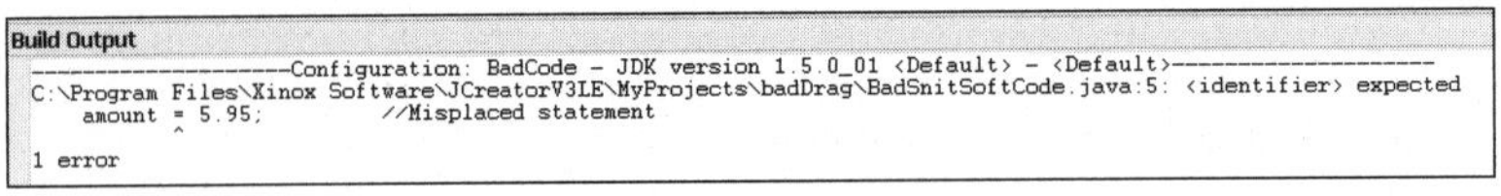

Figure 6-8:
A failed
attempt to
compile
BadSnitSoft
Code.

```
Build Output
            ----------Configuration: BadCode - JDK version 1.5.0_01 <Default> - <Default>----------
C:\Program Files\Xinox Software\JCreatorV3LE\MyProjects\badDrag\BadSnitSoftCode.java:5: <identifier> expected
    amount = 5.95;           //Misplaced statement
           ^
1 error
```

You can't drag statements outside of methods. (Even though a variable declaration ends with a semicolon, a variable declaration isn't considered to be a statement. Go figure!)

The advantage of putting a declaration outside of a method is illustrated in Chapter 19. While you wait impatiently to reach that chapter, notice how I added the word static to each declaration that I pulled out of the main method. I had to do this because the main method's header has the word static in it. Not all methods are static. In fact, most methods aren't static. But, whenever you pull a declaration out of a static method, you have to add the word static at the beginning of the declaration. All the mystery surrounding the word static is resolved in Chapter 18.

Combining variable declarations

The code in Listing 6-1 has only one variable (as if variables are in short supply). You can get the same effect with several variables.

```
class SnitSoftNew {

    public static void main(String args[]) {
        double cdPrice;
        double shippingAndHandling;
        double total;

        cdPrice = 5.95;
        shippingAndHandling = 25.00;
        total = cdPrice + shippingAndHandling;

        System.out.print("We will bill $");
        System.out.print(total);
        System.out.println(" to your credit card.");
    }
}
```

This new code gives you the same output as the code in Listing 6-1. (Refer to Figure 6-1.)

The new code has three declarations — one for each of the program's three variables. Because all three variables have the same type (the type double), I can modify the code and declare all three variables in one fell swoop:

```
double cdPrice, shippingAndHandling, total;
```

So which is better, one declaration or three declarations? Neither is better. It's a matter of personal style.

You can even add initializations to a combined declaration. When you do, each initialization applies to only one variable. For example, with the line

```
double cdPrice, shippingAndHandling = 25.00, total;
```

the value of shippingAndHandling becomes 25.00, but the variables cdPrice and total get no particular value.

Chapter 7

Numbers and Types

In This Chapter

▶ Processing whole numbers

▶ Making new values from old values

▶ Understanding Java's more exotic types

---

*N*ot so long ago, people thought computers did nothing but big, number-crunching calculations. Computers solved arithmetic problems, and that was the end of the story.

In the 1980s, with the widespread use of word-processing programs, the myth of the big metal math brain went by the wayside. But even then, computers made great calculators. After all, computers are very fast and very accurate. Computers never need to count on their fingers. Best of all, computers don't feel burdened when they do arithmetic. I hate ending a meal in a good restaurant by worrying about the tax and tip, but computers don't mind that stuff at all. (Even so, computers seldom go out to eat.)

Using Whole Numbers

Let me tell you, it's no fun being an adult. Right now I have four little kids in my living room. They're all staring at me because I have a bag full of gumballs in my hand. With 30 gumballs in the bag, the kids are all thinking "Who's the best? Who gets more gumballs than the others? And who's going to be treated unfairly?" They insist on a complete, official gumball count, with each kid getting exactly the same number of tasty little treats. I must be careful. If I'm not, then I'll never hear the end of it.

With 30 gumballs and four kids, there's no way to divide the gumballs evenly. Of course, if I get rid of a kid, then I can give ten gumballs to each kid. The trouble is, gumballs are disposable; kids are not. So my only alternative is to divvy up what gumballs I can and dispose of the rest. "Okay, think quick," I say to myself. "With 30 gumballs and four kids, how many gumballs can I promise to each kid?"

I waste no time in programming my computer to figure out this problem for me. When I'm finished, I have the code in Listing 7-1.

Listing 7-1:   How to Keep Four Kids from Throwing Tantrums

```
class KeepingKidsQuiet {

    public static void main(String args[]) {
        int gumballs;
        int kids;
        int gumballsPerKid;

        gumballs = 30;
        kids = 4;
        gumballsPerKid = gumballs / kids;

        System.out.print("Each kid gets ");
        System.out.print(gumballsPerKid);
        System.out.println(" gumballs.");
    }
}
```

A run of the KeepingKidsQuiet program is shown in Figure 7-1. If each kid gets seven gumballs, then the kids can't complain that I'm playing favorites. They'll have to find something else to squabble about.

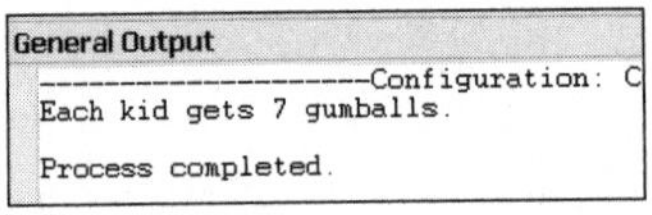

Figure 7-1:
Fair and
square.

```
General Output
-------------------------Configuration: C
Each kid gets 7 gumballs.
Process completed.
```

At the core of the gumball problem, I've got whole numbers — numbers with no digits beyond the decimal point. When I divide 30 by 4, I get 7½, but I can't take the ½ seriously. No matter how hard I try, I can't divide a gumball in half, at least not without hearing "my half is bigger than his half." This fact is reflected nicely in Java. In Listing 7-1, all three variables (gumballs, kids, and gumballsPerKid) are of type int. An int value is a whole number. When you divide one int value by another (as you do with the slash in Listing 7-1), you get another int. When you divide 30 by 4, you get 7 — not 7½. You see this in Figure 7-1. Taken together, the statements

```
gumballsPerKid = gumballs/kids;

System.out.print(gumballsPerKid);
```

put the number 7 on the computer screen.

Reading whole numbers from the keyboard

What a life! Yesterday there were four kids in my living room, and I had 30 gumballs. Today there are six kids in my house, and I have 80 gumballs. How can I cope with all this change? I know! I'll write a program that reads the numbers of gumballs and kids from the keyboard. The program is in Listing 7-2, and a run of the program is shown in Figure 7-2.

Listing 7-2:   A More Versatile Program for Kids and Gumballs

```java
import java.util.Scanner;

class KeepingMoreKidsQuiet {

    public static void main(String args[]) {
        Scanner myScanner = new Scanner(System.in);
        int gumballs;
        int kids;
        int gumballsPerKid;

        System.out.print("How many gumballs? How many kids? ");

        gumballs = myScanner.nextInt();
        kids = myScanner.nextInt();

        gumballsPerKid = gumballs / kids;

        System.out.print("Each kid gets ");
        System.out.print(gumballsPerKid);
        System.out.println(" gumballs.");
    }
}
```

Figure 7-2:
Next thing
you know,
I'll have
seventy
kids and a
thousand
gumballs.

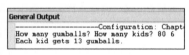

You should notice a couple of things about Listing 7-2. First, you can read an `int` value with the `nextInt` method. Second, you can issue successive calls to `Scanner` methods. In Listing 7-2, I call `nextInt` twice. All I have to do is separate the numbers I type by blank spaces. In Figure 7-2, I put one blank space between my 80 and my 6, but more blank spaces would work as well.

This blank space rule applies to many of the `Scanner` methods. For example, here's some code that reads three numeric values:

```
gumballs = myScanner.nextInt();
costOfGumballs = myScanner.nextDouble();
kids = myScanner.nextInt();
```

Figure 7-3 shows valid input for these three method calls.

Figure 7-3:
Three
numbers
for three
Scanner
method
calls.

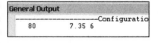

What you read is what you get

When you're writing your own code, you should never take anything for granted. Suppose you accidentally reverse the order of the `gumballs` and `kids` assignment statements in Listing 7-2:

```
//This code is misleading:
System.out.print("How many gumballs? How many kids? ");

kids = myScanner.nextInt();
gumballs = myScanner.nextInt();
```

Then, the line How many gumballs? How many kids? is very misleading. Because the kids assignment statement comes before the gumballs assignment statement, the first number you type becomes the value of kids, and the second number you type becomes the value of gumballs. It doesn't matter that your program displays the message How many gumballs? How many kids?. What matters is the order of the assignment statements in the program.

If the kids assignment statement accidentally comes first, you can get a strange answer, like the zero answer in Figure 7-4. That's how int division works. It just cuts off any remainder. Divide a small number (like 6) by a big number (like 80), and you get 0.

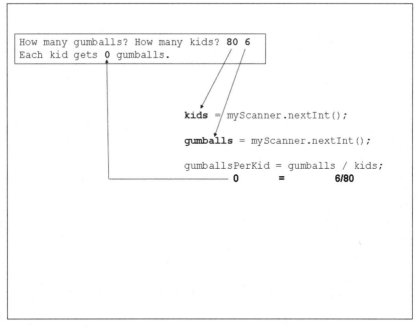

Figure 7-4:
How to make six kids very unhappy.

Creating New Values by Applying Operators

What could be more comforting than your old friend, the plus sign? It was the first thing you learned about in elementary school math. Almost everybody knows how to add two and two. In fact, in English usage, adding two and two is a metaphor for something that's easy to do. Whenever you see a plus sign, one of your brain cells says, "Thank goodness, it could be something much more complicated."

So Java has a plus sign. You can use the plus sign to add two numbers:

```
int apples, oranges, fruit;
apples = 5;
oranges = 16;
fruit = apples + oranges;
```

Of course, the old minus sign is available too:

```
apples = fruit - oranges;
```

Use an asterisk for multiplication, and a forward slash for division:

```
double rate, pay, withholding;
int hours;

rate = 6.25;
hours = 35;
pay = rate * hours;
withholding = pay / 3.0;
```

 When you divide an `int` value by another `int` value, you get an `int` value. The computer doesn't round. Instead, the computer chops off any remainder. If you put `System.out.println(11 / 4)` in your program, the computer prints 2, not 2.75. If you need a decimal answer, make either (or both) of the numbers you're dividing `double` values. For example, if you put `System.out.println(11.0 / 4)` in your program, the computer divides a `double` value, 11.0, by an `int` value, 4. Because at least one of the two values is `double`, the computer prints 2.75.

Finding a remainder

There's a useful arithmetic operator called the *remainder* operator. The symbol for the remainder operator is the percent sign (%). When you put `System.out.println(11 % 4)` in your program, the computer prints 3. It does this because 4 goes into 11 who-cares-how-many times, with a remainder of 3.

The remainder operator turns out to be fairly useful. After all, a remainder is the amount you have left over after you divide two numbers. What if you're making change for $1.38? After dividing 138 by 25, you have 13 cents left over, as shown in Figure 7-5.

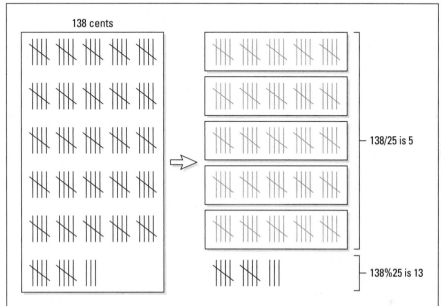

Figure 7-5:
Hey, bud!
Got change
for 138
sticks?

The code in Listing 7-3 makes use of this remainder idea.

Listing 7-3:   Making Change

```
import java.util.Scanner;

class MakeChange {

    public static void main(String args[]) {
        Scanner myScanner = new Scanner(System.in);
        int quarters, dimes, nickels, cents;
        int whatsLeft, total;

System.out.print("How many cents do you have? ");
        total = myScanner.nextInt();

        quarters = total / 25;
        whatsLeft = total % 25;
```

(continued)

Listing 7-3 *(continued)*

```
        dimes = whatsLeft / 10;
        whatsLeft = whatsLeft % 10;

        nickels = whatsLeft / 5;
        whatsLeft = whatsLeft % 5;

        cents = whatsLeft;

        System.out.println();
        System.out.println("From " + total + " cents you get");
        System.out.println(quarters + " quarters");
        System.out.println(dimes + " dimes");
        System.out.println(nickels + " nickels");
        System.out.println(cents + " cents");
    }
}
```

A run of the code in Listing 7-3 is shown in Figure 7-6. You start with a total of 138 cents. The statement

```
quarters = total / 25;
```

divides 138 by 25, giving 5. That means you can make 5 quarters from 138 cents. Next, the statement

```
whatsLeft = total % 25;
```

divides 138 by 25 again, and puts only the remainder, 13, into whatsLeft. Now you're ready for the next step, which is to take as many dimes as you can out of 13 cents.

Figure 7-6:
Change
for $1.38.

```
General Output
-----------------------Configuration:
How many cents do you have? 138

From 138 cents you get
5 quarters
1 dimes
0 nickels
3 cents
```

You keep going like this until you've divided away all the nickels. At that point, the value of whatsLeft is just 3 (meaning 3 cents).

When two or more variables have similar types, you can create the variables with combined declarations. For example, Listing 7-3 has two combined declarations — one for the variables quarters, dimes, nickels, and cents (all of type int); another for the variables whatsLeft and total (both of type int). But to create variables of different types, you need separate declarations. For example, to create an int variable named total and a double variable named amount, you need one declaration int total; and another declaration double amount;.

Listing 7-3 has a call to System.out.println() with nothing in the parentheses. When the computer executes this statement, the cursor jumps to a new line on the screen. (I often use this statement to put a blank line in a program's output.)

The increment and decrement operators

Java has some neat little operators that make life easier (for the computer's processor, for your brain, and for your fingers). Altogether there are four such operators — two increment operators and two decrement operators. The increment operators add one, and the decrement operators subtract one. To see how they work, you need some examples.

Using preincrement

The first example is in Figure 7-7.

```
class AddMoreGumballs {

    public static void main(String args[]) {
        int gumballs=27;

        ++gumballs;
        System.out.println(gumballs);
        System.out.println(++gumballs);
        System.out.println(gumballs);
    }
}
```

gumballs becomes 27

gumballs becomes 28

28 gets displayed

gumballs becomes 29, and 29 gets displayed

29 gets displayed again

Figure 7-7: Using pre-increment.

A run of the program in Figure 7-7 is shown in Figure 7-8. In this horribly uneventful run, the count of gumballs gets displayed three times.

If thine int offends thee, cast it out

The run in Figure 7-6 seems artificial. Why would you start with 138 cents? Why not use the more familiar $1.38? The reason is that the number 1.38 isn't a whole number, and without whole numbers, the remainder operator isn't very useful. For example, the value of `1.38 % 0.25` is `0.1299999999999999`. All those nines are tough to work with.

So if you want to input `1.38`, then the program should take your 1.38 and turn it into 138 cents. The question is, how can you get your program do this?

My first idea is to multiply 1.38 by 100:

```
double amount;
int total;
System.out.print("How much
    money do you have? ");
amount =
    myScanner.nextDouble();
total = amount * 100;    //This
    doesn't quite work.
```

In everyday arithmetic, multiplying by 100 does the trick. But computers are fussy. With a computer, you have to be very careful when you mix `int` values and `double` values. (See the first figure in this sidebar.)

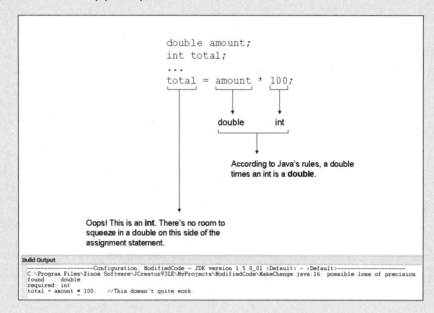

```
double amount;
int total;
...
total = amount * 100;
```

double   int

According to Java's rules, a double times an int is a **double**.

Oops! This is an **int**. There's no room to squeeze in a double on this side of the assignment statement.

Build Output
```
------------Configuration: ModifiedCode - JDK version 1.5.0_01 <Default> - <Default>------------------
C:\Program Files\Xinox Software\JCreatorV3LE\MyProjects\ModifiedCode\MakeChange.java:16: possible loss of precision
found   : double
required: int
total = amount * 100;   //This doesn't quite work.
```

To cram a `double` value into an `int` variable, you need something called *casting*. When you cast a value, you essentially say. "I'm aware that I'm trying to squish a `double` value into an `int` variable. It's a tight fit, but I want to do it anyway."

To do casting, you put the name of a type in parentheses, as follows:

```
total = (int) (amount * 100);
    //This works!
```

This casting notation turns the `double` value 138.00 into the `int` value 138, and everybody's happy. (See the second figure in this sidebar.)

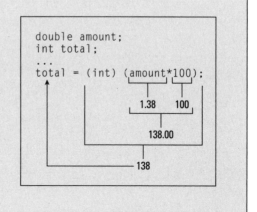

Figure 7-8: A run of the preincrement code (the code in Figure 7-7).

```
General Output
----------------
28
29
29

Process completed.
```

The double plus sign goes under two different names, depending on where you put it. When you put the ++ before a variable, the ++ is called the *preincrement* operator. In the word preincrement, the *pre* stands for *before*. In this setting, the word *before* has two different meanings:

- ✔ You're putting ++ before the variable.

- ✔ The computer adds 1 to the variable's value before the variable gets used in any other part of the statement.

Figure 7-9 has a slow-motion instant replay of the preincrement operator's action. In Figure 7-9, the computer encounters the `System.out.println (++gumballs)` statement. First, the computer adds 1 to `gumballs` (raising the value of `gumballs` to 29). Then the computer executes `System.out.println`, using the new value of `gumballs` (29).

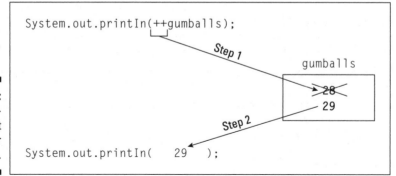

Figure 7-9:
The prein-
crement
operator
in action.

With `System.out.println(++gumballs)`, the computer adds 1 to gumballs *before* printing the new value of `gumballs` on the screen.

Using postincrement

An alternative to preincrement is *postincrement*. With postincrement, the *post*
stands for *after*. The word *after* has two different meanings:

- ✔ You put ++ after the variable.
- ✔ The computer adds 1 to the variable's value after the variable gets used
  in any other part of the statement.

Figure 7-10 has a close-up view of the postincrement operator's action. In Figure 7-10, the computer encounters the `System.out.println(gumballs++)`
statement. First, the computer executes `System.out.println`, using the *old*
value of `gumballs` (28). Then the computer adds 1 to `gumballs` (raising the
value of `gumballs` to 29).

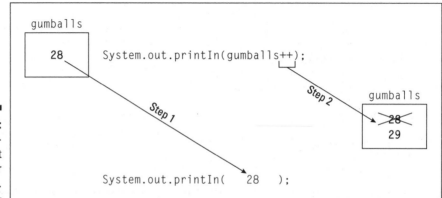

Figure 7-10:
The postin-
crement
operator
in action.

Look at the bold line of code in Figure 7-11. The computer prints the old value of `gumballs` (28) on the screen. Only after printing this old value does the computer add 1 to `gumballs` (raising the `gumballs` value from 28 to 29).

Statements and expressions

Any part of a computer program that has a value is called an *expression*. If you write

```
gumballs = 30;
```

then 30 is an expression (an expression whose value is the quantity 30). If you write

```
amount = 5.95 + 25.00;
```

then `5.95 + 25.00` is an expression (because 5.95 + 25.00 has the value 30.95). If you write

```
gumballsPerKid = gumballs /
    kids;
```

then `gumballs / kids` is an expression. (The value of the expression `gumballs / kids` depends on whatever values the variables `gumballs` and `kids` have when the statement with the expression in it is executed.)

This brings us to the subject of the pre- and postincrement and decrement operators. There are two ways to think about these operators: the way everyone understands it, and the right way. The way I explain it in most of this section (in terms of time, with *before* and *after*) is the way everyone understands the concept. Unfortunately, the way everyone understands the concept isn't really the right way. When you see ++ or --, you can think in terms of time sequence. But occasionally some programmer uses ++ or -- in a convoluted way, and the notions of before and after break down. So if you're ever in a tight spot, you should think about these operators in terms of statements and expressions.

First, remember that a statement tells the computer to do something, and an expression has a value. (Statements are described in Chapter 4, and

expressions are described earlier in this sidebar.) Which category does `gumballs++` belong to? The surprising answer is both. The Java code `gumballs++` is both a statement and an expression.

Suppose that, before executing the code `System.out.println(gumballs++)`, the value of `gumballs` is 28:

✔ As a statement, `gumballs++` tells the computer to add 1 to `gumballs`.

✔ As an expression, the value of `gumballs++` is 28, not 29.

So even though `gumballs` gets 1 added to it, the code `System.out.println(gumballs++)` really means `System.out.println(28)`. (See the figure in this sidebar.)

Now, almost everything you just read about `gumballs++` is true about `++gumballs`. The only difference is, as an expression, `++gumballs` behaves in a more intuitive way. Suppose that, before executing the code `System.out.println(++gumballs)`, the value of `gumballs` is 28:

✔ As a statement, `++gumballs` tells the computer to add 1 to `gumballs`.

✔ As an expression, the value of `++gumballs` is 29.

So with `System.out.println(++gumballs)`, the variable `gumballs` gets 1 added to it, and the code `System.out.println(++gumballs)` really means `System.out.println(29)`.

```
class AddEvenMoreGumballs {

    public static void main(String args[]) {
        int gumballs=27;

        gumballs++;
        System.out.println(gumballs);
        System.out.println(gumballs++);
        System.out.println(gumballs);
    }
}
```

| gumballs becomes 27 |

| gumballs becomes 28 |

| 28 gets displayed |

| 28 gets displayed, **and then** gumballs **becomes 29**. |

| 29 gets displayed |

Figure 7-11: Using postincrement.

With `System.out.println(gumballs++)`, the computer adds 1 to `gumballs` *after* printing the old value that `gumballs` already had.

A run of the code in Figure 7-11 is shown in Figure 7-12. Compare Figure 7-12 with the run in Figure 7-8.

✔ With preincrement in Figure 7-8, the second number that gets displayed is 29.

✔ With postincrement in Figure 7-12, the second number that gets displayed is 28.

In Figure 7-12, the number 29 doesn't show up on the screen until the end of the run, when the computer executes one last `System.out.println (gumballs)`.

Figure 7-12: A run of the postincrement code (the code in Figure 7-11).

```
General Output
-----------------
28
28
29
Process completed.
```

Are you trying to decide between using preincrement or postincrement? Ponder no longer. Most programmers use postincrement. In a typical Java program, you often see things like gumballs++. You seldom see things like ++gumballs.

In addition to preincrement and postincrement, Java has two operators that use --. These operators are called *predecrement* and *postdecrement:*

 ✔ With predecrement (--gumballs), the computer subtracts 1 from the variable's value before the variable gets used in the rest of the statement.

 ✔ With postdecrement (gumballs--), the computer subtracts 1 from the variable's value after the variable gets used in the rest of the statement.

Assignment operators

If you read the previous section — the section about operators that add 1 — you may be wondering if you can manipulate these operators to add 2, or add 5, or add 1000000. Can you write gumballs++++, and still call yourself a Java programmer? Well, you can't. If you try it, then the compiler will give you an error message:

```
unexpected type
required: variable
found   : value
       gumballs++++;
              ^
```

So how can you add values other than 1? As luck would have it, Java has plenty of *assignment operators* you can use. With an assignment operator, you can add, subtract, multiply, or divide by anything you want. You can do other cool operations too.

For example, you can add 1 to the kids variable by writing

```
kids += 1;
```

Is this better than kids++ or kids = kids + 1? No, it's not better. It's just an alternative. But you can add 5 to the kids variable by writing

```
kids += 5;
```

You can't easily add 5 with pre- or postincrement. And what if the kids get stuck in an evil scientist's cloning machine? The statement

```
kids *= 2;
```

multiplies the number of kids by 2.

With the assignment operators, you can add, subtract, multiply, or divide a variable by any number. The number doesn't have to be a literal. You can use a number-valued expression on the right side of the equal sign:

```
double amount = 5.95;
double shippingAndHandling = 25.00, discount = 0.15;

amount += shippingAndHandling;
amount -= discount * 2;
```

The code above adds 25.00 (`shippingAndHandling`) to the value of `amount`. Then, the code subtracts 0.30 (`discount * 2`) from the value of `amount`. How generous!

Size Matters

Here are today's new vocabulary words:

> **foregift** (fore-gift) *n.* A premium that a lessee pays to the lessor upon the taking of a lease.

> **hereinbefore** (here-in-be-fore) *adv.* In a previous part of this document.

Now imagine yourself scanning some compressed text. In this text, all blanks have been removed to conserve storage space. You come upon the following sequence of letters:

> hereinbeforegiftedit

The question is, what do these letters mean? If you knew each word's length, you could answer the question.

> here in be foregift edit

> hereinbefore gifted it

> herein before gift Ed it

A computer faces the same kind of problem. When a computer stores several numbers in memory or on a disk, the computer doesn't put blank spaces between the numbers. So imagine that a small chunk of the computer's memory looks like the stuff in Figure 7-13. (The computer works exclusively with zeros and ones, but Figure 7-13 uses ordinary digits. With ordinary digits, it's easier to see what's going on.)

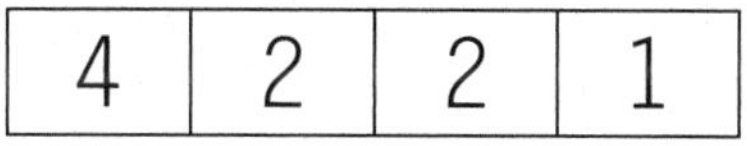

Figure 7-13:
Storing the
digits 4221.

| 4 | 2 | 2 | 1 |

What number or numbers are stored in Figure 7-13? Is it two numbers, 42 and 21? Or is it one number, 4,221? And what about storing four numbers, 4, 2, 2, and 1? It all depends on the amount of space each number consumes.

Imagine a variable that stores the number of paydays in a month. This number never gets bigger than 31. You can represent this small number with just eight zeros and ones. But what about a variable that counts stars in the universe? That number could easily be more than a trillion, and to represent one trillion accurately, you need 64 zeros and ones.

At this point, Java comes to the rescue. Java has four types of whole numbers. Just as in Listing 7-1, I declare

```
int gumballsPerKid;
```

I can also declare

```
byte paydaysInAMonth;
short sickDaysDuringYourEmployment;
long numberOfStars;
```

Each of these types (`byte`, `short`, `int`, and `long`) has its own range of possible values. (See Table 7-1.)

Java has two types of decimal numbers (numbers with digits to the right of the decimal point). Just as in Listing 6-1, I declare

```
double amount;
```

I can also declare

```
float monthlySalary;
```

Given the choice between `double` and `float`, I always choose `double`. A variable of type `double` has a greater possible range of values and much greater accuracy. (See Table 7-1.)

Table 7-1	Java's Primitive Numeric Types
Type Name	*Range of Values*
Whole Number Types	
Byte	−128 to 127
Short	−32768 to 32767
Int	−2147483648 to 2147483647
Long	−9223372036854775808 to 9223372036854775807
Decimal Number Types	
Float	-3.4×10^{38} to 3.4×10^{38}
Double	-1.8×10^{308} to 1.8×10^{308}

Table 7-1 lists six of Java's *primitive* types (also known as *simple* types). Java has only eight primitive types, so only two of Java's primitive types are missing from Table 7-1.

Chapter 8 describes the two remaining primitive types. Chapter 17 introduces types that aren't primitive.

As a beginning programmer, you don't have to choose among the types in Table 7-1. Just use int for whole numbers and double for decimal numbers. If, in your travels, you see something like short or float in someone else's program, just remember the following:

✔ The types byte, short, int, and long represent whole numbers.

✔ The types float and double represent decimal numbers.

Most of the time, that's all you need to know.

Chapter 8

Numbers? Who Needs Numbers?

I don't particularly like fax machines. They're so inefficient. Send a short fax and what do you have? You have two slices of tree — one at the sending end, and another at the receiving end. You also have millions of dots — dots that scan tiny little lines across the printed page. The dots distinguish patches of light from patches of darkness. What a waste!

Compare a fax with an e-mail message. Using e-mail, I can send a 25-word contest entry with just 2500 zeros and ones, and I don't waste any paper. Best of all, an e-mail message doesn't describe light dots and dark dots. An e-mail message contains codes for each of the letters — a short sequence of zeros and ones for the letter A, a different sequence of zeros and ones for the letter B, and so on. What could be simpler?

Now imagine sending a one-word fax. The word is "true," which is understood to mean, "true, I accept your offer to write *Beginning Programming with Java For Dummies,* 2nd Edition." A fax with this message sends a picture of the four letters t-r-u-e, with fuzzy lines where dirt gets on the paper and little white dots where the cartridge runs short on toner.

But really, what's the essence of the "true" message? There are just two possibilities, aren't there? The message could be "true" or "false," and to represent those possibilities, I need very little fanfare. How about 0 for "false" and 1 for "true?"

> They ask, "Do you accept our offer to write *Beginning Programming with Java For Dummies,* 2nd Edition?"
>
> "1," I reply.

Too bad I didn't think of that a few months ago. Anyway, this chapter deals with letters, truth, falsehood, and other such things.

Characters

In Chapters 6 and 7, you store numbers in all your variables. That's fine, but there's more to life than numbers. For example, I wrote this book with a computer, and this book contains thousands and thousands of non-numeric things called *characters*.

The Java type that's used to store characters is *char*. Listing 8-1 has a simple program that uses the `char` type, and a run of the Listing 8-1 program is shown in Figure 8-1.

Listing 8-1:   Using the char Type

```
class LowerToUpper {

    public static void main(String args[]) {
        char smallLetter, bigLetter;

        smallLetter = 'b';
        bigLetter = Character.toUpperCase(smallLetter);
        System.out.println(bigLetter);
    }
}
```

Figure 8-1:
Converting
lower- to
uppercase.

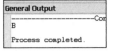

```
General Output
----------------------Con
B
Process completed.
```

In Listing 8-1, the first assignment statement stores the letter b in the `smallLetter` variable. In that statement, notice how b is surrounded by single quote marks. In a Java program, every `char` literal starts and ends with a single quote mark.

When you surround a letter with quote marks, you tell the computer that the letter isn't a variable name. For example, in Listing 8-1, the incorrect statement `smallLetter = b` would tell the computer to look for a variable named b. Because there's no variable named b, you'd get a `cannot find symbol` message.

In the second assignment statement of Listing 8-1, the program calls an API method whose name is `Character.toUpperCase`. The method `Character.toUpperCase` does what its name suggests — the method produces the uppercase equivalent of a lowercase letter. In Listing 8-1, this uppercase equivalent (the letter B) is assigned to the variable `bigLetter`, and the B that's in `bigLetter` is printed on the screen, as illustrated in Figure 8-2.

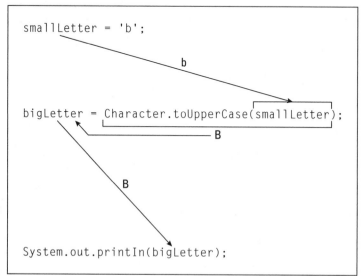

Figure 8-2:
The action in
Listing 8-1.

When the computer displays a `char` value on the screen, the computer does not surround the character with single quote marks.

I digress . . .

A while ago, I wondered what would happen if I called the `Character.to UpperCase` method and fed the method a character that isn't lowercase to begin with. I yanked out the Java API documentation, but I found no useful information. The documentation said that `toUpperCase` "converts the character argument to uppercase using case mapping information from the UnicodeData file." Thanks, but that's not useful to me.

Silly as it seems, I asked myself what I'd do if I were the `toUpperCase` method. What would I say if someone handed me a capital R and told me to capitalize that letter? I'd say, "Take back your stinking capital R." In the lingo of computing, I'd send that person an error message. So I wondered if I'd get an error message when I applied `Character.toUpperCase` to the letter R.

I tried it. I cooked up the experiment in Listing 8-2.

Listing 8-2:   Investigating the Behavior of toUpperCase

```
class MyExperiment {

    public static void main(String args[]) {
        char smallLetter, bigLetter;

        smallLetter = 'R';
        bigLetter = Character.toUpperCase(smallLetter);
        System.out.println(bigLetter);

        smallLetter = '3';
        bigLetter = Character.toUpperCase(smallLetter);
        System.out.println(bigLetter);
    }
}
```

In my experiment, I didn't mix chemicals and blow things up. Here's what I did instead:

✔ **I assigned** `'R'` **to** `smallLetter`.

The `toUpperCase` method took the uppercase R and gave me back another uppercase R. (See Figure 8-3.) I got no error message. This told me what the `toUpperCase` method does with a letter that's already uppercase. The method does nothing.

✔ **I assigned** `'3'` **to** `smallLetter`.

The `toUpperCase` method took the digit 3 and gave me back the same digit 3. (See Figure 8-3.) I got no error message. This told me what the `toUpperCase` method does with a character that's not a letter. It does nothing, zip, zilch, bupkis.

Figure 8-3:
Running
the code in
Listing 8-2.

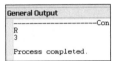

```
General Output
-------------------------Con
R
3
Process completed.
```

I write about this experiment to make an important point. When you don't understand something about computer programming, it often helps to write a test program. Make up an experiment and see how the computer responds.

I guessed that handing a capital R to the `toUpperCase` method would give me an error message, but I was wrong. See? The answers to questions aren't handed down from heaven. The people who created the Java API made decisions. They made some obvious choices, and but they also made some unexpected choices. No one knows everything about Java's features, so don't expect to cram all the answers into your head.

The Java documentation is great, but for every question that the documentation answers, it ignores three other questions. So be bold. Don't be afraid to tinker. Write lots of short, experimental programs. You can't break the computer, so play tough with it. Your inquisitive spirit will always pay off.

Reading and understanding Java's API documentation is an art, not a science. For advice on making the most of these docs, take a look at the Appendix on this book's web site.

One character only, please

A `char` variable stores only one character. So if you're tempted to write the following statements

```
char smallLetters;
smallLetters = 'barry';   //Don't do this
```

please resist the temptation. You can't store more than one letter at a time in a `char` variable, and you can't put more than one letter between a pair of single quotes. If you're trying to store words or sentences (not just single letters), then you need to use something called a *String*. For a look at Java's `String` type, see Chapter 18.

Variables and recycling

In Listing 8-2, I use `smallLetter` twice and I use `bigLetter` twice. That's why they call these things *variables*. First the value of `smallLetter` is R. Later, I vary the value of `smallLetter` so that the value of `smallLetter` becomes 3.

When I assign a new value to `smallLetter`, the old value of `smallLetter` gets obliterated. For example, in Figure 8-4, the second `smallLetter` assignment puts 3 into `smallLetter`. When the computer executes this second assignment statement, the old value R is gone.

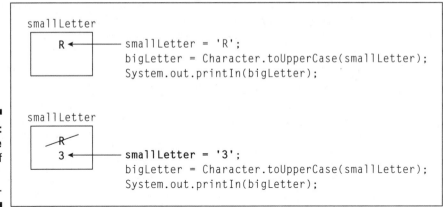

Figure 8-4:
Varying the
value of
small
Letter.

Is that okay? Can you afford to forget the value that smallLetter once had?
Yes, in Listing 8-2, it's okay. After you've assigned a value to bigLetter with
the statement

```
bigLetter = Character.toUpperCase(smallLetter);
```

you can forget all about the existing smallLetter value. You don't need to
do this:

```
// This code is cumbersome.
// The extra variables are unnecessary.
char smallLetter1, bigLetter1;
char smallLetter2, bigLetter2;

smallLetter1 = 'R';
bigLetter1 = Character.toUpperCase(smallLetter1);
System.out.println(bigLetter1);

smallLetter2 = '3';
bigLetter2 = Character.toUpperCase(smallLetter2);
System.out.println(bigLetter2);
```

You don't need to store the old and new values in separate variables. Instead,
you can reuse the variables smallLetter and bigLetter as in Listing 8-2.

This reuse of variables doesn't save you from a lot of extra typing. It doesn't
save much memory space either. But reusing variables keeps the program
uncluttered. When you look at Listing 8-2, you can see at a glance that the
code has two parts, and you see that both parts do roughly the same thing.

The code in Listing 8-2 is simple and manageable. In such a small program, simplicity and manageability don't matter very much. But in a large program, it helps to think carefully about the use of each variable.

When not to reuse a variable

The previous section discusses the reuse of variables to make a program slick and easy to read. This section shows you the flip side. In this section, the problem at hand forces you to create new variables.

Suppose you're writing code to reverse the letters in a four-letter word. You store each letter in its own separate variable. Listing 8-3 shows the code, and Figure 8-5 shows the code in action.

Listing 8-3:   Making a Word Go Backwards

```java
import java.util.Scanner;

class ReverseWord {

    public static void main(String args[]) {
        Scanner myScanner = new Scanner(System.in);
        char c1, c2, c3, c4;

        c1 = myScanner.findInLine(".").charAt(0);
        c2 = myScanner.findInLine(".").charAt(0);
        c3 = myScanner.findInLine(".").charAt(0);
        c4 = myScanner.findInLine(".").charAt(0);

        System.out.print(c4);
        System.out.print(c3);
        System.out.print(c2);
        System.out.print(c1);
        System.out.println();
    }
}
```

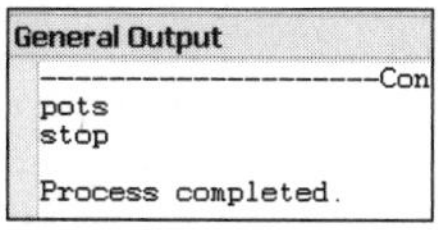

Figure 8-5:
Stop those
pots!

```
General Output
---------------------Con
pots
stop

Process completed.
```

The trick in Listing 8-3 is as follows:

- ✔ Assign values to variables c1, c2, c3, and c4 in that order.
- ✔ Display these variables' values on the screen in reverse order: c4, c3, c2, and then c1, as illustrated in Figure 8-6.

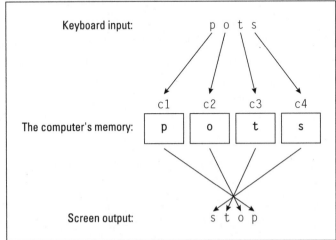

Figure 8-6:
Using four
variables.

If you don't use four separate variables, then you don't get the result that you want. For example, imagine that you store characters in only one variable. You run the program and type the word pots. When it's time to display the word in reverse, the computer remembers the final s in the word pots. But the computer doesn't remember the p, the o, or the t, as shown in Figure 8-7.

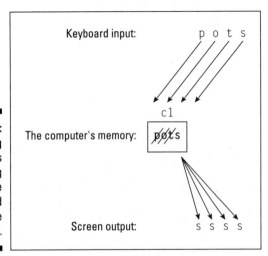

Figure 8-7:
Getting
things
wrong
because
you used
only one
variable.

I wish I could give you twelve simple rules to help you decide when and when not to reuse variables. The problem is, I can't. It all depends on what you're trying to accomplish. So how do you figure out on your own when and when not to reuse variables? Like the guy says to the fellow who asks how to get to Carnegie Hall, "Practice, practice, practice."

Reading characters

The people who created Java's `Scanner` class didn't create a `next` method for reading a single character. So to input a single character, I paste two Java API methods together. I use the `findInLine` and `charAt` methods.

What's behind all this `findInLine(".")`. `charAt(0)` nonsense?

Without wallowing in too much detail, here's how the `findInLine(".").charAt(0)` technique works:

Java's `findInLine` method looks for things in a line of input. The things the method finds depend on the stuff you put in parentheses. For example, a call to `findInLine("\\d\\d\\d")` looks for a group consisting of three digits. With the following line of code

```
System.out.println(myScanner.fi
    ndInLine("\\d\\d\\d"));
```

I can type

```
Testing 123 Testing Testing
```

and the computer responds by displaying

```
123
```

In the call `findInLine("\\d\\d\\d")`, each \\d stands for a single digit. This \\d business is one of many abbreviations in special code called *regular expressions*.

Now here's something strange. In the world of regular expressions, a dot stands for any character at all. (That is, a dot stands for "any character,

not necessarily a dot.") So `findInLine(".")` tells the computer to find the next character of any kind that the user types on the keyboard. When you're trying to input a single character, `findInLine(".")` is mighty useful.

But wait! To grab a single character from the keyboard, I call `findInLine(".").charAt(0)`. What's the role of `charAt(0)` in reading a single character? Unfortunately, any `findInLine` call behaves as if it's finding a bunch of characters, not just a single character. Even when you call `findInLine(".")`, and the computer fetches just one letter from the keyboard, the Java program treats that letter as one of possibly many input characters.

The call to `charAt(0)` takes care of the multi-character problem. This `charAt(0)` call tells Java to pick the initial character from any of the characters that `findInLine` fetches.

Yes, it's complicated. And yes, I don't like having to explain it. But no, you don't have to understand any of the details in this sidebar. Just read the details if you want to read them, and skip the details if you don't care.

Table 5-1 in Chapter 5 introduces this `findInLine(".").charAt(0)` technique for reading a single input character, and Listing 8-3 uses the technique to read one character at a time. (In fact, Listing 8-3 uses the technique four times to read four individual characters.)

Notice the format for the input in Figure 8-5. To enter the characters in the word `pots`, I type four letters, one after another, with no blank spaces between the letters and no quote marks. The `findInLine(".").charAt(0)` technique works that way, but don't blame me or my technique. Other developers' character reading methods work the same way. No matter whose methods you use, reading a character differs from reading a number. Here's how:

✔ **With methods like** `nextDouble` **and** `nextInt`, **you type blank spaces between numbers.**

If I type **80 6**, then two calls to `nextInt` read the number 80, followed by the number 6. If I type **806**, then a single call to `nextInt` reads the number 806 (eight hundred six), as illustrated in Figure 8-8.

✔ **With** `findInLine(".").charAt(0)`, **you don't type blank spaces between characters.**

If I type **po**, then two successive calls to `findInLine(".").charAt(0)` read the letter p, followed by the letter o. If I type **p o**, then two calls to `findInLine(".").charAt(0)` read the letter p, followed by a blank space character. (Yes, the blank space is a character!) Again, see Figure 8-8.

```
firstInt = myScanner.nextInt();
secondInt = myScanner.nextInt();          80  6


onlyInt = myScanner.nextInt();            806


firstChar = myScanner.findInLine(".").charAt(0);
secondChar = myScanner.findInLine(".").charAt(0);   po


firstChar = myScanner.findInLine(".").charAt(0);
secondChar = myScanner.findInLine(".").charAt(0);   p o
```

Figure 8-8:
Reading
numbers and
characters.

To represent a lone character in the text of a computer program, you surround the character with single quote marks. But, when you type a character as part of a program's input, you don't surround the character with quote marks.

Suppose that your program calls `nextInt`, and then `findInLine(".")`. `charAt(0)`. If you type **80x** on the keyboard, you get an error message. (The message says `InputMismatchException`. The `nextInt` method expects you to type a blank space after each `int` value.) Now what happens if, instead of typing **80x**, you type **80 x** on the keyboard? Then the program gets 80 for the `int` value, followed by a blank space for the character value. For the program to get the x, the program has to call `findInLine(".").charAt(0)` one more time. It seems wasteful, but it makes sense in the long run.

The boolean Type

I'm in big trouble. I have 140 gumballs, and 15 kids are running around and screaming in my living room. They're screaming because each kid wants 10 gumballs, and they're running because that's what kids do in a crowded living room. I need a program that tells me if I can give 10 gumballs to each kid.

I need a variable of type *boolean*. A `boolean` variable stores one of two values — `true` or `false` (true, I can give 10 gumballs to each kid; or `false`, I can't give 10 gumballs to each kid). Anyway, the kids are going berserk, so I've written a short program and put it in Listing 8-4. The output of the program is shown in Figure 8-9.

Listing 8-4:   Using the boolean Type

```
class CanIKeepKidsQuiet {

    public static void main(String args[]) {
        int gumballs;
        int kids;
        int gumballsPerKid;
        boolean eachKidGetsTen;

        gumballs = 140;
        kids = 15;
        gumballsPerKid = gumballs / kids;

        System.out.print("True or false? ");
        System.out.println("Each kid gets 10 gumballs.");
        eachKidGetsTen = gumballsPerKid >= 10;
        System.out.println(eachKidGetsTen);
    }
}
```

Figure 8-9:
Oh, no!

```
General Output
----------------Configuration: Chapter
True or false? Each kid gets 10 gumballs.
false
```

In Listing 8-4, the variable eachKidGetsTen is of type boolean. So the value stored in the eachKidGetsTen variable can be either true or false. (I can't store a number or a character in the eachKidGetsTen variable.)

To find a value for the variable eachKidGetsTen, the program checks to see if gumballsPerKid is greater than or equal to ten. (The symbols >= stand for "greater than or equal to." What a pity! There's no _ key on the standard computer keyboard.) Because gumballsPerKid is only nine, gumballsPerKid _ 10 is false. So eachKidGetsTen becomes false. Yikes! The kids will tear the house apart! (Before they do, take a look at Figure 8-10.)

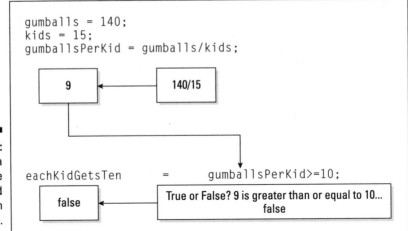

Figure 8-10:
Assigning a
value to the
eachKid
GetsTen
variable.

Expressions and conditions

In Listing 8-4, the code gumballsPerKid >= 10 is an expression. The expression's value depends on the value stored in the variable gumballsPerKid. On a bad day, the value of gumballsPerKid >= 10 is false. So the variable eachKidGetsTen is assigned the value false.

An expression like gumballsPerKid >= 10, whose value is either true or false, is sometimes called a *condition*.

Values like `true` and `false` may look as if they contain characters, but they really don't. Internally, the Java Virtual Machine doesn't store `boolean` values with the letters t-r-u-e or f-a-l-s-e. Instead, the JVM stores codes, like 0 for false and 1 for true. When the computer displays a `boolean` value (as in `System.out.println(eachKidGetsTen)`), the Java virtual machine converts a code like 0 into the five-letter word `false`.

Comparing numbers; comparing characters

In Listing 8-4, I compare a variable's value with the number 10. I use the >= operator in the expression

```
gumballsPerKid >= 10
```

Of course, the greater-than-or-equal comparison gets you only so far. Table 8-1 shows you the operators you can use to compare things with one another.

Table 8-1		Comparison Operators
Operator Symbol	**Meaning**	**Example**
==	is equal to	`yourGuess == winningNumber`
!=	is not equal to	`5 != numberOfCows`
<	is less than	`strikes < 3`
>	is greater than	`numberOfBoxtops > 1000`
<=	is less than or equal to	`numberOfCows + numberOfBulls <= 5`
>=	is greater than or equal to	`gumballsPerKid >= 10`

With the operators in Table 8-1, you can compare both numbers and characters.

Notice the double equal sign in the first row of Table 8-1. Don't try to use a single equal sign to compare two values. The expression `yourGuess = winningNumber` (with a single equal sign) doesn't compare `yourGuess` with `winningNumber`. Instead `yourGuess = winningNumber` changes the value of `yourGuess`. (It assigns the value of `winningNumber` to the variable `yourGuess`.)

You can compare other things (besides numbers and characters) with the == and != operators. But when you do, you have to be careful. For more information, see Chapter 18.

Comparing numbers

Nothing is more humdrum than comparing numbers. "True or false? Five is greater than or equal to ten." False. Five is neither greater than nor equal to ten. See what I mean? Bo-ring.

Comparing whole numbers is an open-and-shut case. But unfortunately, when you compare decimal numbers, there's a wrinkle. Take a program for converting from Celsius to Fahrenheit. Wait! Don't take just any such program; take the program in Listing 8-5.

Listing 8-5:   It's Warm and Cozy in Here

```
import java.util.Scanner;

class CelsiusToFahrenheit {

    public static void main(String args[]) {
        Scanner myScanner = new Scanner(System.in);
        double celsius, fahrenheit;

        System.out.print("Enter the Celsius temperature: ");
        celsius = myScanner.nextDouble();

        fahrenheit = 9.0 / 5.0 * celsius + 32.0;

        System.out.print("Room temperature? ");
        System.out.println(fahrenheit == 69.8);
    }
}
```

If you run the code in Listing 8-5 and input the number 21, the computer finds the value of `9.0 / 5.0 * 21 + 32.0`. Believe it or not, you want to check the computer's answer. (Who knows? Maybe the computer gets it wrong!) You need to do some arithmetic, but please don't reach for your calculator. A calculator is just a small computer, and machines of that kind stick up for one another. To check the computer's work, you need to do the arithmetic by hand. What? You say you're math phobic? Well, don't worry. I've done all the math in Figure 8-11.

If you do the arithmetic by hand, then the value you get for `9.0 / 5.0 * 21 + 32.0` is exactly 69.8. So run the code in Listing 8-5, and give `celsius` the value 21. You should get `true` when you display the value of `fahrenheit == 69.8`, right?

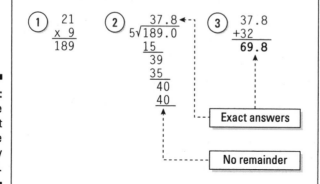

Figure 8-11:
The Fahrenheit temperature is exactly 69.8.

Well, no. Take a look at the run in Figure 8-12. When the computer evaluates `fahrenheit == 69.8`, the value turns out to be `false`, not `true`. What's going on here?

Figure 8-12:
A run of the code in Listing 8-5.

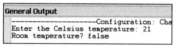

```
General Output
------------------------------Configuration: Cha
Enter the Celsius temperature: 21
Room temperature? false
```

A little detective work can go a long way. So review the facts:

> ✓ **Fact:** The value of `fahrenheit` should be exactly 69.8.
>
> ✓ **Fact:** If `fahrenheit` is 69.8, then `fahrenheit == 69.8` is `true`.
>
> ✓ **Fact:** In Figure 8-12, the computer displays the word `false`. So the expression `fahrenheit == 69.8` isn't `true`.

How do you reconcile these facts? There can be little doubt that `fahrenheit == 69.8` is `false`, so what does that say about the value of `fahrenheit`? Nowhere in Listing 8-5 is the value of `fahrenheit` displayed. Could that be the problem?

At this point, I use a popular programmer's trick. I add statements to display the value of `fahrenheit`.

```
fahrenheit = 9.0 / 5.0 * celsius + 32.0;
System.out.print("fahrenheit: ");     //Added
System.out.println(fahrenheit);       //Added
```

Automated debugging

If your program isn't working correctly, you can try something called a *debugger*. A debugger automatically adds invisible `print` and `println` calls to your suspicious code. In fact, debuggers have all kinds of features to help you diagnose problems. For example, a debugger can pause a run of your program and accept special commands to display variables' values. With some debuggers, you can pause a run and change a variable's value (just to see if things go better when you do).

The debugger *jdb* comes with the free JDK download from Sun Microsystems. The only problem is, jdb is entirely text-based. When you use jdb, you leave your mouse behind. Instead of clicking your mouse, you debug a program by typing commands.

Of course, typing commands can be tedious. So some integrated development environments enhance jdb with additional graphical tools. For example, the Pro version of JCreator provides menus for issuing jdb commands. (See the figure.)

In this book, I don't promote the use of an automated debugger. But for any large programming project, automated debugging is an essential tool. So if you plan to write bigger and better programs, please give jdb a try. To get started, visit `www.jcreator.com` and download JCreator Pro.

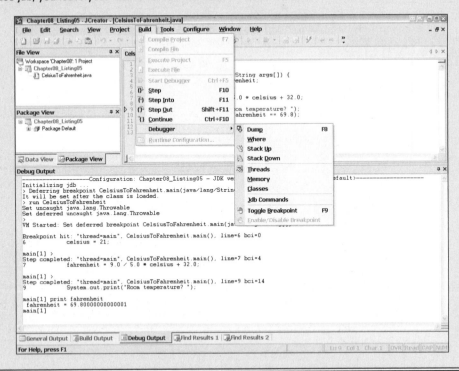

A run of the enhanced code is shown in Figure 8-13. As you can see, the computer misses its mark. Instead of the expected value 69.8, the computer's value for `9.0 / 5.0 * 21 + 32.0` is 69.80000000000001. That's just the way the cookie crumbles. The computer does all its arithmetic with zeros and ones, so the computer's arithmetic doesn't look like the base-10 arithmetic in Figure 8-11. The computer's answer isn't wrong. The answer is just slightly inaccurate.

Figure 8-13:
The
Fahrenheit
variable's
full value.

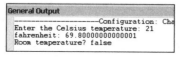

```
General Output
------------------------Configuration: Cha
Enter the Celsius temperature: 21
fahrenheit: 69.80000000000001
Room temperature? false
```

So be careful when you compare two numbers for equality (with ==) or for inequality (with !=). When you compare two `double` values, the values are almost never dead-on equal to one another.

If your program isn't doing what you think it should do, then check your suspicions about the values of variables. Add `print` and `println` statements to your code.

Comparing characters

The comparison operators in Table 8-1 work overtime for characters. Roughly speaking, the operator < means "comes earlier in the alphabet." But you have to be careful of the following:

✔ Because B comes alphabetically before H, the condition `'B' < 'H'` is true. That's not surprising.

✔ Because b comes alphabetically before h, the condition `'b' < 'h'` is true. That's no surprise either.

✔ Every uppercase letter comes before any of the lowercase letters, so the condition `'b' < 'H'` is *false*. Now that's a surprise. (See Figure 8-14.)

In practice, you seldom have reason to compare one letter with another. But in Chapter 18, you can read about Java's `String` type. With the `String` type, you can compare words, names, and other good stuff. At that point, you have to think carefully about alphabetical ordering, and the ideas in Figure 8-14 come in handy.

Figure 8-14:
The ordering
of the letters.

ABCDEFGHIJKLMNOPQRSTUVWXYZabcdefghijklmnopqrstuvwxyz
lesser ⟵―――――――――――――――――――――――――――⟶ greater

Under the hood, the letters A through Z are stored with numeric codes 65 through 90. The letters a through z are stored with codes 97 through 122. That's why each uppercase letter is "less than" any of the lowercase letters.

The Remaining Primitive Types

In Chapter 7, I tell you that Java has eight primitive types, but Table 7-1 lists only six out of eight types. Table 8-2 describes the remaining two types — the types char and boolean. Table 8-2 isn't too exciting, but I can't just leave you with the incomplete story in Table 7-1.

Table 8-2	Java's Primitive Non-numeric Types
Type Name	*Range of Values*
Character Type	
char	Thousands of characters, glyphs, and symbols
Logical Type	
boolean	Only true or false

If you dissect parts of the Java virtual machine, you find that Java considers char to be a numeric type. That's because Java represents characters with something called *Unicode* — an international standard for representing alphabets of the world's many languages. For example the Unicode representation of an uppercase letter C is 67. The representation of a Hebrew letter aleph is 1488. And (to take a more obscure example) the representation for the voiced retroflex approximant in phonetics is 635. But don't worry about all this. The only reason I'm writing about the char type's being numeric is to save face among my techie friends.

Part III
Controlling the Flow

In this part . . .

A computer program is like a role-playing video game. It's not the kind of game that involves shooting, punching, or racing. It's a game that involves strategies. Find the golden ring to open the secret passageway. Save the princess by reciting the magic words. It's that sort of thing.

So in this part of the book, you create passageways. As your program weaves its way from one virtual room to another, the computer gets closer and closer to the solution of an important problem.

Hey, admit it. This sounds like fun!

Chapter 9

Forks in the Road

. . . .

In This Chapter

▶ Writing statements that choose between alternatives

▶ Putting statements inside one another

▶ Writing several kinds of decision making statements

. . . .

Here's an excerpt from *Beginning Programming with Java For Dummies,* 2nd Edition, Chapter 2:

> **If your computer already has a Java 5.0 compiler,** you can skip the next section's steps.*

The excerpt illustrates two important points: First, you may not have to follow some of the steps in Chapter 2. Second, your choice of action can depend on something being true or false.

> **If it's true** that your computer already has a Java 5.0 compiler, skip certain steps in Chapter 2.

So picture yourself walking along a quiet country road. You're enjoying a pleasant summer day. It's not too hot, and a gentle breeze from the north makes you feel fresh and alert. You're holding a copy of this book, opened to the start of Chapter 2. You read the paragraph about having a Java 5.0 compiler, and then you look up.

You see a fork in the road. You see two signs — one pointing to the right; the other pointing to the left. One sign reads, "Have a Java 5.0 compiler? True." The other sign reads, "Have a Java 5.0 compiler? False." You evaluate the compiler situation and march on, veering right or left depending on your software situation. A diagram of this story is shown in Figure 9-1.

---

* This excerpt is reprinted with permission from Wiley Publishing, Inc. If you can't find a copy of Beginning Programming with Java For Dummies, 2nd Edition in your local bookstore, visit www. wiley.com.

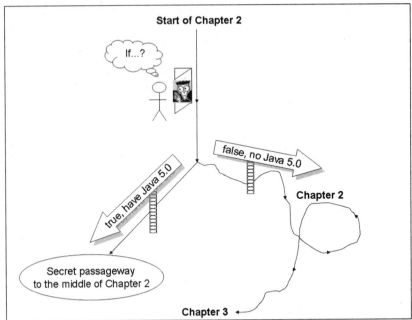

Figure 9-1:
Which way
to go?

Life is filled with forks in the road. Take an ordinary set of directions for heating up a frozen snack:

✔ **Microwave cooking directions:**

> Place on microwave safe plate.

> Microwave on high for 2 minutes.

> Turn product.

> Microwave on high for 2 more minutes.

✔ **Conventional oven directions:**

> Preheat oven to 350 degrees.

> Place product on baking sheet.

> Bake for 25 minutes.

Again, you choose between alternatives. If you use a microwave oven, do this. Otherwise, do that.

In fact, it's hard to imagine useful instructions that don't involve choices. If you're a homeowner with two dependents earning more than $30,000 per year, check here. If you don't remember how to use curly braces in Java programs, see Chapter 4. Did the user correctly type his or her password? If yes, then let the user log in; if no, then kick the bum out. If you think the market will go up, then buy stocks; otherwise, buy bonds. And if you buy stocks, which should you buy? And when should you sell?

This chapter deals with decision-making, which plays a fundamental role in the creation of instructions. With the material in this chapter, you expand your programming power by leaps and bounds.

Making Decisions (Java if Statements)

When you work with computer programs, you make one decision after another. Almost every programming language has a way of branching in one of two directions. In Java (and in many other languages) the branching feature is called an *if statement*. Check out Listing 9-1 to see an if statement.

Listing 9-1:   An if Statement

```
if (randomNumber > 5) {
    System.out.println("Yes. Isn't it obvious?");
} else {
    System.out.println("No, and don't ask again.");
}
```

The if statement in Listing 9-1 represents a branch, a decision, two alternative courses of action. In plain English, this statement has the following meaning:

```
If the randomNumber variable's value is greater than 5,
    display "Yes. Isn't it obvious?" on the screen.
Otherwise,
    display "No, and don't ask again." on the screen.
```

Pictorially, you get the fork shown in Figure 9-2.

Looking carefully at if statements

An if statement can take the following form:

```
if (Condition) {
    SomeStatements
} else {
    OtherStatements
}
```

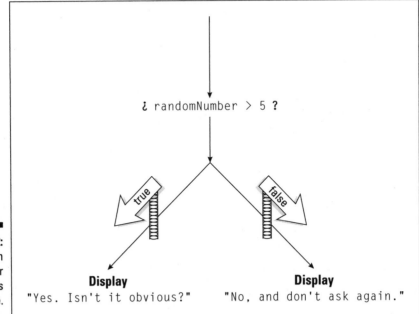

Figure 9-2:
A random
number
decides
your fate.

To get a real-life if statement, substitute meaningful text for the three place-holders `Condition`, `SomeStatements`, and `OtherStatements`. Here's how I make the substitutions in Listing 9-1:

- ✔ I substitute `randomNumber > 5` for `Condition`.
- ✔ I substitute `System.out.println("Yes. Isn't it obvious?");` for `SomeStatements`.
- ✔ I substitute `System.out.println("No, and don't ask again.");` for `OtherStatements`.

The substitutions are illustrated in Figure 9-3.

Sometimes I need alternate names for parts of an if statement. I call them the *if clause* and the *else clause*.

```
if (Condition) {
    if clause
} else {
    else clause
}
```

An if statement is an example of a *compound statement* — a statement that includes other statements within it. The if statement in Listing 9-1 includes two println calls and these calls to println are statements.

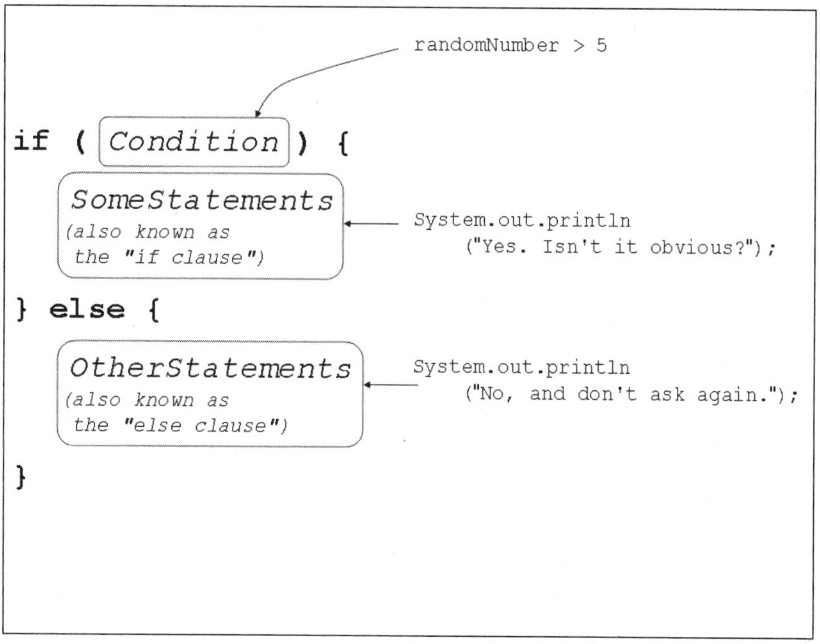

```
                                      randomNumber > 5

   if ( [Condition] ) {

         [SomeStatements
          (also known as         ◄───  System.out.println
          the "if clause")                 ("Yes. Isn't it obvious?");

   } else {

         [OtherStatements        ◄───  System.out.println
          (also known as                   ("No, and don't ask again.");
          the "else clause")

   }
```

Figure 9-3:
An if
statement
and its
format.

Notice how I use parentheses and semicolons in the if statement of Listing 9-1. In particular, notice the following:

- ✔ The condition must be in parentheses.
- ✔ Statements inside the if clause end with semicolons. So do statements inside the else clause.
- ✔ There's no semicolon immediately after the condition.
- ✔ There's no semicolon immediately after the word else.

As a beginning programmer, you may think these rules are arbitrary. But they're not. These rules belong to a very carefully crafted grammar. They're like the grammar rules for English sentences, but they're even more logical! (Sorry, Christine.)

Table 9-1 shows you the kinds of things that can go wrong when you break the if statement's punctuation rules. The table's last two items are the most notorious. In these two situations, the compiler doesn't catch the error. This lulls you into a false sense of security. The trouble is, when you run the program, the code's behavior isn't what you expect it to be.

Table 9-1	Common if Statement Error Messages	
Error	*Example*	*Message or result*
Missing parentheses surrounding the condition	`if randomNumber > 5 {`	`'(' expected`
Missing semicolon after a statement that's inside the `if` clause or the `else` clause	`System.out. println()`	`';' expected`
Semicolon immediately condition	`if (randomNumber > 5);`	`'else' without` after the `'if'`
Semicolon immediately after the word `else`	`} else;`	The program compiles without errors, but the statement after the word `else` is always executed, whether the condition is `true` or `false`.
Missing curly braces	`if (randomNumber > 5)`	The program sometimes compiles without errors, but the program's run may not do what you expect it to do. (So the bottom line is, don't omit the curly braces.)
	`System.out. println("Yes"); else System.out.println ("No");`	

As you compose your code, it helps to think of an `if` statement as one indivisible unit. Instead of typing the whole first line (condition and all), try typing the `if` statement's skeletal outline.

```
if () {            //To do: Fill in the condition.
                   //To do: Fill in SomeStatements.
} else {
                   //To do: Fill in OtherStatements.
}
```

With the entire outline in place, you can start working on the items on your to-do list. When you apply this kind of thinking to a compound statement, it's harder to make a mistake.

A complete program

Listing 9-2 contains a complete program with a simple if statement. The listing's code behaves like an electronic oracle. Ask the program a yes or no question, and the program answers you back. Of course, the answer to your question is randomly generated. But who cares? It's fun to ask anyway.

Listing 9-2: I Know Everything

```java
import java.util.Scanner;
import java.util.Random;

class AnswerYesOrNo {

    public static void main(String args[]) {
        Scanner myScanner = new Scanner(System.in);
        Random myRandom = new Random();
        int randomNumber;

        System.out.print("Type your question, my child:  ");
        myScanner.nextLine();

        randomNumber = myRandom.nextInt(10) + 1;

        if (randomNumber > 5) {
            System.out.println("Yes. Isn't it obvious?");
        } else {
            System.out.println("No, and don't ask again.");
        }
    }
}
```

Figure 9-4 shows several runs of the program in Listing 9-2. The program's action has four parts:

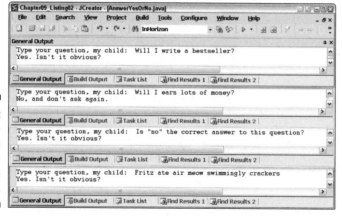

Figure 9-4:
The all-
knowing
Java
program in
action.

1. **Prompt the user.**

   Call `System.out.print`, telling the user to type a question.

2. **Get the user's question from the keyboard.**

   In Figure 9-4, I run the `AnswerYesOrNo` program four times, and I type a different question each time. Meanwhile, back in Listing 9-2, the statement

   ```
   myScanner.nextLine();
   ```

   swallows up my question, and does absolutely nothing with it. This is an anomaly, but you're smart so you can handle it.

   Normally, when a program gets input from the keyboard, the program does something with the input. For instance, the program can assign the input to a variable:

   ```
   amount = myScanner.nextDouble();
   ```

   Alternatively, the program can display the input on the screen:

   ```
   System.out.println(myScanner.nextLine());
   ```

   But the code in Listing 9-2 is different. When this `AnswerYesOrNo` program runs, the user has to type something. (The call to `getLine` waits for the user to type some stuff, and then press Enter.) But the `AnswerYesOrNo` program has no need to store the input for further analysis. (The computer does what I do when my wife asks me if I plan to clean up after myself. I ignore the question and make up an arbitrary answer.) So the program doesn't do anything with the user's input. The call to `myScanner.nextLine` just sits there in a statement of its own, doing nothing, behaving like a big black hole. It's unusual for a program to do this, but an electronic oracle is an unusual thing. It calls for some slightly unusual code.

3. **Get a random number — any `int` value from 1 to 10.**

   Okay, wise guys. You've just trashed the user's input. How will you answer yes or no to the user's question?

   No problem! None at all! You'll display an answer randomly. The user won't know the difference. (Hah, hah!) You can do this as long as you can generate random numbers. The numbers from 1 to 10 will do just fine.

   In Listing 9-2, the stuff about `Random` and `myRandom` looks very much like the familiar `Scanner` code. From a beginning programmer's point of view, `Random` and `Scanner` work almost the same way. Of course, there's an important difference. A call to the `Random` class's `nextInt(10)` method doesn't fetch anything from the keyboard. Instead, this `nextInt(10)` method gets a number out of the blue.

   The name `Random` is defined in the Java API. The call to `myRandom.nextInt(10)` in Listing 9-2 gets a number from 0 to 9. Then my code adds 1 (making a number from 1 to 10) and assigns that number to the

Randomness makes me dizzy

When you call `myRandom.nextInt(10) + 1`, you get a number from 1 to 10. As a test, I wrote a program that calls the `myRandom.nextInt(10) + 1` twenty times.

```java
import java.util.Random;
class TwentyNumbers {
    public static void
    main(String args[]) {
        Random myRandom = new
Random();

    System.out.print(myRandom.n
extInt(10) + 1);
        System.out.print(" ");

    System.out.print(myRandom.n
extInt(10) + 1);
        System.out.print(" ");

    System.out.print(myRandom.n
extInt(10) + 1);
            //...And so on.
```

I ran the program several times, and got the results shown in the figure below. (Actually, I copied the results from JCreator's General Output pane to Windows Notepad.) Stare briefly at the figure and notice two trends:

- There's no obvious way to predict what number comes next.

- No number occurs much more often than any of the others.

```
6 2 2 2 4 3 4 3 6 5 10 8 5 6 2 2 6 6 9 5
7 2 1 6 4 10 10 5 7 7 4 9 7 9 6 8 7 8 3 10
3 4 8 7 6 8 1 5 7 2 3 5 7 1 8 2 6 5 8 3
2 1 10 6 2 2 4 3 3 6 5 2 7 4 4 8 8 9 7 4
7 5 8 4 7 3 2 9 7 6 7 7 3 6 5 3 10 4 8 3
9 4 9 1 4 4 7 2 7 1 4 1 9 8 2 7 7 2 5 1
1 1 2 3 10 5 2 9 7 7 7 6 2 3 9 6 9 10 10 2
5 10 1 10 9 6 2 3 10 1 4 9 3 10 1 5 7 9 3 10
```

The Java virtual machine jumps through hoops to maintain these trends. That's because cranking out numbers in a random fashion is a very tricky business. Here are some interesting facts about the process:

- Scientists and non-scientists use the term *random number.* But in reality, there's no such thing as a single random number. After all, how random is a number like 9?

A number is *random* only when it's one in a very disorderly collection of numbers. More precisely, a number is *random* if the process used to generate the number follows the two trends listed above. When they're being careful, scientists avoid the term *random number,* and use the term *randomly generated number* instead.

- It's hard to generate numbers randomly. Computer programs do the best they can, but ultimately, today's computer programs follow a pattern, and that pattern isn't truly random.

To generate numbers in a truly random fashion, you need a big tub of ping-pong balls, like the kind they use in state lottery drawings. The problem is, most computers don't come with big tubs of ping-pong balls among their peripherals. So strictly speaking, the numbers generated by Java's `Random` class aren't random. Instead, scientists call these numbers *pseudorandom.*

- It surprises us all, but knowing one randomly generated value is of no help in predicting the next randomly generated value.

For example, if you toss a coin twice, and get heads each time, are you more likely to get tails on the third flip? No. It's still fifty-fifty.

If you have three sons, and you're expecting a fourth child, is the fourth child more likely to be a girl? No. A child's gender has nothing to do with the genders of the older children. (I'm ignoring any biological effects, which I know absolutely nothing about. Wait! I do know some biological trivia: A newborn child is more likely to be a boy than a girl. For every 21 newborn boys, there are only 20 newborn girls. Boys are weaker, so we die off faster. That's why nature makes more of us at birth.)

variable `randomNumber`. When that's done, you're ready to answer the user's question.

In Java's API, the word `Random` is the name of a Java class, and `nextInt` is the name of a Java method. For more information on the relationship between classes and methods, see Chapters 17, 18, and 19.

4. **Answer yes or no.**

Calling `myRandom.nextInt(10)` is like spinning a wheel on a TV game show. The wheel has slots numbered 1 to 10. The `if` statement in Listing 9-2 turns your number into a yes or no alternative. If you roll a number that's greater than 5, the program answers *yes*. Otherwise (if you roll a number that's less than or equal to 5), the program answers *no*.

You can trust me on this one. I've made lots of important decisions based on my `AnswerYesOrNo` program.

Indenting if statements in your code

Notice how, in Listing 9-2, the `println` calls inside the `if` statement are indented. Strictly speaking, you don't have to indent the statements that are inside an `if` statement. For all the compiler cares, you can write your whole program on a single line or place all your statements in an artful, misshapen zigzag. The problem is, if you don't indent your statements in some logical fashion, then neither you nor anyone else can make sense of your code. In Listing 9-2, the indenting of the `println` calls helps your eye (and brain) see quickly that these statements are subordinate to the overall if/else flow.

In a small program, unindented or poorly indented code is barely tolerable. But in a complicated program, indentation that doesn't follow a neat, logical pattern is a big, ugly nightmare.

Always indent your code to make the program's flow apparent at a glance.

Variations on the Theme

I don't like to skin cats. But I've heard that, if I ever need to skin one, I have a choice of several techniques. I'll keep that in mind the next time my cat Muon mistakes the carpet for a litter box.*

*Rick Ross, who read about skinning cats in one of my other books, sent me this information via e-mail: "... on page 10 you refer to 'skinning the cat' and go on to discuss litter boxes and whatnot. Please note that the phrase 'more than one way to skin a cat' refers to the difficulty in removing the inedible skin from catfish, and that there is more than one way to do the same. These range from nailing the critter's tail to a board and taking a pair of pliers to peel it down, to letting the furry kind of cat have the darn thing and just not worrying about it. I grew up on The River (the big one running north/south down the US that begins with 'M' and has so many repeated letters), so it's integral to our experience there. A common misconception (if inhumane and revolting). Just thought you'd want to know."

Anyway, whether you're skinning catfish, skinning kitties, or writing computer programs, the same principle holds true. You always have alternatives. Listing 9-2 shows you one way to write an if statement. The rest of this chapter (and all of Chapter 10) show you some other ways to create if statements.

. . . Or else what?

You can create an if statement without an else clause. For example, imagine a Web page on which one in ten randomly chosen visitors receives a special offer. To keep visitors guessing, I call the Random class's nextInt method, and make the offer to anyone whose number is lucky 7.

- ✔ If myRandom.nextInt(10) + 1 generates the number 7, display a special offer message.

- ✔ If myRandom.nextInt(10) + 1 generates any number other than 7, do nothing. Don't display a special offer message, and don't display a discouraging, "Sorry, no offer for you," message.

The code to implement such a strategy is shown in Listing 9-3. A few runs of the code are shown in Figure 9-5.

Listing 9-3:   Aren't You Lucky?

```
import java.util.Random;

class SpecialOffer {

    public static void main(String args[]) {
        Random myRandom = new Random();
        int randomNumber = myRandom.nextInt(10) + 1;

        if (randomNumber == 7) {
            System.out.println("An offer just for you!");
        }

        System.out.println(randomNumber);
    }
}
```

The if statement in Listing 9-3 has no else clause. This if statement has the following form:

```
if (Condition) {
    SomeStatements
}
```

When randomNumber is 7, the computer displays An offer just for you! When randomNumber isn't 7, the computer doesn't display An offer just for you! The action is illustrated in Figure 9-6.

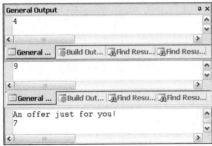

Figure 9-5:
Three runs
of the code
in Listing 9-3.

Always (I mean *always*) use a double equal sign when you compare two numbers or characters in an `if` statement's condition. Never (that's *never, ever, ever*) use a single equal sign to compare two values. A single equal sign does assignment, not comparison.

In Listing 9-3, I took the liberty of adding an extra `println`. This `println` (at the end of the `main` method) displays the random number generated by my call to `nextInt`. On a Web page with special offers, you probably wouldn't see the randomly generated number, but I can't test my `SpecialOffer` code without knowing what numbers the code generates.

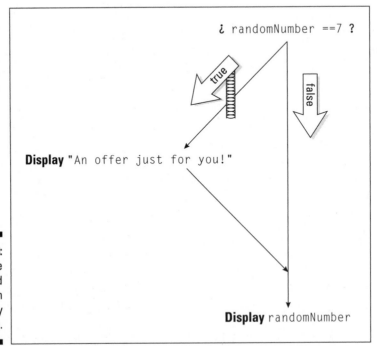

Figure 9-6:
If you have
nothing good
to say, then
don't say
anything.

Anyway, notice that the value of randomNumber is displayed in every run. The println for randomNumber isn't inside the if statement. (This println comes after the if statement.) So the computer always executes this println. Whether randomNumber == 7 is true or false, the computer takes the appropriate if action, and then marches on to execute System.out. println(randomNumber).

Packing more stuff into an if statement

Here's an interesting situation: You have two baseball teams — the Hankees and the Socks. You want to display the teams' scores on two separate lines, with the winner's score coming first. (On the computer screen, the winner's score is displayed above the loser's score. In case of a tie, you display the two identical scores, one above the other.) Listing 9-4 has the code.

Listing 9-4:   May the Best Team Be Displayed First

```
import java.util.Scanner;
import static java.lang.System.in;
import static java.lang.System.out;

class TwoTeams {

    public static void main(String args[]) {
        Scanner myScanner = new Scanner(in);
        int hankees, socks;

        out.print("Hankees and Socks scores?  ");
        hankees = myScanner.nextInt();
        socks = myScanner.nextInt();
        out.println();

        if (hankees > socks) {
            out.print("Hankees: ");
            out.println(hankees);
            out.print("Socks:    ");
            out.println(socks);
        } else {
            out.print("Socks:    ");
            out.println(socks);
            out.print("Hankees: ");
            out.println(hankees);
        }
    }
}
```

Figure 9-7 has a few runs of the code. (To show a few runs in one figure, I copied the results from JCreator's General Output pane to Windows Notepad.)

```
Hankees and Socks scores?  9 4

Hankees: 9
Socks:   4


Hankees and Socks scores?  3 8

Socks:   8
Hankees: 3


Hankees and Socks scores?  0 0

Socks:   0
Hankees: 0
```

Figure 9-7:
See? The
code in
Listing 9-4
really
works!

With curly braces, a bunch of `print` and `println` calls are tucked away safely inside the `if` clause. Another group of `print` and `println` calls are squished inside the `else` clause. This creates the forking situation shown in Figure 9-8.

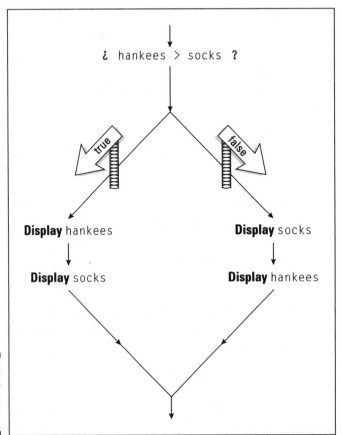

Figure 9-8:
Cheer for
your favorite
team.

Statements and blocks

An elegant way to think about `if` statements is to realize that you can put only one statement inside each clause of an `if` statement.

```
if (Condition)
    aStatement
else
    anotherStatement
```

On first reading of this one-statement rule, you're probably thinking that there's a misprint. After all, in Listing 9-4, each clause (the `if` clause and the `else` clause) seems to contain four statements, not just one.

But technically, the `if` clause in Listing 9-4 has only one statement, and the `else` clause in Listing 9-4 has only one statement. The trick is, when you surround a bunch of statements with curly braces, you get what's called a *block,* and a block behaves, in all respects, like a single statement. In fact, the official Java documentation lists a block as a kind of statement (one of many different kinds of statements). So in Listing 9-4, the block

```
{
    System.out.print("Hankees:
    ");
    System.out.println(hankees);
    System.out.print("Socks:
    ");
    System.out.println(socks);
}
```

is a single statement. It's a statement that has within it, four smaller statements. So this big block, this single statement, serves as the one and only statement inside the `if` clause in Listing 9-4.

That's how the one-statement rule works. In an `if` statement, when you want the computer to execute several statements, you combine those statements into one big statement. To do this, you make a block using curly braces.

Some handy import declarations

When I wrote this section's example, I was tired of writing the word `System`. After all, Listing 9-4 has ten `System.out.print` lines. By this point in the book, shouldn't my computer remember what `out.print` means?

Of course, computers don't work that way. If you want a computer to "know" what `out.print` means, you have to code that knowledge somewhere inside the Java compiler.

Fortunately for me, the ability to abbreviate things like `System.out.print` is part of Java 5.0. (This relatively new version of Java wasn't available until September 2004. An older Java compiler just chokes on the code in Listing 9-4.) This ability to abbreviate things is called *static import*. It's illustrated in the second and third lines of Listing 9-4.

Whenever I start a program with the line

```
import static java.lang.System.out;
```

I can replace `System.out` with plain `out` in the remainder of the program. The same holds true of `System.in`. With an import declaration near the top of Listing 9-4, I can replace `new Scanner(System.in)` with the simpler `new Scanner(in)`.

You may be wondering what all the fuss is about. If I can abbreviate `java.util.Scanner` by writing `Scanner`, what's so special about abbreviating `System.out`? And why do I have to write `out.print`? Can I trim `System.out.print` down to the single word `print`? Look again at the first few lines of Listing 9-4. When do I need the word `static`? And what's the difference between `java.util` and `java.lang`?

I'm sorry. My response to these questions won't thrill you. The fact is, I can't explain away any of these issues until Chapter 18. Before I can explain static import declarations, I need to introduce some ideas. I need to describe classes, packages, and static members.

So until you reach Chapter 18, please bear with me. Just paste three import declarations to the top of your Java programs, and trust that everything will work well.

You can abbreviate `System.out` with the single word `out`. And you can abbreviate `System.in` with the single word `in`. Just be sure to copy the `import` declarations *exactly* as you see them in Listing 9-4. With any deviation from the lines in Listing 9-4, you may get a compiler error.

Chapter 10

Which Way Did He Go?

In This Chapter

▶ Untangling complicated conditions

▶ Writing cool conditional code

▶ Intertwining your if statements

* * *

*I*t's tax time again. At the moment, I'm working on Form 12432-89B. Here's what it says:

> If you're married with fewer than three children, and your income is higher than the EIQ (Estimated Income Quota), or if you're single and living in a non-residential area (as defined by Section 10, Part iii of the Uniform Zoning Act), and you're either self-employed as an LLC (Limited Liability Company) or you qualify for veterans benefits, then skip Steps 3 and 4 or 4, 5, and 6, depending on your answers to Questions 2a and 3d.

No wonder I have no time to write! I'm too busy interpreting these tax forms.

Anyway, this chapter deals with the potential complexity of if statements. This chapter has nothing as complex as Form 12432-89B, but if you ever encounter something that complicated, you'll be ready for it.

Forming Bigger and Better Conditions

In Listing 9-2, the code chooses a course of action based on one call to the Random class's nextInt method. That's fine for the electronic oracle program described in Chapter 9, but what if you're rolling a pair of dice? In Backgammon and other dice games, rolling 3 and 5 isn't the same as rolling 4 and 4, even though the total for both rolls is 8. The next move varies, depending on whether or not you roll doubles. To get the computer to roll two dice, you execute myRandom.nextInt(6) + 1 two times. Then you combine the two rolls into a larger, more complicated if statement.

So to simulate a Backgammon game (and many other, more practical situations) you need to combine conditions.

```
If die1 + die2 equals 8 and die1 equals die2, ...
```

You need things like *and* and *or* — things that can wire conditions together. Java has operators to represent these concepts, which are described in Table 10-1 and illustrated in Figure 10-1.

Table 10-1		Logical Operators	
Operator Symbol	*Meaning*	*Example*	*Illustration*
&&	and	4 < age && age < 8	Figure 10-1(a)
||	or	age < 4 || 8 < age	Figure 10-1(b)
!	not	!eachKidGetsTen	Figure 10-1(c)

Combined conditions, like the ones in Table 10-1, can be mighty confusing. That's why I tread carefully when I use such things. Here's a short explanation of each example in the table:

✔ 4 < age && age < 8

> The value of the age variable is greater than 4 *and* is less than 8. The numbers 5, 6, 7, 8, 9 . . . are all greater than 4. But among these numbers, only 5, 6, and 7 are less than 8. So only the numbers 5, 6, and 7 satisfy this combined condition.

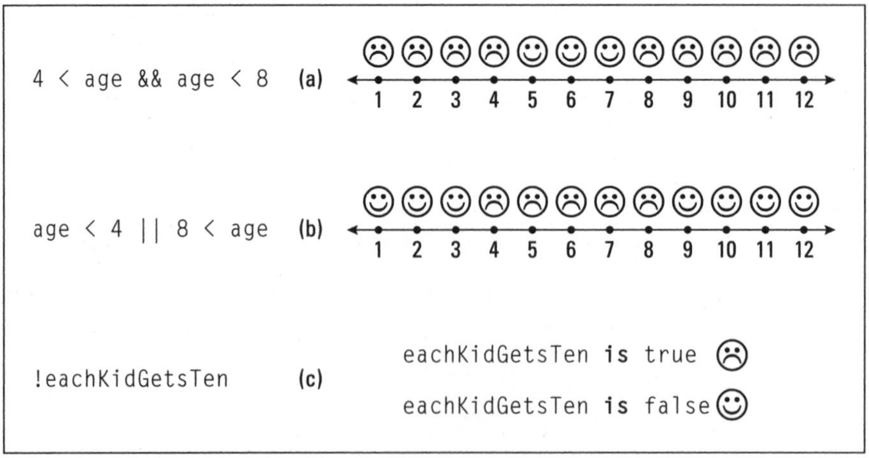

Figure 10-1: When you satisfy a condition, you're happy.

4 < age && age < 8   (a)

age < 4 || 8 < age   (b)

!eachKidGetsTen   (c)

eachKidGetsTen is true ☹

eachKidGetsTen is false ☺

✔ `age < 4 || 8 < age`

The value of the `age` variable is less than 4 *or* is greater than 8. To create the or condition, you use two pipe symbols. On many U.S. English keyboards, you can find the pipe symbol immediately above the Enter key (the same key as the backslash, but shifted).

In this combined condition, the value of the `age` variable is either less than 4 or is greater than 8. So for example, if a number is less than 4, then the number satisfies the condition. Numbers like 1, 2, and 3 are all less than 4, so these numbers satisfy the combined condition.

Also, if a number is greater than 8, then the number satisfies the combined condition. Numbers like 9, 10, and 11 are all greater than 8, so these numbers satisfy the condition.

✔ `!eachKidGetsTen`

If I weren't experienced with computer programming languages, I'd be confused by the exclamation point. I'd think that `!eachKidGetsTen` means, "Yes, each kid *does* get ten." But that's not what this expression means. This expression says, "The variable `eachKidGetsTen` does *not* have the value `true`." In Java and other programming languages, an exclamation point stands for *negative,* for *no way,* for *not.*

Listing 8-4 has a `boolean` variable named `eachKidGetsTen`. A `boolean` variable's value is either `true` or `false`. Because `!` means *not,* the expressions `eachKidGetsTen` and `!eachKidGetsTen` have opposite values. So when `eachKidGetsTen` is true, `!eachKidGetsTen` is false (and vice versa).

Java's `||` operator is *inclusive.* This means that you get `true` whenever the thing on the left side is `true`, the thing on the right side is `true`, or both things are `true`. For example, the condition `2 < 10 || 20 < 30` is true.

In Java, you can't combine comparisons the way you do in ordinary English. In English, you may say, "We'll have between three and ten people at the dinner table." But in Java, you get an error message if you write `3 <= people <= 10`. To do this comparison, you need to something like `3 <= people && people <= 10`.

Combining conditions: An example

Here's a handy example of the use of logical operators. A movie theater posts its prices for admission.

Regular price: $9.25

Kids under 12: $5.25

Seniors (65 and older): $5.25

Because the kids' and seniors' prices are the same, you can combine these prices into one category. (That's not always the best programming strategy, but do it anyway for this example.) To find a particular moviegoer's ticket price, you need one or more if statements. There are many ways to structure the conditions, and I chose one of these ways for the code in Listing 10-1.

Listing 10-1:   Are You Paying Too Much?

```java
import java.util.Scanner;

class TicketPrice {

    public static void main(String args[]) {
        Scanner myScanner = new Scanner(System.in);
        int age;
        double price = 0.00;

        System.out.print("How old are you? ");
        age = myScanner.nextInt();

        if (age >= 12 && age < 65) {
            price = 9.25;
        }
        if (age < 12 || age >= 65) {
            price = 5.25;
        }

        System.out.print("Please pay $");
        System.out.print(price);
        System.out.print(". ");
        System.out.println("Enjoy the show!");
    }
}
```

Several runs of the TicketPrice program (Listing 10-1) are shown in Figure 10-2. (For your viewing pleasure, I've copied the runs from JCreator's General Output pane to Windows Notepad.) When you turn 12, you start paying full price. You keep paying full price until you become 65. At that point, you pay the reduced price again.

- ✔ The first if statement's condition tests for the regular price group. Anyone who's at least 12 years of age *and* is under 65 belongs in this group.

- ✔ The second if statement's condition tests for the fringe ages. A person who's under 12 *or* is 65 or older belongs in this category.

```
How old are you? 11
Please pay $5.25. Enjoy the show!

How old are you? 12
Please pay $9.25. Enjoy the show!

How old are you? 35
Please pay $9.25. Enjoy the show!

How old are you? 64
Please pay $9.25. Enjoy the show!

How old are you? 65
Please pay $5.25. Enjoy the show!
```

Figure 10-2:
Admission
prices for
*Beginning
Programm-
ing with
Java For
Dummies:
The Movie.*

The pivotal part of Listing 10-1 is the lump of `if` statements in the middle, which are illustrated in Figure 10-3.

Figure 10-3:
The
meanings
of the
conditions in
Listing 10-1.

```
age >= 12 && age < 65
```

```
age < 12 || age >= 65
```

When you form the opposite of an existing condition, you can often follow the pattern in Listing 10-1. The opposite of `>=` is `<`. The opposite of `<` is `>=`. The opposite of `&&` is `||`.

If you change the dollar amounts in Listing 10-1, you can get into trouble. For example, with the statement `price = 5.00`, the program displays `Please pay $5.0. Enjoy the show!` This happens because Java doesn't store the two zeros to the right of the decimal point (and Java doesn't know or care that 5.00 is a dollar amount). To fix this kind of thing, see the discussion of `NumberFormat.getCurrencyInstance` in Chapter 18.

When to initialize?

Take a look at Listing 10-1, and notice the `price` variable's initialization.

```
double price = 0.00;
```

This line declares the `price` variable and sets the variable's starting value to `0.00`. When I omit this initialization, I get an error message:

```
variable price might not have been initialized
        System.out.print(price);
                ^
```

What's the deal here? I don't initialize the `age` variable, but the compiler doesn't complain about that. Why is the compiler fussing over the `price` variable?

The answer is in the placement of the code's assignment statements. Consider the following two facts:

✔ **The statement that assigns a value to** `age` (`age = myScanner.nextInt()`) **is not inside an** `if` **statement.**

That assignment statement always gets executed and (as long as nothing extraordinary happens) the variable `age` is sure to be assigned a value.

✔ **Both statements that assign a value to** `price` (`price = 9.25` **and** `price = 5.25`) **are inside** `if` **statements.**

If you look at Figure 10-3, you see that every age group is covered. No one shows up at the ticket counter with an age that forces both `if` conditions to be `false`. So whenever you run the `TicketPrice` program, either the first or the second `price` assignment is executed.

The problem is that the compiler isn't smart enough to check all this. The compiler just sees the structure in Figure 10-4 and becomes scared that the computer won't take either of the `true` detours.

If (for some unforeseen reason) both of the `if` statements' conditions are `false`, then the variable `price` doesn't get assigned a value. So without an initialization, `price` has no value. (More precisely, `price` has no value that's intentionally given to it in the code.)

Eventually, the computer reaches the `System.out.print(price)` statement. It can't display `price` unless `price` has a meaningful value. So at that point, the compiler throws up its virtual hands in disgust.

More and more conditions

Last night I had a delicious meal at the neighborhood burger joint. As part of a promotion, I got a discount coupon along with the meal. The coupon is good for $2.00 off the price of a ticket at the local movie theater.

To make use of the coupon in the `TicketPrice` program, I have to tweak the code in Listing 10-1. The revised code is in Listing 10-2. In Figure 10-5, I take that new code around the block a few times.

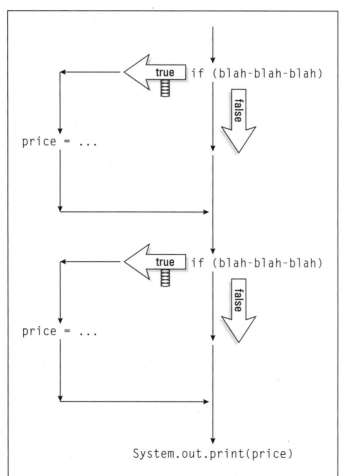

Figure 10-4:
The choices
in Listing
10-1.

Listing 10-2: Do You Have a Coupon?

```java
import java.util.Scanner;

class TicketPriceWithDiscount {

    public static void main(String args[]) {
        Scanner myScanner = new Scanner(System.in);
        int age;
        double price = 0.00;
        char reply;
```

(continued)

Listing 10-2 *(continued)*

```
        System.out.print("How old are you? ");
        age = myScanner.nextInt();

        System.out.print("Have a coupon? (Y/N) ");
        reply = myScanner.findInLine(".").charAt(0);

        if (age >= 12 && age < 65) {
            price = 9.25;
        }
        if (age < 12 || age >= 65) {
            price = 5.25;
        }

        if (reply == 'Y' || reply == 'y') {
            price -= 2.00;
        }
        if (reply != 'Y' && reply != 'y' &&
            reply!='N' && reply!='n') {
            System.out.println("Huh?");
        }

        System.out.print("Please pay $");
        System.out.print(price);
        System.out.print(". ");
        System.out.println("Enjoy the show!");
    }
}
```

```
How old are you? 51
Have a coupon? (Y/N) Y
Please pay $7.25. Enjoy the show!

How old are you? 51
Have a coupon? (Y/N) y
Please pay $7.25. Enjoy the show!

How old are you? 51
Have a coupon? (Y/N) N
Please pay $9.25. Enjoy the show!

How old are you? 51
Have a coupon? (Y/N) X
Huh?
Please pay $9.25. Enjoy the show!
```

Figure 10-5:
Running
the code in
Listing 10-2.

Listing 10-2 has two if statements whose conditions involve characters:

✔ In the first such statement, the computer checks to see if the reply variable stores the letter Y *or* the letter y. If either is the case, then it subtracts 2.00 from the price. (For information on operators like -=, see Chapter 7.)

✔ The second such statement has a hefty condition. The condition tests to see if the `reply` variable stores any reasonable value at all. If the reply *isn't* Y, *and isn't* y, *and isn't* N, *and isn't* n, then the computer expresses its concern by displaying, "Huh?" (As a paying customer, the word "Huh?" on the automated ticket teller's screen will certainly get your attention.)

When you create a big multipart condition, you always have several ways to think about the condition. For example, you can rewrite the last condition in Listing 10-2 as `if (!(reply == 'Y' || reply == 'y' || reply == 'N' || reply == 'n'))`. "*If it's not the case that* the `reply` is *either* Y, y, N, *or* n, then display 'Huh?'" So which way of writing the condition is better — the way I do it in Listing 10-2, or the way I do it in this tip? It depends on your taste. Whatever makes the logic easiest for you to understand is the best way.

Using boolean variables

No matter how good a program is, you can always make it a little bit better. Take the code in Listing 10-2. Does the forest of `if` statements make you nervous? Do you slow to a crawl when you read each condition? Wouldn't it be nice if you could glance at a condition and make sense of it very quickly?

To some extent, you can. If you're willing to create some additional variables, you can make your code easier to read. Listing 10-3 shows you how.

Listing 10-3:   George Boole Would Be Proud

```
import java.util.Scanner;

class NicePrice {

    public static void main(String args[]) {
        Scanner myScanner = new Scanner(System.in);
        int age;
        double price = 0.00;
        char reply;
        boolean isKid, isSenior, hasCoupon, hasNoCoupon;

        System.out.print("How old are you? ");
        age = myScanner.nextInt();

        System.out.print("Have a coupon? (Y/N) ");
        reply = myScanner.findInLine(".").charAt(0);

        isKid = age < 12;
        isSenior = age >= 65;
        hasCoupon = reply == 'Y' || reply == 'y';
        hasNoCoupon = reply == 'N' || reply == 'n';
```

(continued)

Listing 10-3 *(continued)*

```
        if (!isKid && !isSenior) {
            price = 9.25;
        }
        if (isKid || isSenior) {
            price = 5.25;
        }

        if (hasCoupon) {
            price -= 2.00;
        }
        if (!hasCoupon && !hasNoCoupon) {
            System.out.println("Huh?");
        }

        System.out.print("Please pay $");
        System.out.print(price);
        System.out.print(". ");
        System.out.println("Enjoy the show!");
    }
}
```

Runs of the Listing 10-3 code look like the stuff in Figure 10-5. The only difference between Listings 10-2 and 10-3 is the use of boolean variables. In Listing
10-3, you get past all the less than signs and double equal signs before the
start of any if statements. By the time you encounter the two if statements,
the conditions can use simple words — words like isKid, isSenior, and
hasCoupon. With all these boolean variables, expressing each if statement's
condition is a snap. You can read more about boolean variables in Chapter 8.

Adding a boolean variable can make your code more manageable. But some
programming languages don't have boolean variables, so many programmers prefer to create if conditions on the fly. That's why I mix the two techniques (conditions with and without boolean variables) in this book.

Mixing different logical operators together

If you read about Listing 10-2, you know that my local movie theater offers
discount coupons. The trouble is, I can't use a coupon along with any other discount. I tried to convince the ticket taker that I'm under 12 years of age, but he
didn't buy it. When that didn't work, I tried combining the coupon with the
senior citizen discount. That didn't work either.

The theater must use some software that checks for people like me. It looks
something like the code in Listing 10-4. To watch the code run, take a look at
Figure 10-6.

Listing 10-4:   No Extra Break for Kids or Seniors

```java
import java.util.Scanner;

class CheckAgeForDiscount {

    public static void main(String args[]) {
        Scanner myScanner = new Scanner(System.in);
        int age;
        double price = 0.00;
        char reply;

        System.out.print("How old are you? ");
        age = myScanner.nextInt();

        System.out.print("Have a coupon? (Y/N) ");
        reply = myScanner.findInLine(".").charAt(0);

        if (age >= 12 && age < 65) {
            price = 9.25;
        }
        if (age < 12 || age >= 65) {
            price = 5.25;
        }

        if ((reply == 'Y' || reply == 'y') &&
            (age >= 12 && age < 65)) {
            price -= 2.00;
        }

        System.out.print("Please pay $");
        System.out.print(price);
        System.out.print(". ");
        System.out.println("Enjoy the show!");
    }
}
```

Figure 10-6: Running the code in Listing 10-4.

```
How old are you? 7
Have a coupon? (Y/N) Y
Please pay $5.25. Enjoy the show!

How old are you? 25
Have a coupon? (Y/N) y
Please pay $7.25. Enjoy the show!

How old are you? 25
Have a coupon? (Y/N) n
Please pay $9.25. Enjoy the show!

How old are you? 85
Have a coupon? (Y/N) y
Please pay $5.25. Enjoy the show!

How old are you? 85
Have a coupon? (Y/N) Y
Please pay $5.25. Enjoy the show!
```

Listing 10-4 is a lot like its predecessors, Listings 10-1 and 10-2. The big differ-ence is the bolded if statement. This if statement tests two things, and each thing has two parts of its own:

1. **Does the customer have a coupon?**

   That is, did the customer reply with either Y *or* with y?

2. **Is the customer in the regular age group?**

   That is, is the customer at least 12 years old *and* younger than 65?

In Listing 10-4, I join items 1 and 2 using the && operator. I do this because both items (item 1 *and* item 2) must be true in order for the customer to qualify for the $2.00 discount, as illustrated in Figure 10-7.

Using parentheses

Listing 10-4 demonstrates something important about conditions. Sometimes, you need parentheses to make a condition work correctly. Take, for example, the following incorrect if statement:

```
//This code is incorrect:
if (reply == 'Y' || reply == 'y' &&
    age >= 12 && age < 65) {
    price -= 2.00;
}
```

```
How old are you? 85
Have a coupon? (Y/N) Y

price = 5.25;
      .
      .
      .
if ( ( reply=='Y' || reply=='y' ) && ( age >= 12 && age < 65 ) )
       └──────┘    └──────────┘        └──────────┘  └──────────┘
         true         false                true          false
     └────────────────────────┘        └──────────────────────────┘
                true                              false
     └──────────────────────────────────────────────────────────┘
                             false

    price -= 2.00;

Please pay $5.25. Enjoy the show!
```

Figure 10-7:
Both the
reply and
the age
criteria must
be true.

Compare this code with the correct code in Listing 10-4. This incorrect code has no parentheses to group `reply == 'Y'` with `reply == 'y'`, or to group `age >= 12` with `age < 65`. The result is the bizarre pair of runs in Figure 10-8.

```
How old are you? 85
Have a coupon? (Y/N) y
Please pay $5.25. Enjoy the show!

How old are you? 85
Have a coupon? (Y/N) Y
Please pay $3.25. Enjoy the show!
```

In Figure 10-8, notice how the y and Y inputs yield different ticket prices, even though the age is 85 in both runs. This happens because, without parentheses, any `&&` operator gets evaluated before any `||` operator. (That's the rule in the Java programming language — evaluate `&&` before `||`.) When `reply` is Y, the condition in the bad `if` statement takes the following form:

```
reply == 'Y' || some-other-stuff-that-doesn't-matter
```

Whenever `reply == 'Y'` is `true`, the whole condition is automatically `true`, as illustrated in Figure 10-9.

Building a Nest

The year is 1968, and *The Prisoner* is on TV. In the last episode, the show's hero meets his nemesis "Number One." At first Number One wears a spooky happy-face/sad-face mask, and when the mask comes off, there's a monkey mask underneath. To find out what's behind the monkey mask, you have to watch the series on DVD. But in the meantime, notice the layering; a mask within a mask. You can do the same kind of thing with if statements. This section's example shows you how.

But first, take a look at Listing 10-4. In that code, the condition age >= 12 && age < 65 is tested twice. Both times, the computer sends the numbers 12, 65, and the age value through its jumble of circuits, and both times, the computer gets the same answer. This is wasteful, but waste isn't your only concern.

What if you decide to change the age limit for senior tickets? From now on, no one under 100 gets a senior discount. You fish through the code and see the first age >= 12 && age < 65 test. You change 65 to 100, pat yourself on the back, and go home. The problem is, you've changed one of the two age >= 12 && age < 65 tests, but you haven't changed the other. Wouldn't it be better to keep all the age >= 12 && age < 65 testing in just one place?

Listing 10-5 comes to the rescue. In Listing 10-5, I smoosh all my if statements together into one big glob. The code is dense, but it gets the job done nicely.

Listing 10-5:   Nested if Statements

```java
import java.util.Scanner;

class AnotherAgeCheck {

    public static void main(String args[]) {
        Scanner myScanner = new Scanner(System.in);
        int age;
        double price = 0.00;
        char reply;

        System.out.print("How old are you? ");
        age = myScanner.nextInt();

        System.out.print("Have a coupon? (Y/N) ");
        reply = myScanner.findInLine(".").charAt(0);

        if (age >= 12 && age < 65) {
            price = 9.25;
            if (reply == 'Y' || reply == 'y') {
                price -= 2.00;
            }
        } else {
            price = 5.25;
        }
```

```
        System.out.print("Please pay $");
        System.out.print(price);
        System.out.print(". ");
        System.out.println("Enjoy the show!");
    }
}
```

Nested if statements

A run of the code in Listing 10-5 looks identical to a run for Listing 10-4. You can see several runs in Figure 10-6. The main idea in Listing 10-5 is to put an if statement inside another if statement. After all, Chapter 9 says that an if statement can take the following form:

```
if (Condition) {
    SomeStatements
} else {
    OtherStatements
}
```

Who says *SomeStatements* can't contain an if statement? For that matter, *OtherStatements* can also contain an if statement. And, yes, you can create an if statement within an if statement within an if statement. There's no predefined limit on the number of if statements that you can have.

```
if (age >= 12 && age < 65) {
    price = 9.25;
    if (reply == 'Y' || reply == 'y') {
        if (isSpecialFeature) {
            price -= 1.00;
        } else {
            price -= 2.00;
        }
    }
} else {
    price = 5.25;
}
```

When you put one if statement inside another, you create *nested* if statements. Nested statements aren't difficult to write, as long as you take things slowly, and keep a clear picture of the code's flow in your mind. If it helps, draw yourself a diagram like the one shown in Figure 10-10.

When you nest statements, you must be compulsive about the use of indentation and braces (see Figure 10-11). When code has misleading indentation, no one (not even the programmer who wrote the code) can figure out how the code works. A nested statement with sloppy indentation is a programmer's nightmare.

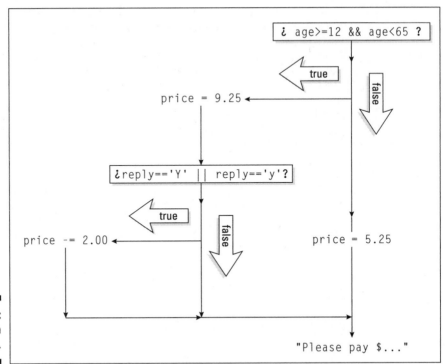

Figure 10-10:
The flow in
Listing 10-5.

```
                                    if (age >= 12 && age < 65)
                                    ┌  {
Two statements                      │      price = 9.25;
in an if clause;  ←                 │      if (reply=='Y' || reply=='y')   One statement
braces required.                    │          price -= 2.00;          ┐→ in an if clause;
                                    └  }                                  braces optional.
One statement in      else
an else clause;  ←┌       price = 5.25;
braces optional.  └
```

Figure 10-11:
Be careful
about
adding the
proper
indentation
and braces.

Cascading if statements

Here's a riddle: You have two baseball teams — the Hankees and the Socks.
You want to display the teams' scores on two separate lines, with the winner's
score coming first. (On the computer screen, the winner's score is displayed
above the loser's score.) What happens when the scores are tied?

Do you give up? The answer is, there's no right answer. What happens depends on the way you write the program. Take a look back at Listing 9-4 in Chapter 9. When the scores are equal, the condition hankees > socks is false. So the program's flow of execution drops down to the else clause. That clause displays the Socks score first and the Hankees score second. (Refer to Figure 9-7.)

The program doesn't have to work this way. If I take Listing 9-4 and change hankees > socks to hankees >= socks then, in case of a tie, the Hankees score comes first.

Suppose you want a bit more control. When the scores are equal, you want an It's a tie message. To do this, think in terms of a three-pronged fork. You have a prong for a Hankees win, another prong for a Socks win, and a third prong for a tie. You can write this code in several different ways, but one way that makes lots of sense is in Listing 10-6. For three runs of the code in Listing 10-6, see Figure 10-12.

Listing 10-6:   In Case of a Tie . . .

```
import java.util.Scanner;
import static java.lang.System.out;

class WinLoseOrTie {

    public static void main(String args[]) {
        Scanner myScanner = new Scanner(System.in);
        int hankees, socks;

        out.print("Hankees and Socks scores?  ");
        hankees = myScanner.nextInt();
        socks = myScanner.nextInt();
        out.println();

        if (hankees > socks) {
            out.println("Hankees win...");
            out.print("Hankees: ");
            out.println(hankees);
            out.print("Socks:   ");
            out.println(socks);
        } else if (socks > hankees) {
            out.println("Socks win...");
            out.print("Socks:   ");
            out.println(socks);
            out.print("Hankees: ");
            out.println(hankees);
```

(continued)

Listing 10-6 *(continued)*

```
        } else {
            out.println("It's a tie...");
            out.print("Hankees: ");
            out.println(hankees);
            out.print("Socks:   ");
            out.println(socks);
        }
    }
}
```

```
Hankees and Socks scores?  9 4

Hankees win...
Hankees: 9
Socks:   4


Hankees and Socks scores?  3 8

Socks win...
Socks:   8
Hankees: 3


Hankees and Socks scores?  0 0

It's a tie...
Hankees: 0
Socks:   0
```

Figure 10-12:
Go, team,
go!

Listing 10-6 illustrates a way of thinking about a problem. You have one question with more than two answers. (In this section's baseball problem, the question is "Who wins?" and the answers are "Hankees," "Socks," or "Neither.") The problem begs for an if statement, but an if statement has only two branches — the true branch and the false branch. So you combine alternatives to form *cascading if statements*.

In Listing 10-6, the format for the cascading if statements is

```
if (Condition1) {
    SomeStatements
} else if (Condition2) {
    OtherStatements
} else {
    EvenMoreStatements
}
```

In general, you can use else if as many times as you want:

```
if (hankeesWin) {
    out.println("Hankees win...");
    out.print("Hankees: ");
    out.println(hankees);
    out.print("Socks:   ");
    out.println(socks);
} else if (socksWin) {
    out.println("Socks win...");
    out.print("Socks:   ");
    out.println(socks);
    out.print("Hankees: ");
    out.println(hankees);
} else if (isATie) {
    out.println("It's a tie...");
    out.print("Hankees: ");
    out.println(hankees);
    out.print("Socks:   ");
    out.println(socks);
} else if (gameCancelled) {
    out.println("Sorry, sports fans.");
} else {
    out.println("The game isn't over yet.");
}
```

Nothing is special about cascading if statements. This isn't a new programming language feature. Cascading if statements take advantage of a loophole in Java — a loophole about omitting curly braces in certain circumstances. Other than that, cascading if statements just gives you a new way to think about decisions within your code.

Note: Listing 10-6 uses a static import declaration to avoid needless repetition of the words System.out. To read a little bit about the static import declaration (along with an apology for my not explaining this concept more thoroughly), see Chapter 9. Then to get the real story on static import declarations, see Chapter 18.

Enumerating the Possibilities

Chapter 8 describes Java's boolean type — the type with only two values (true and false). The boolean type is very handy, but sometimes you need more values. After all, a traffic light's values can be green, yellow, or red. A playing card's suit can be spade, club, heart, or diamond. And a weekday can be Monday, Tuesday, Wednesday, Thursday, or Friday.

Life is filled with small sets of possibilities, and Java has a feature that can reflect these possibilities. The feature is called an enum type. It's new in Java version 5.0.

Creating an enum type

The story in Listing 10-6 has three possible endings — the Hankees win, the Socks win, or the game is tied. You can represent the possibilities with a one-line Java program. The program is in Listing 10-7.

Listing 10-7: Three Possibilities

```
enum WhoWins {home, visitor, neither}
```

This week's game is played at Hankeeville's SnitSoft Stadium, so the value home represents a win for the Hankees, and the value visitor represents a win for the Socks.

I wonder what thoughts you have on your first encounter with Listing 10-7. "What good is a one-line program?" you ask. "Three values? Who cares?" you say. "Does this code do anything useful?" you think. "Does the code do anything at all?"

One of the goals in computer programming is for each program's structure to mirror whatever problem the program solves. When a program reminds you of its underlying problem, the program is easy to understand, and inexpensive to maintain. For instance, a program to tabulate customer accounts should use names like customer and account. And a program that deals with three possible outcomes (home wins, visitor wins, and tie) should have a variable with three possible values. So in Listing 10-7, I create a type to store three values.

The WhoWins type defined in Listing 10-7 is called an *enum type*. Think of the new WhoWins type as a boolean on steroids. Instead of two values (true and false) the WhoWins type has three values (home, visitor, and neither). You can create a variable of type WhoWins

```
WhoWins who;
```

and then assign a value to the new variable.

```
who = WhoWins.home;
```

The fact that you define WhoWins in a file all its own may be a bit unsettling, so I deal with that issue in the this chapter's final section.

Using an enum type

Listing 10-8 shows you how to use the brand new WhoWins type.

Listing 10-8:   Proud Winners and Sore Losers

```java
import java.util.Scanner;
import static java.lang.System.out;

class Scoreboard {

    public static void main(String args[]) {
        Scanner myScanner = new Scanner(System.in);
        int hankees, socks;
        WhoWins who;

        out.print("Hankees and Socks scores?   ");
        hankees = myScanner.nextInt();
        socks = myScanner.nextInt();
        out.println();

        if (hankees > socks) {
            who = WhoWins.home;
            out.println("The Hankees win :-)");
        } else if (socks > hankees) {
            who = WhoWins.visitor;
            out.println("The Socks win :-(");
        } else {
            who = WhoWins.neither;
            out.println("It's a tie :-|");
        }

        out.println();
        out.println("Today's game is brought to you by");
        out.println("SnitSoft, the number one software");
        out.println("vendor in the Hankeeville area.");
        out.println("SnitSoft is featured proudly in");
        out.println("Chapter 6. And remember, four out");
        out.println("of five doctors recommend SnitSoft");
        out.println("to their patients.");
        out.println();

        if (who == WhoWins.home) {
            out.println("We beat 'em good. Didn't we?");
        }
        if (who == WhoWins.visitor) {
            out.println("The umpire made an unfair call.");
        }
        if (who == WhoWins.neither) {
            out.println("The game goes into overtime.");
        }
    }
}
```

Three runs of the program in Listing 10-8 are pictured in Figure 10-13.

```
Hankees and Socks scores?  9 4

The Hankees win :-)

Today's game is brought to you by
SnitSoft, the number one software
vendor in the Hankeeville area.
SnitSoft is featured proudly in
Chapter 6. And remember, four out
of five doctors recommend SnitSoft
to their patients.

We beat 'em good. Didn't we?

Hankees and Socks scores?  3 8

The Socks win :-(

Today's game is brought to you by
SnitSoft, the number one software
vendor in the Hankeeville area.
SnitSoft is featured proudly in
Chapter 6. And remember, four out
of five doctors recommend SnitSoft
to their patients.

The umpire made an unfair call.

Hankees and Socks scores?  0 0

It's a tie :-|

Today's game is brought to you by
SnitSoft, the number one software
vendor in the Hankeeville area.
SnitSoft is featured proudly in
Chapter 6. And remember, four out
of five doctors recommend SnitSoft
to their patients.

The game goes into overtime.
```

Figure 10-13:
Joy in
Hankeeville?

Here's what happens in Listing 10-8:

- ✔ **I create a variable to store values of type** `WhoWins`.

  Just as the line

  ```
  double amount;
  ```

  declares `amount` to store `double` values (values like 5.95 and 30.95), the line

  ```
  WhoWins who;
  ```

  declares `who` to store `WhoWins` values (values like `home`, `visitor`, and `neither`).

- ✔ **I assign a value to the** `who` **variable.**

  I execute one of the

  ```
  who = WhoWins.something;
  ```

  assignment statements. The statement that I execute depends on the outcome of the `if` statement's `hankees > socks` comparison.

Notice how I refer to each of the `WhoWins` values in Listing 10-8. I write `WhoWins.home`, `WhoWins.visitor`, or `WhoWins.neither`. If I forget the `WhoWins` prefix and type

```
who = home;   //This assignment doesn't work!
```

then the compiler gives me a `cannot find symbol` error message. That's just the way enum types work.

✔ **I compare the variable's value with each of the `WhoWins` values.**

In one `if` statement, I check the `who == WhoWins.home` condition. In the remaining two `if` statements I check for the other `WhoWins` values.

Near the end of Listing 10-8, I could have done without enum values. I could have tested things like `hankees > socks` a second time.

```
if (hankees > socks) {
    out.println("The Hankees win :-)");
}

// And later in the program...

if (hankees > socks) {
    out.println("We beat 'em good. Didn't we?");
}
```

But that tactic would be clumsy. In a more complicated program, I may end up checking `hankees > socks` a dozen times. It would be like asking the same question over and over again.

Instead of repeatedly checking the `hankees > socks` condition, I store the game's outcome as an enum value. Then I check the enum value as many times as I want. That's a very tidy way to solve the repeated checking problem.

Creating a project with two Java source files

You can't run Listing 10-8 without Listing 10-7. And Listing 10-7 does nothing on its own. To do anything useful, you have to put these two files in the same JCreator project. Here's how:

1. **Create a new JCreator project.**

   For details, see Chapter 3.

2. **Right-click the new project's name in the File View tree. Then, in the resulting context menu, select Add⇨New Class.**

   JCreator's Class Wizard appears.

3. In the wizard's Name field, type the name of your enum type.

To create the code in Listing 10-7, type the name **WhoWins**.

4. Click Finish.

The wizard disappears to reveal JCreator's work area. The editor pane has a new WhoWins.java tab. Delete any code that you see in the WhoWins.java pane, and replace that code with the line in Listing 10-7. (See Figure 10-14.)

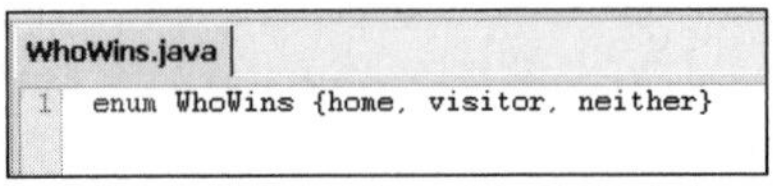

Figure 10-14:
Editing the
WhoWins.
java file.

```
WhoWins.java
 1   enum WhoWins {home, visitor, neither}
```

5. Follow the usual steps to add a new Scoreboard class.

In Scoreboard.java file's editor pane, type the code in Listing 10-8.

6. Choose Build➪Compile Project.

7. Choose Build➪Execute Project.

Voila! The code runs as it does in Figure 10-13.

Chapter 11

How to Flick a Virtual Switch

*I*magine playing *Let's Make a Deal* with ten different doors. "Choose door number 1, door number 2, door number 3, door number 4. . . . Wait! Let's break for a commercial. When we come back, I'll say the names of the other six doors."

Meet the switch Statement

The code back in Listing 9-2 in Chapter 9 simulates a simple electronic oracle. Ask the program a question, and the program randomly generates a yes or no answer. But, as toys go, the code in Listing 9-2 isn't much fun. The code has only two possible answers. There's no variety. Even the earliest talking dolls could say about ten different sentences.

Suppose that you want to enhance the code of Listing 9-2. The call to `myRandom.nextInt(10) + 1` generates numbers from 1 to 10. So maybe you can display a different sentence for each of the ten numbers. A big pile of `if` statements should do the trick:

```
if (randomNumber == 1) {
    System.out.println("Yes. Isn't it obvious?");
}
if (randomNumber == 2) {
    System.out.println("No, and don't ask again.");
}
if (randomNumber == 3) {
    System.out.print("Yessir, yessir!");
    System.out.println(" Three bags full.");
}
```

```
  if (randomNumber == 4)
    .
    .
    .
if (randomNumber < 1 || randomNumber > 10) {
    System.out.print("Sorry, the electronic oracle");
    System.out.println(" is closed for repairs.");
}
```

But that approach seems wasteful. Why not create a statement that checks the value of `randomNumber` just once and then takes an action based on the value that it finds? Fortunately, just such a statement exists: the *switch* statement. Listing 11-1 has an example of a `switch` statement.

Listing 11-1: An Answer for Every Occasion

```java
import java.util.Scanner;
import java.util.Random;
import static java.lang.System.out;

class TheOldSwitcheroo {

    public static void main(String args[]) {
        Scanner myScanner = new Scanner(System.in);
        Random myRandom = new Random();
        int randomNumber;

        out.print("Type your question, my child:  ");
        myScanner.nextLine();

        randomNumber = myRandom.nextInt(10) + 1;

        switch (randomNumber) {
        case 1:
            out.println("Yes. Isn't it obvious?");
            break;

        case 2:
            out.println("No, and don't ask again.");
            break;

        case 3:
            out.print("Yessir, yessir!");
            out.println(" Three bags full.");
            break;

        case 4:
            out.print("What part of 'no'");
            out.println(" don't you understand?");
            break;
```

```
    case 5:
        out.println("No chance, Lance.");
        break;

    case 6:
        out.println("Sure, whatever.");
        break;

    case 7:
        out.print("Yes, but only if");
        out.println(" you're nice to me.");
        break;

    case 8:
        out.println("Yes (as if I care).");
        break;

    case 9:
        out.print("No, not until");
        out.println(" Cromwell seizes Dover.");
        break;

    case 10:
        out.print("No, not until");
        out.println(" Nell squeezes Rover.");
        break;

    default:
        out.print("You think you have");
        out.print(" problems?");
        out.print(" My random number");
        out.println(" generator is broken!");
        break;
    }

    out.println("Goodbye");
  }
}
```

The cases in a switch statement

Figure 11-1 shows three runs of the program in Listing 11-1. Here's what happens during one of these runs:

✔ The user types a heavy question, and the variable `randomNumber` gets a value. In the second run of Figure 11-1, this value is 2.

✔ Execution of the code in Listing 11-1 reaches the top of the `switch` statement, so the computer starts checking this statement's `case` clauses. The value 2 doesn't match the topmost `case` clause (the `case 1` clause), so the computer moves on to the next `case` clause.

🖙 The value in the next `case` clause (the number 2) matches the value of the `randomNumber` variable, so the computer executes the statements in this `case 2` clause. These two statements are

```
out.println("No, and don't ask again.");
break;
```

The first of the two statements displays `No, and don't ask again` on the screen. The second statement is called a *break* statement. (What a surprise!) When the computer encounters a `break` statement, the computer jumps out of whatever `switch` statement it's in. So in Listing 11-1, the computer skips right past `case 3`, `case 4`, and so on. The computer jumps to the statement just after the end of the `switch` statement.

🖙 The computer displays `Goodbye`, because that's what the statement after the `switch` statement tells the computer to do.

Figure 11-1: Running the code of Listing 11-1.

```
Type your question, my child:  Is the Continuum Hypothesis true?
Sure, whatever.
Goodbye

Type your question, my child:  Does P=NP?
No, and don't ask again.
Goodbye

Type your question, my child:  Does Turing machine T halt on input i?
Yes, but only if you're nice to me.
Goodbye
```

The overall idea behind the program in Listing 11-1 is illustrated in Figure 11-2.

The default in a switch statement

What if something goes terribly wrong during a run of the Listing 11-1 program? Suppose the expression `myRandom.nextInt(10) + 1` generates a number that's not in the 1 to 10 range. Then the computer responds by dropping past all the `case` clauses. Instead of landing on a `case` clause, the computer jumps to the `default` clause. In the `default` clause, the computer displays `You think you have problems?...`, and then breaks out of the `switch` statement. After the computer is out of the `switch` statement, the computer displays `Goodbye`.

You don't really need to put a `break` at the very end of a `switch` statement. In Listing 11-1, the last `break` (the `break` that's part of the `default` clause) is just for the sake of overall tidiness.

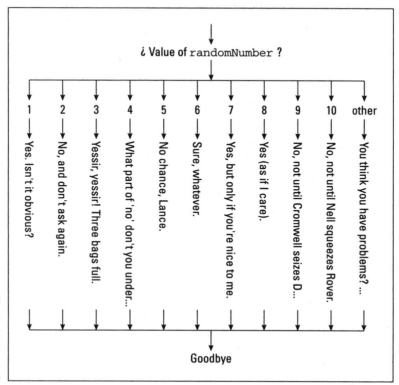

Figure 11-2:
A fork with
eleven
prongs.

¿ Value of randomNumber ?

| 1 | 2 | 3 | 4 | 5 | 6 | 7 | 8 | 9 | 10 | other |

1 — Yes. Isn't it obvious?

2 — No, and don't ask again.

3 — Yessir, yessir! Three bags full.

4 — What part of 'no' don't you under...

5 — No chance, Lance.

6 — Sure, whatever.

7 — Yes, but only if you're nice to me.

8 — Yes (as if I care).

9 — No, not until Cromwell seizes D...

10 — No, not until Nell squeezes Rover.

other — You think you have problems? ...

Goodbye

Picky details about the switch statement

A switch statement can take the following form:

```
switch (Expression) {
case FirstValue:
    Statements

case SecondValue:
    MoreStatements

// ... more cases...

default:
    EvenMoreStatements
}
```

Here are some tidbits about switch statements:

✔ The *Expression* doesn't have to have an int value. It can be char, byte, short, or int. For example, the following code works nicely:

```
char letterGrade;
letterGrade = myScanner.findInLine(".").charAt(0);

switch (letterGrade) {
case 'A':
    System.out.println("Excellent");
    break;

case 'B':
    System.out.println("Good");
    break;

case 'C':
    System.out.println("Average");
    break;
}
```

✔ The *Expression* doesn't have to be a single variable. It can be any expression of type `char`, `byte`, `short`, or `int`. For example, you can simulate the rolling of two dice with the following code:

```
int die1, die2;

die1 = myRandom.nextInt(6) + 1;
die2 = myRandom.nextInt(6) + 1;

switch (die1 + die2) {
    //...etc.
```

✔ The cases in a `switch` statement don't have to be in order. Here's some acceptable code:

```
switch (randomNumber) {
case 2:
    System.out.println("No, and don't ask again.");
    break;

case 1:
    System.out.println("Yes. Isn't it obvious?");
    break;

case 3:
    System.out.print("Yessir, yessir!");
    System.out.println(" Three bags full.");
    break;

//...etc.
```

This mixing of cases may slow you down when you're trying to read a program, but it's legal nonetheless.

✔ You don't need a `case` for each expected value of the *Expression*. You can leave some expected values to the `default`. Here's an example:

```
switch (randomNumber) {
case 1:
    System.out.println("Yes. Isn't it obvious?");
    break;

case 5:
    System.out.println("No chance, Lance.");
    break;

case 7:
    System.out.print("Yes, but only if");
    System.out.println(" you're nice to me.");
    break;

case 10:
    System.out.print("No, not until");
    System.out.println(" Nell squeezes Rover.");
    break;

default:
    System.out.print("Sorry,");
    System.out.println(" I just can't decide.");
    break;
}
```

✔ The `default` clause is optional.

```
switch (randomNumber) {
case 1:
    System.out.println("Yes. Isn't it obvious?");
    break;

case 2:
    System.out.println("No, and don't ask again.");
    break;

case 3:
    System.out.print("I'm too tired.");
    System.out.println(" Go ask somebody else.");
}
System.out.println("Goodbye");
```

If you have no `default` clause, and a value that's not covered by any of the cases comes up, then the `switch` statement does nothing. For example, if `randomNumber` is 4, then the code shown above displays `Goodbye`, and nothing else.

✔ In some ways, `if` statements are more versatile than `switch` statements. For example, you can't use a condition in a `switch` statement's *Expression*:

```
//You can't do this:
switch (age >= 12 && age < 65)
```

You can't use a condition as a `case` value either:

```
//You can't do this:
switch (age) {
case age <= 12: //...etc.
```

To break or not to break

In every Java programmer's life, a time comes when he or she forgets to use `break` statements. At first, the resulting output is confusing, but then the programmer remembers fall-through. The term *fall-through* describes what happens when you end a `case` without a `break` statement. What happens is that execution of the code falls right through to the next `case` in line. Execution keeps falling through until you eventually reach a `break` statement or the end of the entire `switch` statement.

If you don't believe me, just look at Listing 11-2. This listing's code has a `switch` statement gone bad:

Listing 11-2:   Please, Gimme a Break!

```
/*
 * This isn't good code. The programmer forgot some
 * of the break statements.
 */
import java.util.Scanner;
import java.util.Random;
import static java.lang.System.out;

class BadBreaks {

    public static void main(String args[]) {
        Scanner myScanner = new Scanner(System.in);
        Random myRandom = new Random();
        int randomNumber;

        out.print("Type your question, my child:   ");
        myScanner.nextLine();

        randomNumber = myRandom.nextInt(10) + 1;

        switch (randomNumber) {
        case 1:
            out.println("Yes. Isn't it obvious?");

        case 2:
            out.println("No, and don't ask again.");
```

```
        case 3:
            out.print("Yessir, yessir!");
            out.println(" Three bags full.");

        case 4:
            out.print("What part of 'no'");
            out.println(" don't you understand?");
            break;

        case 5:
            out.println("No chance, Lance.");

        case 6:
            out.println("Sure, whatever.");

        case 7:
            out.print("Yes, but only if");
            out.println(" you're nice to me.");

        case 8:
            out.println("Yes (as if I care).");

        case 9:
            out.print("No, not until");
            out.println(" Cromwell seizes Dover.");

        case 10:
            out.print("No, not until");
            out.println(" Nell squeezes Rover.");

        default:
            out.print("You think you have");
            out.print(" problems?");
            out.print(" My random number");
            out.println(" generator is broken!");
        }

        out.println("Goodbye");
    }
}
```

I've put two runs of this code in Figure 11-3. In the first run, the randomNumber is 7. The program executes cases 7 through 10, and the default. In the second run, the randomNumber is 3. The program executes cases 3 and 4. Then, because case 4 has a break statement, the program jumps out of the switch and displays Goodbye.

The switch statement in Listing 11-2 is missing some break statements. Even without these break statements, the code compiles with no errors. But when you run the code in Listing 11-2, you don't get the results that you want.

```
Type your question, my child:  Do good things happen to good people?
Yes, but only if you're nice to me.
Yes (as if I care).
No, not until Cromwell seizes Dover.
No, not until Nell squeezes Rover.
You think you have problems? My random number generator is broken!
Goodbye

Type your question, my child:  Is your switch statement missing some breaks?
Yessir, yessir! Three bags full.
What part of 'no' don't you understand?
Goodbye
```

Figure 11-3:
Please
make up
your mind.

Using Fall-through to Your Advantage

Often, when you're using a switch statement, you don't want fall-through, so you pepper break statements throughout the switch. But, sometimes, fall-through is just the thing you need.

Take the number of days in a month. Is there a simple rule for this? Months containing the letter "r" have 31 days? Months in which "i" comes before "e" except after "c" have 30 days?

You can fiddle with if conditions all you want. But to handle all the possibilities, I prefer a switch statement. Listing 11-3 demonstrates the idea.

Listing 11-3:   Finding the Number of Days in a Month

```java
import java.util.Scanner;

class DaysInEachMonth {

    public static void main(String args[]) {
        Scanner myScanner = new Scanner(System.in);
        int month, numberOfDays = 0;
        boolean isLeapYear;

        System.out.print("Which month? ");
        month = myScanner.nextInt();

        switch (month) {
        case 1:
        case 3:
        case 5:
        case 7:
        case 8:
        case 10:
        case 12:
            numberOfDays = 31;
            break;

        case 4:
        case 6:
```

```
     case 9:
     case 11:
         numberOfDays = 30;
         break;

     case 2:
         System.out.print("Leap year (true/false)? ");
         isLeapYear = myScanner.nextBoolean();
         if (isLeapYear) {
            numberOfDays = 29;
         } else {
            numberOfDays = 28;
         }
     }

     System.out.print(numberOfDays);
     System.out.println(" days");
   }
}
```

Figure 11-4 shows several runs of the program in Listing 11-3. For month number 6, the computer jumps to case 6. There are no statements inside the case 6 clause, so that part of the program's run is pretty boring.

Figure 11-4:
How many days until the next big deadline?

```
Which month? 1
31 days

Which month? 6
30 days

Which month? 2
Leap year (true/false)? false
28 days

Which month? 2
Leap year (true/false)? true
29 days
```

But with no break in the case 6 clause, the computer marches right along to case 9. Once again, the computer finds no statements and no break, so the computer ventures to the next case, which is case 11. At that point, the computer hits pay dirt. The computer assigns 30 to numberOfDays, and breaks out of the entire switch statement. (See Figure 11-5.)

February is the best month of all. For one thing, the February case in Listing 11-3 contains a call to the Scanner class's nextBoolean method. The method expects me to type either true or false. The code uses whatever word I type to assign a value to a boolean variable. (In Listing 11-3, I assign true or false to the isLeapYear variable.)

February also contains its own if statement. In Chapter 10, I nest if statements within other if statements. But in February, I nest an if statement within a switch statement. That's cool.

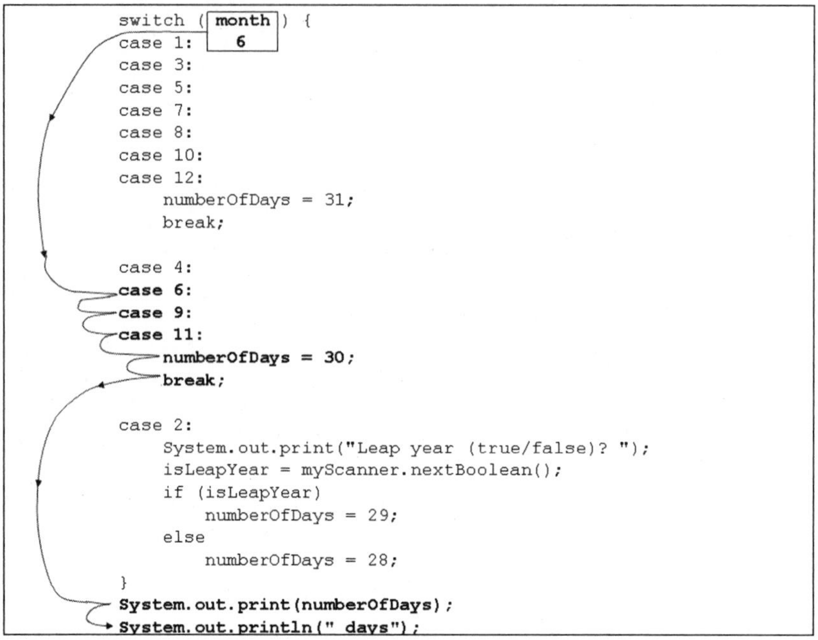

```
switch ( month ) {
    case 1:        6
    case 3:
    case 5:
    case 7:
    case 8:
    case 10:
    case 12:
        numberOfDays = 31;
        break;

    case 4:
    case 6:
    case 9:
    case 11:
        numberOfDays = 30;
        break;

    case 2:
        System.out.print("Leap year (true/false)? ");
        isLeapYear = myScanner.nextBoolean();
        if (isLeapYear)
            numberOfDays = 29;
        else
            numberOfDays = 28;
    }
    System.out.print(numberOfDays);
    System.out.println(" days");
```

Figure 11-5:
Follow the
bouncing
ball.

Using a Conditional Operator

Java has a neat feature that I can't resist writing about. Using this feature, you
can think about alternatives in a very natural way.

And what do I mean by "a natural way?" If I think out loud as I imitate the if
statement near the end of Listing 11-3, I come up with this:

```
//The thinking in Listing 11-3:
What should I do next?
If this is a leap year,
    I'll make the numberOfDays be 29;
Otherwise,
    I'll make the numberOfDays be 28.
```

I'm wandering into an if statement without a clue about what I'm doing next.
That seems silly. It's February, and everybody knows what you do in
February. You ask how many days the month has.

In my opinion, the code in Listing 11-3 doesn't reflect the most natural way to
think about February. So here's a more natural way:

```
//A more natural way to think about the problem:
The value of numberOfDays is...
    Wait! Is this a leap year?
        If yes, 29
        If no, 28
```

In this second, more natural way of thinking, I know from the start that I'm picking a number of days. So by the time I reach a fork in the road (Is this a leap year?), the only remaining task is to choose between 29 and 28.

I can make the choice with finesse:

```
case 2:
    System.out.print("Leap year (true/false)? ");
    isLeapYear = myScanner.nextBoolean();
    numberOfDays = isLeapYear ? 29 : 28;
```

The ? : combination is called a *conditional operator*. In Figure 11-6, I show you how my natural thinking about February can morph into the conditional operator's format.

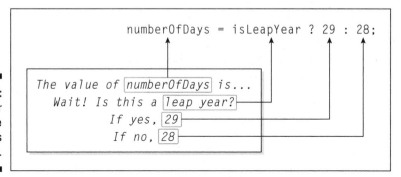

Figure 11-6:
From your mind to the computer's code.

Taken as a whole, isLeapYear ? 29 : 28 is an expression with a value. And what value does this expression have? Well, the value of isLeapYear ? 29 : 28 is either 29 or 28. It depends on whether isLeapYear is or isn't true. That's how the conditional operator works:

- ✔ If the stuff before the question mark is true, then the whole expression's value is whatever comes between the question mark and the colon.

- ✔ If the stuff before the question mark is false, then the whole expression's value is whatever comes after the colon.

Figure 11-7 gives you a goofy way to visualize these ideas.

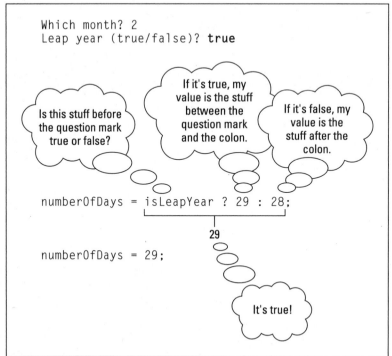

Figure 11-7:
Have you
ever seen an
expression
talking to
itself?

So the conditional operator's overall effect is as if the computer is executing

```
numberOfDays = 29;
```

or

```
numberOfDays = 28;
```

One way or another, `numberOfDays` gets a value, and the code solves the problem with style.

Chapter 12

Around and Around It Goes

. . . .

In This Chapter

▶ Creating program loops

▶ Formulating solutions to problems with loops

▶ Diagnosing loop problems

. . . .

*C*hapter 8 has code to reverse the letters in a four-letter word that the user enters. In case you jumped over Chapter 8 or you just don't want to flip back, here's a quick recap of the code:

```
c1 = myScanner.findInLine(".").charAt(0);
c2 = myScanner.findInLine(".").charAt(0);
c3 = myScanner.findInLine(".").charAt(0);
c4 = myScanner.findInLine(".").charAt(0);

System.out.print(c4);
System.out.print(c3);
System.out.print(c2);
System.out.print(c1);
```

The code is just dandy for words with exactly four letters, but how do you reverse a five-letter word? As the code stands, you have to add two new statements:

```
c1 = myScanner.findInLine(".").charAt(0);
c2 = myScanner.findInLine(".").charAt(0);
c3 = myScanner.findInLine(".").charAt(0);
c4 = myScanner.findInLine(".").charAt(0);
c5 = myScanner.findInLine(".").charAt(0);

System.out.print(c5);
System.out.print(c4);
System.out.print(c3);
System.out.print(c2);
System.out.print(c1);
```

What a drag! You add statements to a program whenever the size of a word changes! You remove statements when the input shrinks! That can't be the best way to solve the problem. Maybe you can command a computer to add statements automatically. (But then again, maybe you can't.)

As luck would have it, you can do something that's even better. You can write a statement once, and tell the computer to execute the statement many times. How many times? You can tell the computer to execute a statement as many times as it needs to be executed.

That's the big idea. The rest of this chapter has the details.

Repeating Instructions Over and Over Again (Java while Statements)

Here's a simple dice game: Keep rolling two dice until you roll 7 or 11. Listing 12-1 has a program that simulates the action in the game, and Figure 12-1 shows two runs of the program.

Listing 12-1: Roll 7 or 11

```java
import java.util.Random;
import static java.lang.System.out;

class SimpleDiceGame {

    public static void main(String args[]) {
        Random myRandom = new Random();
        int die1 = 0, die2 = 0;

        while (die1 + die2 != 7 && die1 + die2 != 11) {
            die1 = myRandom.nextInt(6) + 1;
            die2 = myRandom.nextInt(6) + 1;

            out.print(die1);
            out.print(" ");
            out.println(die2);
        }

        out.print("Rolled ");
        out.println(die1 + die2);
    }
}
```

At the core of Listing 12-1 is a thing called a *while statement* (also known as a *while loop*). A while statement has the following form:

```java
while (Condition) {
    Statements
}
```

```
3 1
4 3
Rolled 7

2 1
4 6
5 3
6 4
4 6
1 5
2 2
1 5
1 3
2 6
1 4
6 5
Rolled 11
```

Figure 12-1: Momma needs a new pair of shoes.

Rephrased in English, the `while` statement in Listing 12-1 would say

```
while the sum of the two dice isn't 7 and isn't 11
keep doing all the stuff in curly braces: {



}
```

The stuff in curly braces (the stuff that is repeated over and over again) is the code that gets two new random numbers and displays those random numbers' values. The statements in curly braces are repeated as long as `die1 + die2 != 7 && die1 + die2 != 11` keeps being true.

Each repetition of the statements in the loop is called an *iteration* of the loop. In Figure 12-1, the first run has two iterations, and the second run has twelve iterations.

When `die1 + die2 != 7 && die1 + die2 != 11` is no longer true (that is, when the `sum` is either 7 or 11), then the repeating of statements stops dead in its tracks. The computer marches on to the statements that come after the loop.

Following the action in a loop

To trace the action of the code in Listing 12-1, I'll borrow numbers from the first run in Figure 12-1:

- ✔ At the start, the values of `die1` and `die2` are both 0.

- ✔ The computer gets to the top of the `while` statement, and checks to see if `die1 + die2 != 7 && die1 + die2 != 11` is true. (See Figure 12-2.) The condition is true so the computer takes the `true` path in Figure 12-3.

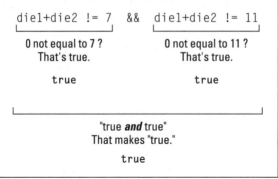

Figure 12-2:
Two wrongs
don't make
a right, but
two trues
make a true.

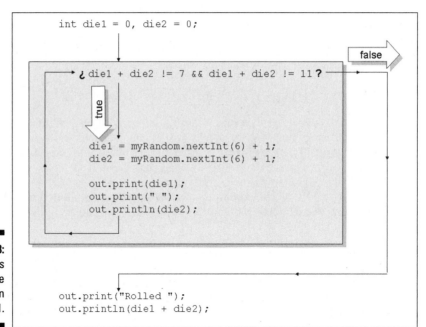

Figure 12-3:
Paths
through the
code in
Listing 12-1.

The computer performs an iteration of the loop. During this iteration, the computer gets new values for `die1` and `die2`, and prints those values on the screen. In the first run of Figure 12-1, the new values are 3 and 1.

✔ The computer returns to the top of the `while` statement, and checks to see if `die1 + die2 != 7 && die1 + die2 != 11` is still true. The condition is true so the computer takes the `true` path in Figure 12-3.

The computer performs another iteration of the loop. During this iteration, the computer gets new values for `die1` and `die2`, and prints those values on the screen. In Figure 12-1, the new values are 4 and 3.

✔ The computer returns to the top of the `while` statement, and checks to see if `die1 + die2 != 7 && die1 + die2 != 11` is still true. Lo and behold! This condition has become false! (See Figure 12-4.) The computer takes the `false` path in Figure 12-3.

The computer leaps to the statements after the loop. The computer displays `Rolled 7`, and ends its run of the program.

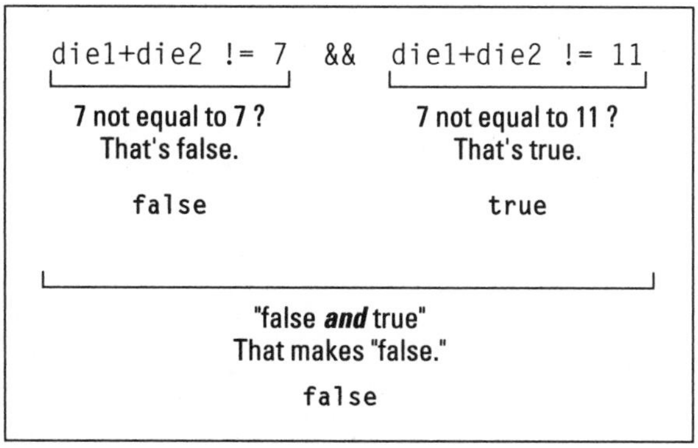

```
die1+die2 != 7    &&   die1+die2 != 11
└──────┬──────┘        └──────┬──────┘

   7 not equal to 7 ?         7 not equal to 11 ?
      That's false.              That's true.

        false                       true

   └──────────────────────┬──────────────────────┘

              "false and true"
              That makes "false."

                   false
```

Figure 12-4:
Look! I rolled
a seven!

No early bailout

In Listing 12-1, when the computer finds `die1 + die2 != 7 && die1 + die2 != 11` to be true, the computer marches on and executes all five statements inside the loop's curly braces. The computer executes

```
die1 = myRandom.nextInt(6) + 1;
die2 = myRandom.nextInt(6) + 1;
```

Maybe (just maybe), the new values of `die1` and `die2` add up to 7. Even so, the computer doesn't jump out in mid-loop. The computer finishes the iteration, and executes

```
out.print(die1);
out.print(" ");
out.println(die2);
```

one more time. The computer performs the test again (to see if `die1 + die2 != 7 && die1 + die2 != 11` is still true) only after it fully executes all five statements in the loop.

Statements and blocks (Plagiarizing my own sentences from Chapter 9)

Java's `while` statements have a lot in common with `if` statements. Like an `if` statement, a `while` statement is a *compound statement*. That is, a `while` statement includes other statements within it. Also, both `if` statements and `while` statements typically include *blocks* of statements. When you surround a bunch of statements with curly braces, you get what's called a *block*, and a block behaves, in all respects, like a single statement.

In a typical `while` statement, you want the computer to repeat several smaller statements over and over again. To repeat several smaller statements, you combine those statements into one big statement. To do this, you make a block using curly braces.

In Listing 12-1, the block

```
{
    die1 = myRandom.nextInt(6)
+ 1;
    die2 = myRandom.nextInt(6)
+ 1;

    out.print(die1);
    out.print(" ");
    out.println(die2);
}
```

is a single statement. It's a statement that has, within it, five smaller statements. So this big block, (this single statement) serves as one big statement inside the `while` statement in Listing 12-1.

That's the story about `while` statements and blocks. To find out how this stuff applies to `if` statements, see the "Statements and blocks" sidebar near the end of Chapter 9.

Thinking about Loops (What Statements Go Where)

Here's a simplified version of the card game Twenty-One: You keep taking cards until the total is 21 or higher. Then, if the total is 21, you win. If the total is higher, you lose. (By the way, each face card counts as a 10.) To play this game, you want a program whose runs look like the runs in Figure 12-5.

In most sections of this book, I put a program's listing before the description of the program's features. But this section is different. This section deals with strategies for composing code. So in this section, I start by brainstorming about strategies.

Finding some pieces

How do you write a program that plays a simplified version of Twenty-One? I start by fishing for clues in the game's rules, spelled out in this section's first paragraph. The big fishing expedition is illustrated in Figure 12-6.

```
Card      Total
8         8
6         14
3         17
4         21
You win :-)


Card      Total
1         1
7         8
3         11
4         15
2         17
2         19
3         22
You lose :-(
```

Figure 12-5: You win sum; you lose sum.

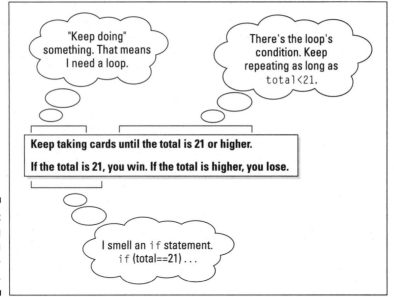

Figure 12-6: Thinking about a programming problem.

With the reasoning in Figure 12-6, I need a loop and an if statement:

```
while (total < 21) {
    //do stuff
}

if (total == 21) {
    //You win
} else {
    //You lose
}
```

What else do I need to make this program work? Look at the sample output in Figure 12-5. I need a heading with the words `Card` and `Total`. That's a call to `System.out.println`:

```
System.out.println("Card     Total");
```

I also need several lines of output — each containing two numbers. For example, in Figure 12-5, the line 6 14 displays the values of two variables. One variable stores the most recently picked card; the other variable stores the total of all cards picked so far:

```
System.out.print(card);
System.out.print("       ");
System.out.println(total);
```

Now I have four chunks of code, but I haven't decided how they all fit together. Well, you can go right ahead and call me crazy. But at this point in the process, I imagine those four chunks of code circling around one another, like part of a dream sequence in a low-budget movie. As you may imagine, I'm not very good at illustrating circling code in dream sequences. Even so, I handed my idea to the art department at Wiley Publishing, and they came up with the picture in Figure 12-7.

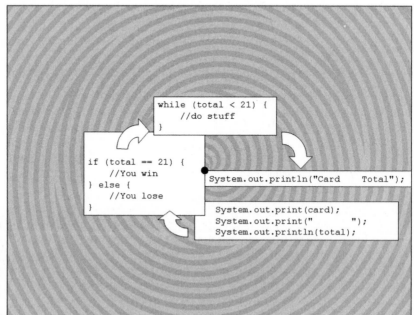

Figure 12-7: ... and where they stop, nobody knows.

Assembling the pieces

Where should I put each piece of code? The best way to approach the problem is to ask how many times each piece of code should be executed:

- **The program displays** card **and** total **values more than once.** For example, in the first run of Figure 12-5, the program displays these values four times (first 8 8, then 6 14, and so on). To get this repeated display, I put the code that creates the display inside the loop:

```
while (total < 21) {
    System.out.print(card);
    System.out.print("          ");
    System.out.println(total);
}
```

- **The program displays the** Card Total **heading only once per run.** This display comes before any of the repeated number displays, so I put the heading code before the loop:

```
System.out.println("Card      Total");

while (total < 21) {
    System.out.print(card);
    System.out.print("          ");
    System.out.println(total);
}
```

- **The program displays** You win **or** You lose **only once per run.** This message display comes after the repeated number displays. So I put the win/lose code after the loop:

```
//Preliminary draft code - NOT ready for prime time:
System.out.println("Card      Total");

while (total < 21) {
    System.out.print(card);
    System.out.print("          ");
    System.out.println(total);
}

if (total == 21) {
    System.out.println("You win :-)");
} else {
    System.out.println("You lose :-(");
}
```

Getting values for variables

I almost have a working program. But if I take the code that I've developed for a mental test run, I face a few problems. To see what I mean, picture yourself in the computer's shoes for a minute. (Well, a computer doesn't have shoes. Picture yourself in the computer's boots.)

You start at the top of the code shown previously (the code that starts with the `Preliminary draft` comment). In the code's first statement, you display the words `Card Total`. So far, so good. But then you encounter the `while` loop, and test the condition `total < 21`. Well, is `total` less than 21, or isn't it? Honestly, I'm tempted to make up an answer, because I'm embarrassed about not knowing what the `total` variable's value is. (I'm sure the computer is embarrassed too.)

The variable `total` must have a known value before the computer reaches the top of the `while` loop. Because a player starts with no cards at all, the initial `total` value should be 0. That settles it. I declare `int total = 0` at the top of the program.

But what about my friend, the `card` variable? Should I set `card` to zero also? No. There's no zero-valued card in a deck (at least, not when I'm playing fair). Besides, `card` should get a new value several times during the program's run.

Wait! In the previous sentence, the phrase *several times* tickles a neuron in my brain. It stimulates the *inside a loop* reflex. So I place an assignment to the `card` variable inside my `while` loop:

```
//This is a DRAFT - still NOT ready for prime time:
int card, total = 0;

System.out.println("Card     Total");

while (total < 21) {
    card = myRandom.nextInt(10) + 1;

    System.out.print(card);
    System.out.print("       ");
    System.out.println(total);
}

if (total == 21) {
    System.out.println("You win :-)");
} else {
    System.out.println("You lose :-(");
}
```

The code still has an error, and I can probably find the error with more computer role-playing. But instead, I get daring. I run this beta code to see what happens. Figure 12-8 shows part of a run.

Unfortunately, the run in Figure 12-8 doesn't stop on its own. This kind of processing is called an *infinite loop*. The loop runs and runs until someone trips over the computer's extension cord.

```
General Output
────────────────
Card      Total
5         0
10         0
3         0
4         0
8         0
5         0
5         0
1         0
6         0
7         0
2         0
1         0
3         0
4         0
8         0
3         0
```

Figure 12-8:
An incorrect
run.

You can stop a program's run dead in its tracks. If you use JCreator, choose Tools⇨Stop Tool from the main menu. With many other environments, pressing Ctrl+C stops the execution of a runaway program.

From infinity to affinity

For some problems, an infinite loop is normal and desirable. Consider, for example, a real-time mission-critical application — air traffic control, or the monitoring of a heart-lung machine. In these situations, a program should run and run and run.

But a game of Twenty-One should end pretty quickly. In Figure 12-8, the game doesn't end because the total never reaches 21 or higher. In fact, the total is always zero. The problem is that my code has no statement to change the total variable's value. I should add each card's value to the total:

```
total += card;
```

Again, I ask myself where this statement belongs in the code. How many times should the computer execute this assignment statement? Once at the start of the program? Once at the end of the run? Repeatedly?

The computer should repeatedly add a card's value to the running total. In fact, the computer should add to the total each time a card gets drawn. So the assignment statement above should be inside the while loop, right alongside the statement that gets a new card value:

```
card = myRandom.nextInt(10) + 1;
total += card;
```

With this revelation, I'm ready to see the complete program. The code is in Listing 12-2, and two runs of the code are shown in Figure 12-5.

Escapism

You can use a neat trick to make a program's output line up correctly. In Figure 12-5, the numbers 8 8, then 6 14 (and so on) are displayed. I want these numbers to be right under the heading words Card and Total. Normally, you can get perfect vertical columns by pressing the tab key, but a computer program creates the output in Figure 12-5. How can you get a computer program to press the tab key?

In Java, there's a way. You can put \t inside double quote marks.

```
System.out.println("Card\tTotal
    ");

System.out.print(card);
```

```
System.out.print("\t");
System.out.println(total);
```

In the first statement, the computer displays Card, then jumps to the next tab stop on the screen, and then displays Total. In the next three statements, the computer displays a card number (like the number 6), then jumps to the next tab stop (directly under the word Total), and then displays a total value (like the number 14).

The \t combination of characters is an example of an *escape sequence*. Another of Java's escape sequences, the combination \n, moves the cursor to a new line. In other words, System.out.print("Hello\n") does the same thing as System.out.println("Hello").

Listing 12-2: A Simplified Version of the Game Twenty-One

```
import java.util.Random;

class PlayTwentyOne {

    public static void main(String args[]) {
        Random myRandom = new Random();
        int card, total = 0;

        System.out.println("Card     Total");

        while (total < 21) {
            card = myRandom.nextInt(10) + 1;
            total += card;

            System.out.print(card);
            System.out.print("        ");
            System.out.println(total);
        }

        if (total == 21) {
            System.out.println("You win :-)");
        } else {
            System.out.println("You lose :-(");
        }
    }
}
```

If you've read this whole section, then you're probably exhausted. Creating a loop can be a lot of work. Fortunately, the more you practice, the easier it becomes.

Thinking About Loops (Priming)

I remember when I was a young boy. We lived on Front Street in Philadelphia, near where the El train turned onto Kensington Avenue. Come early morning, I'd have to go outside and get water from the well. I'd pump several times before any water would come out. Ma and Pa called it "priming the pump."

These days I don't prime pumps. I prime `while` loops. Consider the case of a busy network administrator. She needs a program that extracts a username from an e-mail address. For example, the program reads

```
John@BurdBrain.com
```

and writes

```
John
```

How does the program do it? Like other examples in the chapter, this problem involves repetition:

```
Repeatedly do the following:
    Read a character.
    Write the character.
```

The program then stops the repetition when it finds the @ sign. I take a stab at writing this program. My first attempt doesn't work, but it's a darn good start. It's in Listing 12-3.

Listing 12-3:   Trying to Get a Username from an E-mail Address

```
/*
 * This code does NOT work, but I'm not discouraged.
 */
import java.util.Scanner;

class FirstAttempt {

    public static void main(String args[]) {
        Scanner myScanner = new Scanner(System.in);
        char symbol = ' ';
```

(continued)

Listing 12-3 *(continued)*

```
        while (symbol != '@') {
            symbol = myScanner.findInLine(".").charAt(0);
            System.out.print(symbol);
        }

        System.out.println();
    }
}
```

When you run the code in Listing 12-3, you get the output shown in Figure 12-9. The user types one character after another — the letter J, then o, then h, and so on. At first, the program in Listing 12-3 does nothing. (The computer doesn't send any of the user's input to the program until the user presses Enter.) After the user types a whole e-mail address and presses Enter, the program gets its first character (the J in John).

Unfortunately, the program's output isn't what you expect. Instead of just the user name John, you get the username and the @ sign.

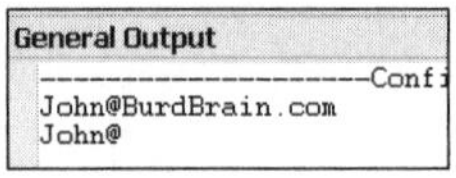

Figure 12-9:
Oops! Got
the @ sign
too.

```
General Output
------------------------Confi
John@BurdBrain.com
John@
```

To find out why this happens, follow the computer's actions as it reads the input John@BurdBrain.com:

```
Set symbol to ' ' (a blank space).

Is that blank space the same as an @ sign?
No, so perform a loop iteration.
    Input the letter 'J'.
    Print the letter 'J'.

Is that 'J' the same as an @ sign?
No, so perform a loop iteration.
    Input the letter 'o'.
    Print the letter 'o'.

Is that 'o' the same as an @ sign?
No, so perform a loop iteration.
    Input the letter 'h'.
    Print the letter 'h'.
```

```
Is that 'h' the same as an @ sign?
No, so perform a loop iteration.
    Input the letter 'n'.
    Print the letter 'n'.

Is that 'n' the same as an @ sign?   //Here's the problem.
No, so perform a loop iteration.
    Input the @ sign.
    Print the @ sign.                //Oops!

Is that @ sign the same as an @ sign?
Yes, so stop iterating.
```

Near the end of the program's run, the computer compares the letter n with the @ sign. Because n isn't an @ sign, the computer dives right into the loop:

- ✔ The first statement in the loop reads an @ sign from the keyboard.

- ✔ The second statement in the loop doesn't check to see if it's time to stop printing. Instead, that second statement just marches ahead and displays the @ sign.

After you've displayed the @ sign, there's no going back. You can't change your mind and undisplay the @ sign. So the code in Listing 12-3 doesn't quite work.

Working on the problem

You learn from your mistakes. The problem with Listing 12-3 is that, between reading and writing a character, the program doesn't check for an @ sign. Instead of doing "Test, Input, Print," it should do "Input, Test, Print." That is, instead of doing this:

```
Is that 'o' the same as an @ sign?
No, so perform a loop iteration.
    Input the letter 'h'.
    Print the letter 'h'.

Is that 'h' the same as an @ sign?
No, so perform a loop iteration.
    Input the letter 'n'.
    Print the letter 'n'.

Is that 'n' the same as an @ sign?   //Here's the problem.
No, so perform a loop iteration.
    Input the @ sign.
    Print the @ sign.                //Oops!
```

the program should do this:

```
    Input the letter 'o'.
Is that 'o' the same as an @ sign?
No, so perform a loop iteration.
    Print the letter 'o'.

    Input the letter 'n'.
Is that 'n' the same as an @ sign?
No, so perform a loop iteration.
    Print the letter 'n'.

    Input the @ sign.
Is that @ sign the same as an @ sign?
Yes, so stop iterating.
```

This cycle is shown in Figure 12-10.

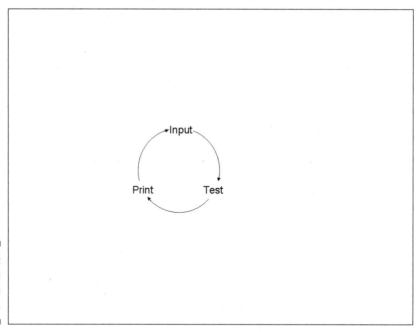

Figure 12-10:
What the
program
needs to do.

You can try to imitate the following informal pattern:

```
    Input a character.
Is that character the same as an @ sign?
If not, perform a loop iteration.
    Print the character.
```

The problem is, you can't create a `while` loop that looks like this:

```
//This is not correct code:
{
    symbol = myScanner.findInLine(".").charAt(0);
while (symbol != '@')
    System.out.print(symbol);
}
```

You can't sandwich a `while` statement's condition between two of the statements that you intend to repeat. So what can you do? You need to follow the flow in Figure 12-11. Because every `while` loop starts with a test, that's where you jump into the circle, First Test, then Print, and finally Input.

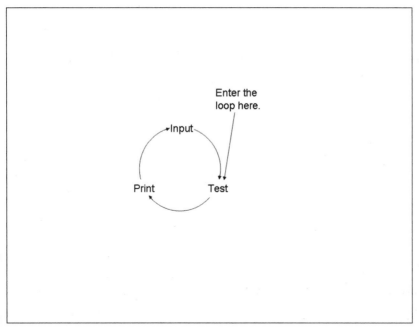

Figure 12-11:
Jumping into
a loop.

Listing 12-4 shows the embodiment of this "test, then print, then input" strategy.

Listing 12-4:   Nice Try, But . . .

```
/*
 * This code almost works, but there's one tiny error:
 */
import java.util.Scanner;
```

(continued)

Listing 12-4 *(continued)*

```
class SecondAttempt {

    public static void main(String args[]) {
        Scanner myScanner = new Scanner(System.in);
        char symbol = ' ';

        while (symbol != '@') {
            System.out.print(symbol);
            symbol = myScanner.findInLine(".").charAt(0);
        }

        System.out.println();
    }
}
```

A run of the Listing 12-4 code is shown in Figure 12-12. The code is almost correct, but I still have a slight problem. Notice the blank space before the user's input. The program races prematurely into the loop. The first time the computer executes the statements

```
System.out.print(symbol);
symbol = myScanner.findInLine(".").charAt(0);
```

the computer displays an unwanted blank space. Then the computer gets the J in John. In some applications, an extra blank space is no big deal. But in other applications, extra output can be disastrous.

Figure 12-12:
The
computer
displays an
extra blank
space.

General Output
```
---------------------Conf:
 John@BurdBrain.com
John
```

Fixing the problem

Disastrous or not, an unwanted blank space is the symptom of a logical flaw. The program shouldn't display results before it has any meaningful results to display. The solution to this problem is called . . . (drumroll, please) . . . *priming the loop.* You pump findInLine(".").charAt(0) once to get some values flowing. Listing 12-5 shows you how to do it.

Listing 12-5:   How to Prime a Loop

```
/*
 * This code works correctly!
 */
import java.util.Scanner;

class GetUserName {

    public static void main(String args[]) {
        Scanner myScanner = new Scanner(System.in);
        char symbol;

        symbol = myScanner.findInLine(".").charAt(0);

        while (symbol != '@') {
            System.out.print(symbol);
            symbol = myScanner.findInLine(".").charAt(0);
        }

        System.out.println();
    }
}
```

Listing 12-5 follows the strategy shown in Figure 12-13. First you get a character (the letter J in John, for example), then you enter the loop. After you're in the loop, you test the letter against the @ sign, and print the letter if it's appropriate to do so. Figure 12-14 shows a beautiful run of the GetUserName program.

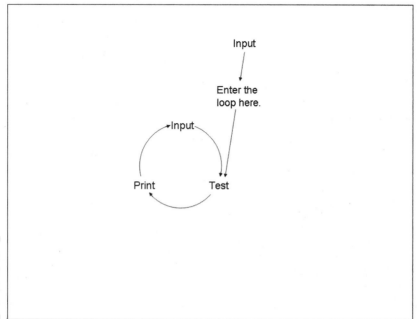

Figure 12-13:
The strategy in Listing 12-5.

Figure 12-14:
A run of the
code in
Listing 12-5.

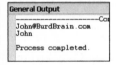

```
General Output
----------------------------Co
John@BurdBrain.com
John

Process completed.
```

The priming of loops in an important programming technique. But it's not the end of the story. In Chapters 14, 15, and 16, you can read about some other useful looping tricks.

Chapter 13

Piles of Files: Dealing with Information Overload

. . . .

In This Chapter

▶ Using data on your hard drive

▶ Writing code to access the hard drive

▶ Troubleshooting input/output behavior

. . . .

*C*onsider these scenarios:

✔ You're a business owner with hundreds of invoices. To avoid boxes full of paper, you store invoice data in a file on your hard drive. You need customized code to sort and classify the invoices.

✔ You're an astronomer with data from scans of the night sky. When you're ready to analyze a chunk of data, you load the chunk onto your computer's hard drive.

✔ You're the author of a popular self-help book. Last year's fad was called the Self Mirroring Method. This year's craze is the Make Your Cake System. You can't modify your manuscript without converting to the publisher's new specifications. The trouble is, there's no existing software to make the task bearable.

Each situation calls for a new computer program, and each program reads from a large data file. On top of all that, each program creates a brand new file containing bright, shiny results.

In previous chapters, the examples get input from the keyboard and send output to the screen. That's fine for small tasks, but you can't have the computer prompt you for each bit of night sky data. For big problems, you need lots of data, and the best place to store the data is on a computer's hard drive.

Running a Disk-Oriented Program

To deal with volumes of data, you need tools for reading from (and writing to) disk files. At the mere mention of disk files, some peoples' hearts start to palpitate with fear. After all, a disk file is elusive and invisible. It's stored somewhere inside your computer, with some magic magnetic process.

The truth is, getting data from a disk is very much like getting data from the keyboard. And printing data to a disk is like printing data to the computer screen.

Consider the scenario when you run the code in the previous chapters. You type some stuff on the keyboard. The program takes this stuff, and spits out some stuff of its own. The program sends this new stuff to the screen. In effect, the flow of data goes from the keyboard, to the computer's innards, and on to the screen, as shown in Figure 13-1.

Of course, the goal in this chapter is the scenario in Figure 13-2. There's a file containing data on your hard drive. The program takes data from the disk file and spits out some brand new data. The program then sends the new data to another file on the hard drive. In effect, the flow of data goes from a disk file, to the computer's innards, and on to another disk file.

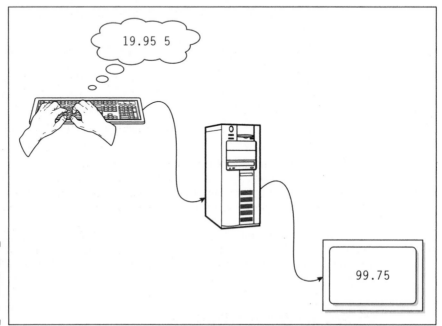

Figure 13-1:
Using the
keyboard
and screen.

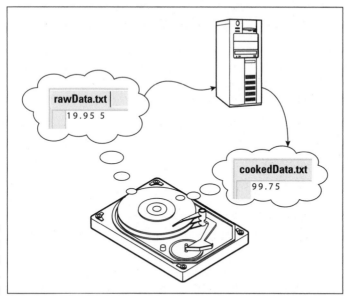

Figure 13-2:
Using disk
files.

The two scenarios in Figures 13-1 and 13-2 are very similar. In fact, it helps to remember these fundamental points:

- ✔ **The stuff in a disk file is no different from the stuff that you type on a keyboard.**

    If a keyboard-reading program expects you to type 19.95 5, then the corresponding disk-reading program expects a file containing those same characters, 19.95 5. If a keyboard-reading program expects you to press Enter and type more characters, then the corresponding disk-reading program expects more characters on the next line in the file.

- ✔ **The stuff in a disk file is no different from the stuff that you see on the screen.**

    If a screen-printing program displays the number 99.75, then the corresponding disk-writing program writes the number 99.75 to a file. If a screen-printing program moves the cursor to the next line, then the corresponding disk-writing program creates a new line in the file.

If you have trouble imagining what you have in a disk file, just imagine the text that you would type on the keyboard, or the text that you would see on the computer screen. That same text can appear in a file on your disk.

A sample program

Listing 13-1 contains a keyboard/screen program. The program multiplies unit price by quantity to get a total price. A run of the code is shown in Figure 13-3.

Listing 13-1: Using the Keyboard and the Screen

```java
import java.util.Scanner;

class ComputeTotal {

    public static void main(String args[]) {
        Scanner myScanner = new Scanner(System.in);
        double unitPrice, quantity, total;

        unitPrice = myScanner.nextDouble();
        quantity = myScanner.nextInt();

        total = unitPrice * quantity;

        System.out.println(total);
    }
}
```

Figure 13-3:
Read
from the
keyboard;
write to the
screen.

```
General Output

19.95 5
99.75
```

The goal is to write a program like the one in Listing 13-1. But instead of talking to your keyboard and screen, this new program talks to your hard drive. The new program reads unit price and quantity from your hard drive, and writes the total back to your hard drive.

Java's API has everything you need for interacting with a hard drive. A nice example is in Listing 13-2.

Listing 13-2: Using Input and Output Files

```java
import java.util.Scanner;
import java.io.File;
import java.io.FileNotFoundException;
import java.io.PrintStream;

class ReadAndWrite {

    public static void main(String args[])
        throws FileNotFoundException {
```

```
       Scanner diskScanner =
           new Scanner(new File("rawData.txt"));
       PrintStream diskWriter =
           new PrintStream("cookedData.txt");
       double unitPrice, quantity, total;

       unitPrice = diskScanner.nextDouble();
       quantity = diskScanner.nextInt();

       total = unitPrice * quantity;

       diskWriter.println(total);
    }
}
```

Creating code that messes with your hard drive

> *"I _____ (print your name)___ agree to pay $_____ each month on the ___th day of the month."*

Fill in the blanks. That's all you have to do. Reading input from a disk can work the same way. Just fill in the blanks in Listing 13-3.

Listing 13-3:   A Template to Read Data from a Disk File

```
/*
 * Before you can compile this code,
 * you must fill in the blanks.
 */
import java.util.Scanner;
import java.io.File;
import java.io.FileNotFoundException;

class _____ {

    public static void main(String args[])
        throws FileNotFoundException {

        Scanner diskScanner =
            new Scanner(new File("_____"));


        _____ = diskScanner.nextInt();
        _____ = diskScanner.nextDouble();
        _____ = diskScanner.nextLine();
        _____ = diskScanner.findInLine(".").charAt(0);
```

(continued)

Listing 13-3 *(continued)*

```
        // Etc.
    }
}
```

To use Listing 13-3, make up a name for your class. Insert that name into the first blank space. Type the name of the input file in the second space (between the quotation marks). Then, to read a whole number from the input file, call `diskScanner.nextInt`. To read a number that has a decimal point, call `diskScanner.nextDouble`. You can call any of the `Scanner` methods in Table 5-1 (the same methods you call when you get keystrokes from the keyboard).

The stuff in Listing 13-3 isn't a complete program. Instead, it's a *code template* — a half-baked piece of code, with spaces for you to fill in.

With the template in Listing 13-3, you can input data from a disk file. With a similar template, you can write output to a file. The template is in Listing 13-4.

Listing 13-4:   A Template to Write Data to a Disk File

```
/*
 * Before you can compile this code,
 * you must fill in the blanks.
 */
import java.io.File;
import java.io.FileNotFoundException;
import java.io.PrintStream;

class _____ {

    public static void main(String args[])
        throws FileNotFoundException {

        PrintStream diskWriter =
            new PrintStream("_____");

        diskWriter.print(_____);
        diskWriter.println(_____);

        // Etc.
    }
}
```

To use Listing 13-4, insert the name of your class into the first blank space. Type the name of the output file in the space between the quotation marks. Then, to write part of a line to the output file, call `diskWriter.print`. To write the remainder of a line to the output file, call `diskWriter.println`.

A quick look at Java's disk access facilities

Templates like the ones in Listings 13-3 and 13-4 are very nice. But knowing how the templates work is even better. Here are a few tidbits describing the inner workings of Java's disk access code.

✔ **A** `PrintStream` **is something you can use for writing output.**

A `PrintStream` is like a `Scanner`. The big difference is, a `Scanner` is for reading input and a `PrintStream` is for writing output. To see what I mean, look at Listing 13-2. Notice the similarity between the statements that use `Scanner` and the statements that use `PrintStream`.

The word `PrintStream` is defined in the Java API.

✔ **In Listing 13-2, the expression** `new File("rawData.txt")` **plays the same role that** `System.in` **plays in so many other programs.**

Just as `System.in` stands for the computer's keyboard, the expression `new File("rawData.txt")` stands for a file on your computer's hard drive. When the computer calls `new File("rawData.txt")`, the computer creates something like `System.in` — something you can stuff inside the `new Scanner( )` parentheses.

The word `File` is defined in the Java API.

✔ **A** `FileNotFoundException` **is something that may go wrong during an attempt to read input from a disk file (or an attempt to write output to a disk file).**

Disk file access is loaded with pitfalls. Even the best programs run into disk access trouble occasionally. So to brace against such pitfalls, Java insists on your adding some extra words to your code.

In Listing 13-2, the added words `throws FileNotFoundException` form a *throws clause*. A throws clause is a kind of disclaimer. Putting a throws clause in your code is like saying "I realize that this code can run into trouble."

Of course in the legal realm, you often have no choice about signing disclaimers. "If you don't sign this disclaimer then the surgeon won't operate on you." Okay, then; I'll sign it. The same is true with a Java throws clause. If you put things like `new PrintStream("cookedData.txt")` in your code, and you don't add something like `throws FileNotFoundException`, then the Java compiler refuses to compile your code.

So when do you need this `throws FileNotFoundException` clause, and when should you do without it? Well, having certain things in your code — things like `new PrintStream("cookedData.txt")` — force you to create a throws clause. You can learn all about the kinds of things that demand throws clauses. But at this point, it's better to concentrate on other programming issues. As a beginning Java programmer, the safest thing to do is to follow the templates in Listings 13-3 and 13-4.

The word `FileNotFoundException` is... you guessed it... defined in the Java API.

✔ **To create this chapter's code, I made up the names** `diskScanner` **and** `diskWriter`.

The words `diskScanner` and `diskWriter` don't come from the Java API. In place of `diskScanner` and `diskWriter` you can use any names you want. All you have to do is to use the names consistently within each of your Java programs.

The Pro version of JCreator has a built-in feature for creating and inserting code templates. To download a trial copy of JCreator Pro, visit `www.JCreator.com`.

If your program gets input from one disk file and writes output to another, then combine the stuff from Listings 13-3 and 13-4. When you do, you get a program like the one in Listing 13-2.

Running the sample program

Testing the code in Listing 13-2 is a three-step process. Here's an outline of the three steps:

1. **Create** `rawData.txt` **file.**

2. **Compile and run the code in Listing 13-2.**

3. **View the contents of the** `cookedData.txt` **file.**

The next few sections cover each step in detail.

Creating an input file

You can use any plain old text editor to create an input file for the code in Listing 13-2. In this section, I show you how to use JCreator's built-in editor.

1. **In the File View pane, right-click the name of a project.**

   In this example, select the project containing the Listing 13-2 code.

2. **In the right-click context menu, choose Add⇨New File.**

   JCreator's File Wizard opens to the File Path tab.

3. **In the Name field, type the name of your new data file.**

   You can type any name that your computer considers to be a valid file name. For this section's example, I used the name `rawData.txt`, but other names, such as `rawData.dat`, `rawData`, or `raw123.01.dataFile` are fine. I try to avoid troublesome names (including short, uninformative names and names containing blank spaces) but the name you choose is entirely up to you (and your computer's operating system, and your boss's whims, and your customer's specifications).

   Always include a dot in File Path tab's Name field. If the file's name has no extension, add a dot at the end of the name. For example, to create a file named `rawData` (not `rawData.txt` or `rawData.dat`), type `rawData.` (that's `rawData` followed by a dot.) If you don't type your own dot anywhere in the Name field, then JCreator adds a default extension to the file's name (turning `rawData` into `rawData.java`).

4. Click Finish.

The file's name appears in JCreator's File View pane. A tab (with the new file's name) appears in JCreator's Editor pane.

5. Type text in the Editor pane.

To create this section's example, I typed the text 19.95 5 as shown in Figure 13-4. To create your own example, type whatever text your program needs during its run.

Figure 13-4:
Editing an
input file.

or - [rawData.txt]

| Project | Build | Tool |

) · (· | 名 diskOutpu

| ₽ × | rawData.txt |

19.95 5

This book's Web site has tips for readers who need to create data files without using JCreator. This includes instructions for Linux, Unix, and Macintosh environments.

Compiling and running the code

Do the same thing you do with any other Java program. Choose Build⇨Compile Project, and then choose Build⇨Execute Project. The result of the run (at least the part of the result that you can see in JCreator's General Output pane) is shown in Figure 13-5.

Figure 13-5:
Compiling
and running
the code in
Listing 13-2.

General Output

————————————Co

Process completed.

I'm the first to admit it — the run in Figure 13-5 is duller than dirt. The total lack of any noticeable output gives some people the willies. The truth is, a program like the one in Listing 13-2 does all of its work behind the scenes. The program has no statements that read from the keyboard and has no statements that print to the screen. So if you have a very loud hard drive, you may hear a little chirping sound when you choose Build⇨Execute Project, but you won't type any program input, and you won't see any program output.

The program sends all its output to a file on your hard drive. So what do you do to see the file's contents?

Viewing the output file

To see the output of the program in Listing 13-2, follow these steps:

1. **In the File View pane, right-click the name of a project.**

   In this example, select the project containing the Listing 13-2 code.

2. **In the right-click context menu, choose Add⇨Add Existing Files.**

   A familiar Open dialog box appears.

3. **In the Open dialog box's Files of Type list, select All Files(*.*).**

   When you select All Files(*.*), additional entries appear in the Open dialog's list of filenames.

4. **In the list of filenames, double-click** cookedData.txt.

   As a result, the name cookedData.txt appears in the File View pane.

5. **Double-click the** cookedData.txt **branch in the File View pane.**

   The contents of cookedData.txt appear in JCreator's editor. (See Figure 13-6.)

Figure 13-6: Viewing an output file.

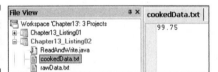

Troubleshooting problems with disk files

When you run the code in Listing 13-2, the computer executes new Scanner (new File("rawData.txt")). If the Java virtual machine can't find the rawData.txt file, then you see a message like the one shown in Figure 13-7. This error message can be very frustrating. In many cases, you know darn well that there's a rawData.txt file on your hard drive. The stupid computer simply can't find it.

Figure 13-7: The computer can't find your file.

```
General Output
-------------------Configuration: Chapter13_Listing02 - JDK version 1.5.0_01 <Default> - <Default>-----------------
Exception in thread "main" java.io.FileNotFoundException: rawData.txt (The system cannot find the file specified)
        at java.io.FileInputStream.open(Native Method)
        at java.io.FileInputStream.<init>(FileInputStream.java:106)
        at java.util.Scanner.<init>(Scanner.java:621)
        at ReadAndWrite.main(ReadAndWrite.java:11)
```

There's no quick, sure-fire way to fix this problem. But you should always check the following things first:

✔ **Check again for a file named** `rawData.txt`.

Open My Computer and poke around for a file with that name.

The filenames displayed in My Computer can be misleading. You may see the name `rawData` even though the file's real name is `rawData.txt`. To fix this problem once and for all, read the sidebar "Those pesky file-name extensions" in Chapter 3.

✔ **Check the spelling of the file's name.**

Make sure that the name in your program is exactly the same as the name of the file on your hard drive. Just one misplaced letter can keep the computer from finding a file.

✔ **If you use Unix or Linux, check the capitalization of the file's name.**

In Unix and Linux, the difference between uppercase and lowercase can baffle the computer.

✔ **Check that the file is in the correct directory.**

Sure, you have a file named `rawData.txt`. But, to find the file, don't expect the computer to search everywhere on your hard drive.

As a general rule, you should have `rawData.txt` and the Listing 13-2 code in the same directory on your hard drive. But file locations can be tricky, especially if you work in an unfamiliar programming environment. In some situations the general rule may not apply to you.

So here's a trick you can use: Compile and run this stripped-down version of the code in Listing 13-2:

```java
import java.io.File;
import java.io.FileNotFoundException;
import java.io.PrintStream;

class JustWrite {

    public static void main(String args[])
        throws FileNotFoundException {

        PrintStream diskWriter =
            new PrintStream("cookedData.txt");
        diskWriter.println(99.75);
    }
}
```

This program has no need for a stinking `rawData.txt` file. If you run this code and get no error messages, then search your hard drive for this program's output (the `cookedData.txt` file). Note the name of the directory that contains the `cookedData.txt` file. When you put `rawData.txt` in this same directory, then any problem you had running the Listing 13-2 code should go away.

✔ **Check the** `rawData.txt` **file's content.**

It never hurts to peek inside the `rawData.txt` file, and make sure that the file contains the numbers `19.95 5`. If `rawData.txt` no longer appears in JCreator's editor pane, find the Listing 13-2 project in the File View tree. Double-clicking the project's `rawData.txt` branch makes that file appear in JCreator's editor pane.

Writing a Disk-Oriented Program

Listing 13-2 is very much like Listing 13-1. In fact, you can go from Listing 13-1 to Listing 13-2 with some simple editing. Here's how:

✔ **Add the following import declarations to the beginning of your code:**

```
import java.io.File;
import java.io.FileNotFoundException;
import java.io.PrintStream;
```

✔ **Add the following throws clause to the method header:**

```
throws FileNotFoundException
```

✔ **In the call to** `new Scanner`, **replace** `System.in` **with a call to** `new File` **as follows:**

```
Scanner aVariableName =
    new Scanner(new File("inputFileName"))
```

✔ **Create a** `PrintStream` **for writing output to a disk file.**

```
PrintStream anotherVariableName =
    new PrintStream("outputFileName");
```

✔ **Use the** `Scanner` **variable name in calls to** `nextInt`, `nextLine`, **and so on.**

For example, to go from Listing 13-1 to Listing 13-2, I change

```
unitPrice = myScanner.nextDouble();
quantity = myScanner.nextInt();
```

to

```
unitPrice = diskScanner.nextDouble();
quantity = diskScanner.nextInt();
```

✔ **Use the** `PrintStream` **variable name in calls to** `print` **and** `println`.

For example, to go from Listing 13-1 to Listing 13-2, I change

```
System.out.println(total);
```

to

```
diskWriter.println(total);
```

Reading from a file

All the `Scanner` methods can read from existing disk files. For instance, to read a word from a file named `mySpeech`, use code of the following kind:

```
Scanner diskScanner =
    new Scanner(new File("mySpeech"));

String oneWord = diskScanner.next();
```

To read a character from a file named `letters.dat`, and then display the character on the screen, you can do something like this:

```
Scanner diskScanner =
    new Scanner(new File("letters.dat"));

System.out.println(diskScanner.findInLine(".").charAt(0));
```

Notice how I read from a file named `mySpeech`, not `mySpeech.txt` or `mySpeech.doc`. Anything that you put after the dot is called a *filename extension*, and for a file full of numbers and other data, the filename extension is optional. Sure, a Java program must be called *something*`.java`, but a data file can be named `mySpeech.txt`, `mySpeech.reallymine.allmine`, or just `mySpeech`. As long as the name in your `new File` call is the same as the filename on your computer's hard drive, everything is okay.

Writing to a file

The `print` and `println` methods can write to disk files. Here are some examples:

- ✔ During a run of the code in Listing 13-2, the variable `total` stores the number 99.75. To deposit 99.75 into the `cookedData.txt` file, you execute

  ```
  diskWriter.println(total);
  ```

  This `println` call writes to a disk file because of the following line in Listing 13-2:

  ```
  PrintStream diskWriter =
      new PrintStream("cookedData.txt");
  ```

- ✔ In another version of the program, you may decide not to use a `total` variable. To write 99.75 to the `cookedData.txt` file, you can call

  ```
  diskWriter.println(unitPrice * quantity);
  ```

- ✔ To display `OK` on the screen, you can make the following method call:

  ```
  System.out.print("OK");
  ```

To write OK to a file named `approval.txt`, you can use the following code:

```
PrintStream diskWriter =
    new PrintStream("approval.txt");

diskWriter.print("OK");
```

✔ You may decide to write OK as two separate characters. To write to the screen, you can make the following calls:

```
System.out.print('O');
System.out.print('K');
```

And to write OK to the `approval.txt` file, you can use the following code:

```
PrintStream diskWriter =
    new PrintStream("approval.txt");

diskWriter.print('O');
diskWriter.print('K');
```

✔ Like their counterparts for System.out, the disk-writing print and println methods differ in their end-of-line behaviors. For example, you want to display the following text on the screen:

```
Hankees  Socks
7        3
```

To do this, you can make the following method calls:

```
System.out.print("Hankees  ");
System.out.println("Socks");
System.out.print(7);
System.out.print("        ");
System.out.println(3);
```

To plant the same text into a file named `scores.dat`, you can use the following code:

```
PrintStream diskWriter =
    new PrintStream("scores.dat");

diskWriter.print("Hankees  ");
diskWriter.println("Socks");
diskWriter.print(7);
diskWriter.print("        ");
diskWriter.println(3);
```

When you make up a new data filename, you don't have to use a particular three-letter extension. In fact, you don't have to use an extension at all. Out of habit, I normally use `.txt` or `.dat`, but I could also use `.text`, `.data`, `.flatworm`, or I could skip the extension entirely.

Name that file

What if a file that contains data is not in your program's project directory? If that's the case, when you call `new File`, the file's name must include directory names. For example, imagine that your `TallyBudget.java` program is in JCreator's

`MyProjects\Chapter13_Listing09` directory, and that a file named `totals` is in a directory named `c:\advertisements`. (See the following figure.)

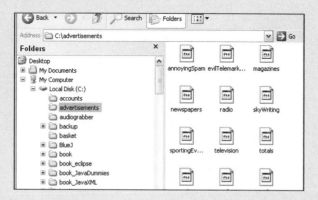

Then, to refer to the `totals` file, you include the directory name, the filename and (to be on the safe side) the drive letter:

```
Scanner diskScanner =
    new Scanner(new
    File("c:\\advertisements\\to
    tals"));
```

Notice how I use double backslashes. To find out why, look at the sidebar entitled "Escapism" in Chapter 12. The string `"\totals"` with a single backslash stands for a tab, followed by `otals`. But in this example, the file's name is `totals`, not `otals`. With a single backslash, the name `...advertisements\totals"` would not work correctly.

Inside quotation marks, you use the double back-slash to indicate what would usually be a single backslash. So the string `"c:\\advertise-ments\\totals"` stands for `c:\advertise-ments\totals`. That's good, because `c:\advertisements\totals` is the way you normally refer to a file in Windows.

Of course, if you use Unix, Linux, or a Macintosh, then you're in luck. This double backslash nonsense doesn't apply to you. Just write

```
Scanner diskScanner =
    new Scanner(new
    File("/home/bburd/advertise-
    ments/totals"));
```

or something similar that reflects your system's directory structure.

Writing, Rewriting, and Re-rewriting

Given my mischievous ways, I tried a little experiment. I asked myself what would happen if I ran the same file-writing program more than once. So I created a tiny program (the program in Listing 13-5) and I ran the program twice. Then I examined the program's output file. The output file (shown in Figure 13-8) contains only two letters.

Listing 13-5:   A Little Experiment

```java
import java.io.File;
import java.io.FileNotFoundException;
import java.io.PrintStream;

class WriteOK {

    public static void main(String args[])
        throws FileNotFoundException {

        PrintStream diskWriter =
            new PrintStream(new File("approval.txt"));

        diskWriter.print  ('O');
        diskWriter.println('K');
    }
}
```

Figure 13-8:
Testing the waters.

Here's the sequence of events from the start to the end of the experiment:

1. Before I run the code in Listing 13-5, my computer's hard drive has no `approval.txt` file.

   That's okay. Every experiment has to start somewhere.

2. I run the code in Listing 13-5.

   The call to `new PrintStream` in Listing 13-5 creates a file named `approval.txt`. Initially, the new `approval.txt` file contains no characters. Later in Listing 13-5, calls to `print` and `println` put characters in the file. So after running the code, the `approval.txt` file contains two letters — the letters `OK`.

3. I run the code from Listing 13-5 a second time.

   At this point, I could imagine seeing OKOK in the approval.txt file. But that's not what I see in Figure 13-8. After running the code twice, the approval.txt file contains just one OK. Here's why:

   - The call to new PrintStream in Listing 13-5 deletes my existing approval.txt file. The call creates a new, empty approval.txt file.

   - After creating a new approval.txt file, the print method call drops the letter O into the new file.

   - The println method call adds the letter K to the same approval.txt file.

So that's the story. Each time you run the program, it trashes whatever approval.txt file is already on the hard drive. Then the program adds data to a newly created approval.txt file.

Chapter 14

Creating Loops within Loops

· ·

· ·

If you're an editor at Wiley Publishing, please don't read the next few paragraphs. In the next few paragraphs, I give away an important trade secret (something you really don't want me to do).

I'm about to describe a surefire process for writing a best-selling *For Dummies* book. Here's the process:

Write several words to create a sentence. Do this several times to create a paragraph.

```
Repeat the following to form a paragraph:
   Repeat the following to form a sentence:
      Write a word.
```

Repeat the above instructions several times to make a section. Make several sections, and then make several chapters.

```
Repeat the following to form a best-selling For Dummies book:
   Repeat the following to form a chapter:
      Repeat the following to form a section:
         Repeat the following to form a paragraph:
            Repeat the following to form a sentence:
               Write a word.
```

This process involves a loop within a loop within a loop within a loop within a loop. It's like a verbal M.C. Escher print. Is it useful, or is it frivolous?

Well, in the world of computer programming, this kind of thing happens all the time. Most five-layered loops are hidden behind method calls, but two-layered loops within loops are everyday occurrences. So this chapter tells you how to compose a loop within a loop. It's very useful stuff.

By the way, if you're a Wiley Publishing editor, you can start reading again from this point onward.

Paying Your Old Code a Little Visit

The program in Listing 12-5 extracts a username from an e-mail address. For example, the program reads

```
John@BurdBrain.com
```

from the keyboard, and writes

```
John
```

to the screen. Let me tell you . . . in this book, I have some pretty lame excuses for writing programs, but this simple e-mail example tops the list! Why would you want to type something on the keyboard, only to have the computer display part of what you typed? There must be a better use for code of this kind.

Sure enough, there is. The BurdBrain.com network administrator has a list of 10,000 employees' e-mail addresses. More precisely, the administrator's hard drive has a file named email.txt. This file contains 10,000 e-mail addresses, with one address on each line, as shown in Figure 14-1.

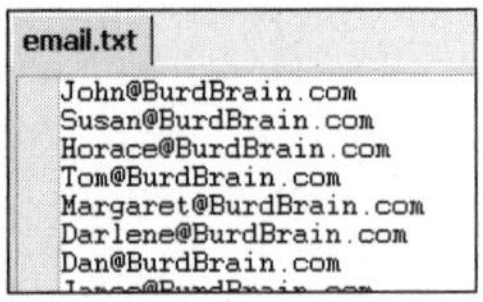

Figure 14-1:
A list of
e-mail
addresses.

```
email.txt
    John@BurdBrain.com
    Susan@BurdBrain.com
    Horace@BurdBrain.com
    Tom@BurdBrain.com
    Margaret@BurdBrain.com
    Darlene@BurdBrain.com
    Dan@BurdBrain.com
    Janea@BurdBrain.com
```

The company's e-mail software has an interesting feature. To send e-mail within the company, you don't need to type an entire e-mail address. For example, to send e-mail to John, you can type the username John instead of John@BurdBrain.com. (This @BurdBrain.com part is called the *host name*.)

So the company's network administrator wants to distill the content of the email.txt file. She wants a new file, usernames.txt, that contains user-names with no host names, as shown in Figure 14-2.

Figure 14-2:
Usernames
extracted
from the list
of e-mail
addresses.

```
usernames.txt
  John
  Susan
  Horace
  Tom
  Margaret
  Darlene
  Dan
```

Reworking some existing code

To solve the administrator's problem, you need to modify the code in Listing 12-5. The new version gets an e-mail address from a disk file and writes a username to another disk file. The new version is in Listing 14-1.

Listing 14-1:   From One File to Another

```java
import java.util.Scanner;
import java.io.File;
import java.io.FileNotFoundException;
import java.io.PrintStream;

class ListOneUsername {

    public static void main(String args[])
        throws FileNotFoundException {

        Scanner diskScanner =
            new Scanner(new File("email.txt"));
        PrintStream diskWriter =
            new PrintStream("usernames.txt");
        char symbol;

        symbol = diskScanner.findInLine(".").charAt(0);

        while (symbol != '@') {
            diskWriter.print(symbol);
            symbol = diskScanner.findInLine(".").charAt(0);
        }

        diskWriter.println();
    }
}
```

Listing 14-1 does almost the same thing as its forerunner in Listing 12-5. The only difference is that the code in Listing 14-1 doesn't interact with the user. Instead, the code in Listing 14-1 interacts with disk files.

Running your code

Here's how you run the code in Listing 14-1:

1. **Put the file** `email.txt` **in your project directory along with the** `ListOneUsername.java` **file (the code from Listing 14-1).**

   In the `email.txt` file, put just one e-mail address. Any address will do, as long as the address contains an @ sign.

2. **Compile and run the code in Listing 14-1.**

   When you run the code, you see nothing interesting in the General Output pane. All you see is the phrase `Process completed`.

3. **View the contents of the** `usernames.txt` **file.**

   If your `email.txt` file contains `John@BurdBrain.com`, then the `usernames.txt` file contains `John`.

For more details on any of these steps, see the discussion accompanying Listings 13-2, 13-3, and 13-4 in Chapter 13.

Creating Useful Code

The previous section describes a network administrator's problem — creating a file filled with usernames from a file filled with e-mail addresses. The code in Listing 14-1 solves part of the problem — it extracts just one e-mail address. That's a good start, but to get just one username, you don't need a computer program. A pencil and paper does the trick.

So don't keep the network administrator waiting any longer. In this section, you develop a program that processes dozens, hundreds, and even thousands of e-mail addresses from a file on your hard drive.

First you need a strategy to create the program. Take the statements in Listing 14-1 and run them over and over again. Better yet, have the statements run themselves over and over again. Fortunately, you already know how to do something over and over again: You use a loop. (See Chapter 12 for the basics on loops.)

So here's the strategy: Take the statements in Listing 14-1 and enclose them in a larger loop:

```
while (not at the end of the email.txt file) {
    Execute the statements in Listing 14-1
}
```

Looking back at the code in Listing 14-1, you see that the statements in that code have a `while` loop of their own. So this strategy involves putting one loop inside another loop:

```
while (not at the end of the email.txt file) {
    //Blah-blah

    while (symbol != '@') {
        //Blah-blah-blah
    }

    //Blah-blah-blah-blah
}
```

Because one loop is inside the other, they're called *nested loops*. The old loop (the `symbol != '@'` loop) is the *inner loop*. The new loop (the end-of-file loop) is called the *outer loop*.

Checking for the end of a file

Now all you need is a way to test the loop's condition. How do you know when you're at the end of the `email.txt` file?

The answer comes from Java's `Scanner` class. This class's `hasNext` method answers `true` or `false` to the following question:

> Does the `email.txt` file have anything to read in it (beyond what you've already read)?

If the program's `findInLine` calls haven't gobbled up all the characters in the `email.txt` file, then the value of `diskScanner.hasNext()` is `true`. So to keep looping while you're not at the end of the `email.txt` file, you do the following:

```
while (diskScanner.hasNext()) {
    Execute the statements in Listing 14-1
}
```

The first realization of this strategy is in Listing 14-2.

Listing 14-2:   The Mechanical Combining of Two Loops

```java
/*
 * This code does NOT work (but
 * you learn from your mistakes).
 */

import java.util.Scanner;
import java.io.File;
import java.io.FileNotFoundException;
import java.io.PrintStream;

class ListAllUsernames {

    public static void main(String args[])
        throws FileNotFoundException {

        Scanner diskScanner =
            new Scanner(new File("email.txt"));
        PrintStream diskWriter =
            new PrintStream("usernames.txt");
        char symbol;

        while (diskScanner.hasNext()) {
            symbol = diskScanner.findInLine(".").charAt(0);

            while (symbol != '@') {
                diskWriter.print(symbol);
                symbol =
                    diskScanner.findInLine(".").charAt(0);
            }

            diskWriter.println();
        }
    }
}
```

When you run the code in Listing 14-2, you get the disappointing response shown in Figure 14-3.

Figure 14-3:
You goofed.

```
General Output
-------------------Configuration: Chapter14_Listing02 - JDK ver
Exception in thread "main" java.lang.NullPointerException
        at ListAllUsernames.main(ListAllUsernames.java:27)
```

How it feels to be a computer

What's wrong with the code in Listing 14-2? To find out, I role-play the computer. "If I were a computer, what would I do when I execute the code in Listing 14-2?"

The first several things that I'd do are pictured in Figure 14-4. I would read the J in John, then write the J in John, and then read the letter o (also in John).

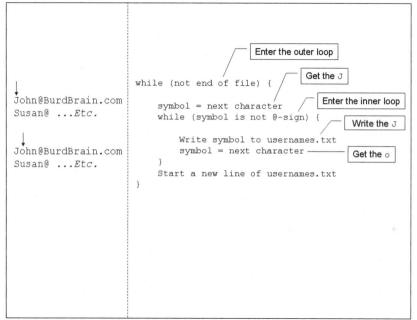

Figure 14-4:
Role-playing the code in Listing 14-2.

After a few trips through the inner loop, I'd get the @ sign in John@BurdBrain. com, as shown in Figure 14-5.

Finding this @ sign would jump me out of the inner loop and back to the top of the outer loop, as shown in Figure 14-6.

I'd get the B in BurdBrain, and sail back into the inner loop. But then (horror of horrors!) I'd write that B to the usernames.txt file. (See Figure 14-7.)

```
                                    while (not end of file) {    ┌──────────────────────┐
                                                                 │  Start another iteration │
                                                                 │   of the inner loop      │
        │                               symbol = next character └──────────────────────┘
John@BurdBrain.com                      while (symbol is not @-sign) {    ┌─────────────┐
Susan@ ...Etc.                                                           │ Write the n │
                                                                          └─────────────┘
                                            Write symbol to usernames.txt
        │                                   symbol = next character ──── ┌─────────────┐
John@BurdBrain.com                      }                                │  Get the @  │
Susan@ ...Etc.                          Start a new line of usernames.txt └─────────────┘

                                    }
```

Figure 14-5:
Reaching
the end
of the
username.

```
                                    while (not end of file) {

                                                                         ┌────────────────────┐
                                        symbol = next character          │ Leave the inner loop │
                                        while (symbol is not @-sign) {    └────────────────────┘

        │                                   Write symbol to usernames.txt
John@BurdBrain.com                          symbol = next character
Susan@ ...Etc.                          }
                                        Start a new line of usernames.txt
                                    }
                                         ┌──────────────────────────────────┐
                                         │ Go back to the top of the outer loop │
                                         └──────────────────────────────────┘
```

Figure 14-6:
Leaving the
inner loop.

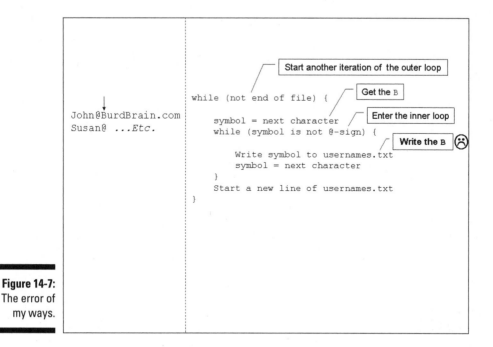

John@BurdBrain.com
Susan@ ...Etc.

Start another iteration of the outer loop

```
while (not end of file) {
    symbol = next character                Get the B
    while (symbol is not @-sign) {          Enter the inner loop
        Write symbol to usernames.txt       Write the B
        symbol = next character
    }
    Start a new line of usernames.txt
}
```

Figure 14-7:
The error of
my ways.

There's the error! You don't want to write host names to the usernames.txt file. When the computer found the @ sign, it should have skipped past the rest of John's e-mail address.

At this point, you have a choice. You can jump straight to the corrected code in Listing 14-3, or you can read on to find out about the error message in Figure 14-3.

Why the computer accidentally pushes past the end of the file

Ah! You decided to read on to see why Figure 14-3 has that nasty error message.

Once again, I role-play the computer. I've completed the steps in Figure 14-7. I shouldn't process BurdBrain.com with the inner loop. But unfortunately, I do.

I keep running and processing more e-mail addresses. When I get to the end of the last e-mail address, I grab the m in BurdBrain.com and go back to test for an @ sign, as shown in Figure 14-8.

Now I'm in trouble. This last m certainly isn't an @ sign. So I jump into the inner loop, and try to get yet another character. (See Figure 14-9.) The email.txt file has no more characters, so Java sends an error message to the computer screen. (The NullPointerException error message is back in Figure 14-3.)

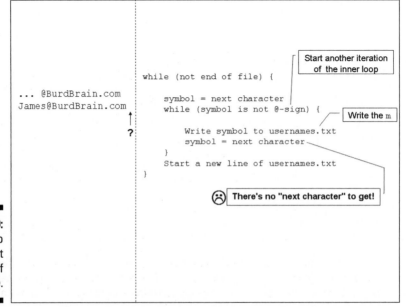

Figure 14-8:
The
journey's
last leg.

Figure 14-9:
Trying to
read past
the end of
the file.

Solving the problem

Listing 14-3 has the solution to the problem described with Figures 14-1 and 14-2. The code in this listing is almost identical to the code in Listing 14-2. The only difference is the added call to nextLine. When the computer reaches an @ sign, this nextLine call gobbles up the rest of the input line. (In other words, the nextLine call gobbles up the rest of the e-mail address. The idea works because each e-mail address is on its own separate line.) After chewing and swallowing @BurdBrain.com, the computer moves gracefully to the next line of input.

Listing 14-3: That's Much Better!

```
/*
 * This code is correct!!
 */

import java.util.Scanner;
import java.io.File;
import java.io.FileNotFoundException;
import java.io.PrintStream;

class ListAllUsernames {

    public static void main(String args[])
        throws FileNotFoundException {

        Scanner diskScanner =
            new Scanner(new File("email.txt"));
        PrintStream diskWriter =
            new PrintStream("usernames.txt");
        char symbol;

        while (diskScanner.hasNext()) {
            symbol = diskScanner.findInLine(".").charAt(0);

            while (symbol != '@') {
                diskWriter.print(symbol);
                symbol =
                    diskScanner.findInLine(".").charAt(0);
            }

            diskScanner.nextLine();
            diskWriter.println();
        }
    }
}
```

To run the code in Listing 14-3, you need an email.txt file — a file like the one shown in Figure 14-1. In the email.txt file, type several e-mail addresses. Any addresses will do, as long as each address contains an @ sign and each address is on its own separate line. Save the `email.txt` file in your project directory along with the `ListAllUsernames.java` file (the code from Listing 14-3). For more details, see the discussion accompanying Listings 13-2, 13-3, and 13-4 in Chapter 13.

With Listing 14-3, you've reached an important milestone. You've analyzed a delicate programming problem and found a complete, working solution. The tools you used included thinking about strategies and role-playing the computer. As time goes on, you can use these tools to solve bigger and better problems.

Chapter 15

The Old Runaround

1 remember it distinctly — the sense of dread I would feel on the way to Aunt Edna's house. She was a kind old woman, and her intentions were good. But visits to her house were always so agonizing.

First we'd sit in the living room and talk about other relatives. That was okay, as long as I understood what people were talking about. Sometimes, the gossip would be about adult topics, and I'd become very bored.

After all the family chatter, my father would help Aunt Edna with her bills. That was fun to watch, because Aunt Edna had a genetically inherited family ailment. Like me and many of my ancestors, Aunt Edna couldn't keep track of paperwork to save her life. It was as if the paper had allergens that made Aunt Edna's skin crawl. After ten minutes of useful bill paying, my father would find a mistake, an improper tally or something else in the ledger that needed attention. He'd ask Aunt Edna about it, and she'd shrug her shoulders. He'd become agitated trying to track down the problem, while Aunt Edna rolled her eyes and smiled with ignorant satisfaction. It was great entertainment.

Then, when the bill paying was done, we'd sit down to eat dinner. That's when I would remember why I dreaded these visits. Dinner was unbearable. Aunt Edna believed in Fletcherism — a health movement whose followers chewed each mouthful of food one hundred times. The more devoted followers used a chart, with a different number for the mastication of each kind of food. The minimal number of chews for any food was 32 — one chomp for each tooth in your mouth. People who did this said they were "Fletcherizing."

Mom and Dad thought the whole Fletcher business was silly, but they respected Aunt Edna and felt that people her age should be humored, not defied. As for me, I thought I'd explode from the monotony. Each meal lasted forever. Each mouthful was an ordeal. I can still remember my mantra — the words I'd say to myself without meaning to do so:

```
I've chewed 0 times so far.
Have I chewed 100 times yet? If not, then
    Chew!
    Add 1 to the number of times that I've chewed.
    Go back to "Have I chewed" to find out if I'm done yet.
```

Repeating Statements a Certain Number Times (Java for Statements)

Life is filled with examples of counting loops. And computer programming mirrors life (. . . or is it the other way around?). When you tell a computer what to do, you're often telling the computer to print three lines, process ten accounts, dial a million phone numbers, or whatever. Because counting loops are so common in programming, the people who create programming languages have developed statements just for loops of this kind. In Java, the statement that repeats something a certain number of times is called a *for* statement. An example of a `for` statement is in Listing 15-1.

Listing 15-1:   Horace Fletcher's Revenge

```java
import static java.lang.System.out;

class AuntEdnaSettlesForTen {

    public static void main(String args[]) {

        for (int count = 0; count < 10; count++) {
            out.print("I've chewed ");
            out.print(count);
            out.println(" time(s).");
        }

        out.println("10 times! Hooray!");
        out.println("I can swallow!");
    }
}
```

Figure 15-1 shows you what you get when you run the program of Listing 15-1:

✔ The `for` statement in Listing 15-1 starts by setting the `count` variable equal to 0.

✔ Then the `for` statement tests to make sure that `count` is less than 10 (which it certainly is).

✔ Then the `for` statement dives ahead and executes the printing statements between the curly braces. At this early stage of the game, the computer prints `I've chewed 0 time(s)`.

✔ Then the `for` statement executes `count++` — that last thing inside the `for` statement's parentheses. This last action adds 1 to the value of `count`.

```
General Output
-------------------------Config
I've chewed 0 time(s).
I've chewed 1 time(s).
I've chewed 2 time(s).
I've chewed 3 time(s).
I've chewed 4 time(s).
I've chewed 5 time(s).
I've chewed 6 time(s).
I've chewed 7 time(s).
I've chewed 8 time(s).
I've chewed 9 time(s).
10 times! Hooray!
I can swallow!
```

Figure 15-1:
Chewing
ten times.

This ends the first iteration of the `for` statement in Listing 15-1. Of course, there's more to this loop than just one iteration:

✔ With `count` now equal to 1, the `for` statement checks again to make sure that `count` is less than 10. (Yes, 1 is smaller than 10.)

✔ Because the test turns out okay, the `for` statement marches back into the curly braced statements and prints `I've chewed 1 time(s)` on the screen.

✔ Then the `for` statement executes that last `count++` inside its parentheses. The statement adds 1 to the value of `count`, increasing the value of `count` to 2.

And so on. This whole thing keeps being repeated over and over again until, after ten iterations, the value of `count` finally reaches 10. When this happens, the check for `count` being less than 10 fails, and the loop's execution ends. The computer jumps to whatever statement comes immediately after the `for` statement. In Listing 15-1, the computer prints `10 times! Hooray! I can swallow!` The whole process is illustrated in Figure 15-2.

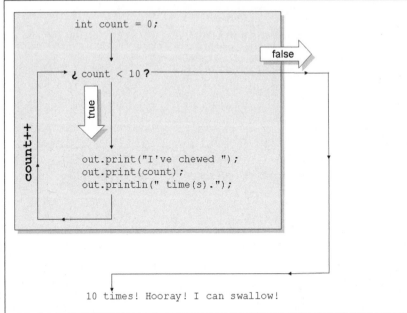

Figure 15-2:
The action
of the for
loop in
Listing 15-1.

The anatomy of a for statement

A typical for statement looks like this:

```
for (Initialization; Condition; Update) {
    Statements
}
```

After the word for, you put three things in parentheses: an *Initialization*, a *Condition*, and an *Update*.

Each of the three items in parentheses plays its own distinct role:

- ✔ **Initialization:** The initialization is executed once, when the run of your program first reaches the for statement.

- ✔ **Condition:** The condition is tested several times (at the start of each iteration).

- ✔ **Update:** The update is also evaluated several times (at the end of each iteration).

If it helps, think of the loop as if its text is shifted all around:

```
//This is NOT real code
int count = 0
for count < 0 {
    out.print("I've chewed ");
    out.print(count);
    out.println(" time(s).");
    count++;
}
```

Versatile looping statements

If you were stuck on a desert island with only one kind of loop, what kind would you want to have? The answer is, you can get along with any kind of loop. The choice between a `while` loop and a `for` loop is about the code's style and efficiency. It's not about necessity.

Anything that you can do with a `for` loop, you can do with a `while` loop as well. Consider, for example, the `for` loop in Listing 15-1. Here's how you can achieve the same effect with a `while` loop:

```
int count = 0;
while (count < 10) {
    out.print("I've chewed ");
    out.print(count);
    out.println(" time(s).");
    count++;
}
```

In the `while` loop, you have explicit statements to declare, initialize, and increment the `count` variable.

The same kind of trick works in reverse. Anything that you can do with a `while` loop, you can do with a `for` loop as well. But turning certain `while` loops into `for` loops seems strained and unnatural. Consider a `while` loop from Listing 12-2:

```
while (total < 21) {
    card = myRandom.nextInt(10)
    + 1;
```

```
    total += card;
    System.out.print(card);
    System.out.print("
    ");
    System.out.println(total);
}
```

Turning this loop into a `for` loop means wasting most of the stuff inside the `for` loop's parentheses:

```
for ( ; total < 21 ; ) {
    card = myRandom.nextInt(10)
    + 1;
    total += card;
    System.out.print(card);
    System.out.print("
    ");
    System.out.println(total);
}
```

The `for` loop above has a condition, but it has no initialization and no update. That's okay. Without an initialization, nothing special happens when the computer first enters the `for` loop. And without an update, nothing special happens at the end of each iteration. It's strange, but it works.

Usually, when you write a `for` statement, you're counting how many times to repeat something. But, in truth, you can do just about any kind of repetition with a `for` statement.

You can't write a real `for` statement this way. (The compiler would throw code like this right into the garbage can.) Even so, this is the order in which the parts of the `for` statement are executed.

The first line of a `for` statement (the word `for` followed by stuff in parentheses) is not a complete statement. So you almost never put a semicolon after the stuff in parentheses. If you make a mistake and type a semicolon, you usually put the computer into an endless, do-nothing loop. The computer's cursor just sits there and blinks until you forcibly stop the program's run.

Initializing a for loop

Look at the first line of the `for` loop in Listing 15-1, and notice the declaration `int count = 0`. That's something new. When you create a `for` loop, you can declare a variable (like `count`) as part of the loop initialization.

If you declare a variable in the initialization of a `for` loop, you can't use that variable outside the loop. For example, in Listing 15-1, try putting `out.println(count)` after the end of the loop:

```
//This code does not compile.
for (int count = 0; count < 10; count++) {
    out.print("I've chewed ");
    out.print(count);
    out.println(" time(s).");
}

out.print(count);    //The count variable doesn't
                     // exist here.
```

With this extra reference to the `count` variable, the compiler gives you an error message. You can see the message in Figure 15-3. If you're not experienced with `for` statements, the message may surprise you. "Whadaya mean 'cannot find symbol'? There's a `count` variable just four lines above that statement." Ah, yes. But the `count` variable is declared in the `for` loop's initialization. Outside the `for` loop, that `count` variable doesn't exist.

Figure 15-3:
What count
variable?
I don't see
a count
variable.

```
Build Output
------------------Configuration: BadCode - JDK version 1.5.0_01 <Default> - <Default>------------------
C:\Program Files\Xinox Software\JCreatorV3LE\MyProjects\BadCode\AuntEdna.java:13: cannot find symbol
symbol  : variable count
location: class AuntEdna
        out.print(count);
1 error
```

To use a variable outside of a `for` statement, you have to declare that variable outside the `for` statement. You can even do this with the `for` statement's counting variable. Listing 15-2 has an example.

Listing 15-2:   Using a Variable Declared Outside of a for Loop

```
import static java.lang.System.out;

class AuntEdnaDoesItAgain {

    public static void main(String args[]) {
        int count;

        for (count = 0; count < 10; count++) {
            out.print("I've chewed ");
            out.print(count);
            out.println(" time(s).");
        }

        out.print(count);
        out.println(" times! Hooray!");
        out.println("I can swallow!");
    }
}
```

A run of the code in Listing 15-2 looks exactly like the run for Listing 15-1. The run is pictured in Figure 15-1. Unlike its predecessor, Listing 15-2 enjoys the luxury of using the `count` variable to display the number 10. It can do this because, in Listing 15-2, the `count` variable belongs to the entire `main` method, and not to the `for` loop alone.

Notice the words `for (count = 0` in Listing 15-2. Because `count` is declared above the `for` statement, you don't declare `count` again in the `for` statement's initialization. I tried declaring `count` twice, as in the following code:

```
//This does NOT work:
int count;

for (int count = 0; count < 10; count++) {
    ...etc.
```

and the compiler told me to clean up my act:

```
count is already defined in main(java.lang.String[])
        for (int count = 0; count < 10; count++) {
             ^
```

Using Nested for Loops

Because you're reading *Beginning Programming with Java For Dummies,* 2nd Edition, I assume that you manage a big hotel. The next chapter tells you everything you need to know about hotel management. But before you begin reading that chapter, you can get a little preview in this section.

I happen to know that your hotel has nine floors, and each floor of your hotel has twenty rooms. On this sunny afternoon, someone hands you a diskette containing a file full of numbers. You copy this hotelData file to your hard drive, and then open the file in JCreator's editor. You see the stuff shown in Figure 15-4.

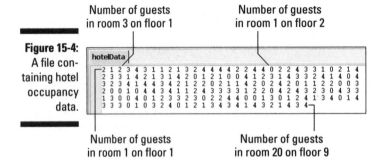

Figure 15-4:
A file containing hotel occupancy data.

This file gives the number of guests in each room. For example, at the start of the file, you see 2 1 2. This means that, on the first floor, Room 1 has 2 guests, Room 2 has 1 guest, and Room 3 has 2 guests. After reading twenty of these numbers, you see 0 2 2. So, on the second floor, Room 1 has 0 guests, Room 2 has 2 guests, and Room 3 has 2 guests. The story continues until the last number in the file. According to that number, Room 20 on the ninth floor has 4 guests.

You'd like a more orderly display of these numbers — a display of the kind in Figure 15-5. So you whip out your keyboard to write a quick Java program.

As in some earlier examples, you decide which statements go where by asking yourself how many times each statement should be executed. For starters, the display in Figure 15-5 has nine lines, and each line has 20 numbers:

```
for (each of 9 floors)
    for (each of 20 rooms on a floor)
        get a number from the file and
        display the number on the screen.
```

Figure 15-5:
A readable
display of
the data in
Figure 15-4.

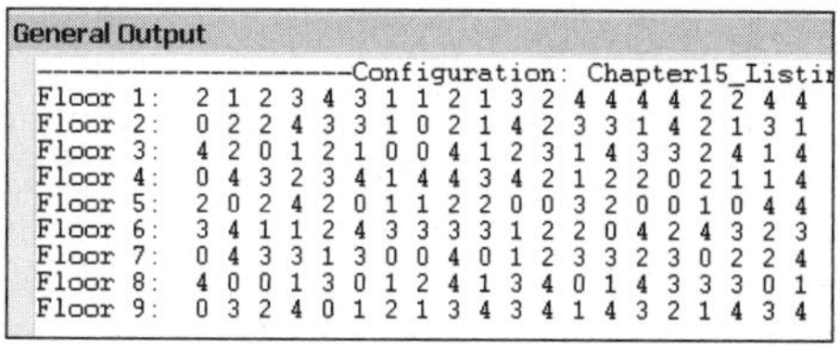

```
General Output
-----------------------Configuration: Chapter15_Listir
Floor 1:   2 1 2 3 4  3 1 1 2 1 3 2 4 4 4 4 2 2 4 4
Floor 2:   0 2 2 4 3  3 1 0 2 1 4 2 3 3 1 4 2 1 3 1
Floor 3:   4 2 0 1 2  1 0 0 4 1 2 3 1 4 3 3 2 4 1 4
Floor 4:   0 4 3 2 3  4 1 4 4 3 4 2 1 2 2 0 2 1 1 4
Floor 5:   2 0 2 4 2  0 1 1 2 2 0 0 3 2 0 0 1 0 4 4
Floor 6:   3 4 1 1 2  4 3 3 3 3 1 2 2 0 4 2 4 3 2 3
Floor 7:   0 4 3 3 1  3 0 0 4 0 1 2 3 3 2 3 0 2 2 4
Floor 8:   4 0 0 1 3  0 1 2 4 1 3 4 0 1 4 3 3 3 0 1
Floor 9:   0 3 2 4 0  1 2 1 3 4 3 4 1 4 3 2 1 4 3 4
```

So your program has a for loop within a for loop — a pair of nested for loops.

Next, you notice how each line begins in Figure 15-5. Each line contains the word Floor, followed by the floor number. Because this Floor display occurs only nine times in Figure 15-5, the statements to print this display belong in the *for each of 9 floors* loop (and not in the *for each of 20 rooms* loop). The statements should be before the *for each of 20 rooms* loop, because this Floor display comes once before each line's twenty number display:

```
for (each of 9 floors)
    display "Floor" and the floor number,
    for (each of 20 rooms on a floor)
        get a number from the file and
        display the number on the screen.
```

You're almost ready to write the code. But there's one detail that's easy to forget. (Well, it's a detail that I always forget.) After displaying 20 numbers, the program advances to a new line. This new-line action happens only nine times during the run of the program, and it always happens *after* the program displays 20 numbers:

```
for (each of 9 floors)
    display "Floor" and the floor number,
    for (each of 20 rooms on a floor)
        get a number from the file and
        display the number on the screen,
    Go to the next line.
```

That does it. That's all you need. The code to create the display of Figure 15-5 is in Listing 15-3.

Listing 15-3: Hey! Is This a For-by-For?

```
import java.util.Scanner;
import java.io.File;
import java.io.FileNotFoundException;
import static java.lang.System.out;

class DisplayHotelData {

    public static void main(String args[])
        throws FileNotFoundException {

        Scanner diskScanner =
            new Scanner(new File("hotelData"));

        for (int floor = 1; floor <= 9; floor++) {
            out.print("Floor ");
            out.print(floor);
            out.print(":  ");

            for (int roomNum = 1; roomNum <= 20; roomNum++) {
                out.print(diskScanner.nextInt());
                out.print(' ');
            }

            out.println();
        }
    }
}
```

The code in Listing 15-3 has the variable `floor` going from 1 to 9, and has the variable `roomNum` going from 1 to 20. Because the `roomNum` loop is inside the `floor` loop, the writing of twenty numbers happens 9 times. That's good. It's exactly what I want.

Repeating Until You Get What You Need (Java do Statements)

I introduce Java's `while` loop in Chapter 12. When you create a `while` loop, you write the loop's condition first. After the condition, you write the code that gets repeatedly executed.

```
while (Condition) {
    Code that gets repeatedly executed
}
```

This way of writing a `while` statement is no accident. The look of the statement emphasizes an important point — that the computer always checks the condition before executing any of the repeated code.

If the loop's condition is never true, then the stuff inside the loop is never executed — not even once. In fact, you can easily cook up a `while` loop whose statements are never executed (although I can't think of a reason why you would ever want to do it):

```
//This code doesn't print anything:
int twoPlusTwo = 2 + 2;
while (twoPlusTwo == 5) {
    System.out.println("Are you kidding?");
    System.out.println("2+2 doesn't equal 5.");
    System.out.print  ("Everyone knows that");
    System.out.println(" 2+2 equals 3.");
}
```

In spite of this silly `twoPlusTwo` example, the `while` statement turns out to be the most useful of Java's looping constructs. In particular, the `while` loop is good for situations in which you must look before you leap. For example: "While money is in my account, write a mortgage check every month." When you first encounter this statement, if your account has a zero balance, you don't want to write a mortgage check — not even one check.

But at times (not many), you want to leap before you look. In a situation when you're asking the user for a response, maybe the user's response makes sense, but maybe it doesn't. Maybe the user's finger slipped, or perhaps the user didn't understand the question. In many situations, it's important to correctly interpret the user's response. If the user's response doesn't make sense, you must ask again.

Getting a trustworthy response

Consider a program that deletes several files. Before deleting anything, the program asks for confirmation from the user. If the user types Y, then delete; if the user types N, then don't delete. Of course, deleting files is serious stuff. Mistaking a bad keystroke for a "yes" answer can delete the company's records. (And mistaking a bad keystroke for a "no" answer can preserve the company's incriminating evidence.) So if there's any doubt about the user's response, the program should ask the user to respond again.

Pause a moment to think about the flow of actions — what should and shouldn't happen when the computer executes the loop. A loop of this kind doesn't need to check anything before getting the user's first response. Indeed, before the user gives the first response, the loop has nothing to check. The loop shouldn't start with "as long as the user's response is invalid, get another response from the user." Instead, the loop should just leap ahead, get a response from the user, and then check the response to see if it made sense. The code to do all this is in Listing 15-4.

Listing 15-4:   Repeat Before You Delete

```
/*
 * DISCLAIMER: Neither the author nor Wiley Publishing, Inc.,
 * nor anyone else even remotely connected with the
 * creation of this book, assumes any responsibility
 * for any damage of any kind due to the use of this code,
 * or the use of any work derived from this code, including
 * any work created partially or in full by the reader.
 *
 * Sign here:_____
 */

import java.util.Scanner;
import java.io.IOException;

class IHopeYouKnowWhatYoureDoing {

    public static void main(String args[])
        throws IOException {

        Scanner myScanner = new Scanner(System.in);
        char reply;

        do {
            System.out.print("Reply with Y or N...");
            System.out.print("  Delete all .keep files? ");
            reply = myScanner.findInLine(".").charAt(0);
        } while (reply != 'Y' && reply != 'N');

        if (reply == 'Y') {
            Runtime.getRuntime().exec("cmd /c del *.keep");
        }
    }
}
```

The code in Listing 15-4 works on all the industrial-strength versions of Microsoft Windows, including Windows NT, 2000, and XP. To get the same effect in Windows 95, 98, or Me, you have to change the last line of code as follows:

```
Runtime.getRuntime().exec("start command /c del *.keep");
```

To work the same magic in Unix or Linux, you can use the following command:

```
Runtime.getRuntime().exec
    (new String[] {"/bin/sh", "-c", "rm -f *.keep"});
```

One way or another, the call to `Runtime.getRuntime...yada-yada` deletes all files whose names end with `.keep`.

In Listing 15-4, the call to `Runtime.getRuntime().exec` enables the Java program to execute an operating system command. This `Runtime` business can be tricky to use, so don't fret over the details. Just take my word for it — the call to `Runtime.getRuntime().exec` in Listing 15-4 deletes files.

The `Runtime.getRuntime().exec` method is one of those "you need a throws clause" methods that I introduce in Chapter 13. Unlike the methods in Chapter 13, the `exec` method forces you to throw an `IOException`. And with a `throws IOException` clause comes an `import java.io.IOException` declaration.

At this point you may be wondering how I know that the `exec` method needs a `throws IOException` clause. How many other Java API methods require throws clauses, and how do you find out about all these things? The answer is, you can find this information in Java's API documentation. For details, see the Appendix on this book's Web site.

Deleting files

A run of the Listing 15-4 program is shown in Figure 15-6. Before deleting a bunch of files, the program asks the user if it's okay to do the deletion. If the user gives one of the two expected answers (Y or N) then the program proceeds according to the user's wishes. But if the user enters any other letter (or any digit, punctuation symbol, or whatever), then the program asks the user for another response.

Figure 15-6:
No! Don't
do it!

```
General Output
--------------------Configuration: Chapter15_List:
Reply with Y or N... Delete all .keep files? U
Reply with Y or N... Delete all .keep files? 8
Reply with Y or N... Delete all .keep files? y
Reply with Y or N... Delete all .keep files? n
Reply with Y or N... Delete all .keep files? Y
```

In Figure 15-6, the user hems and haws for a while, first with the letter U, then the digit 8, and then with lowercase letters. Finally, the user enters Y, and the program deletes the `.keep` files. If you compare the files on your hard drive (before and after the run of the program), you'll see that the program trashes files with names ending in `.keep`.

If you use JCreator, here's how you can tell that files are being deleted:

1. **Create a project containing the code in Listing 15-4.**

   If you downloaded the special edition of JCreator from this book's Web site, you can skip this create-a-project step and use the existing Chapter15_Listing04 project.

2. **In the File View pane, right-click the name of the project.**

   A context menu appears.

3. **In the context menu, choose Add⇨New File.**

   JCreator's File Wizard opens to the File Path tab.

4. **In the Name field, type the name of your new data file.**

   Type `irreplaceableInfo.keep`, or something like that.

5. **Click Finish.**

   The file's name appears in JCreator's File View pane. For this experiment, you don't have to add any text to the file. The file exists only to be deleted.

6. **Repeat Steps 2 through 5 a few more times.**

   Create files named `somethingOrOther.keep` and files that don't have `.keep` in their names.

7. **Compile and run the program.**

   When the program runs, type **Y** to delete the `.keep` files. (The program deletes `.keep` files only in this program's project directory. The program's run has no effect on any files outside of the project directory.)

   After running the program, you want to check to make sure that the program deleted the `.keep` files.

8. **In the File View pane, right-click the name of the project.**

   A context menu appears.

9. **In the context menu, select Refresh From Local.**

   JCreator takes another look at the project directory, and lists the directory's files in the File View's tree. Assuming that the program did its job correctly, files with names ending in `.keep` no longer appear in the tree.

Using Java's do statement

To write the program in Listing 15-4, you need a loop — a loop that repeatedly asks the user if the `.keep` files should be deleted. The loop continues to ask until the user gives a meaningful response. The loop tests its condition at the end of each iteration, after each of the user's responses.

That's why the program in Listing 15-4 has a *do* loop (also known as a *do . . . while* loop). With a do loop, the program jumps right in, executes some statements, and then checks a condition. If the condition is true, then the program goes back to the top of the loop for another go-around. If the condition is false, then the computer leaves the loop (and jumps to whatever code comes immediately after the loop). The action of the loop in Listing 15-4 is illustrated in Figure 15-7.

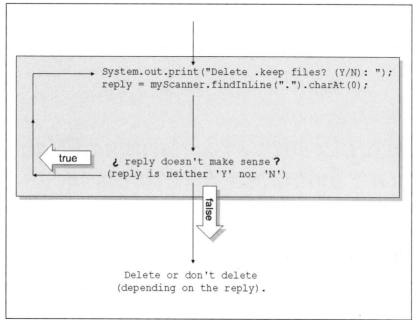

Figure 15-7: Here we go loop, do loop.

A closer look at the do statement

The format of a do loop is

```
do {
    Statements
} while (Condition)
```

Writing the *Condition* at the end of the loop reminds me that the computer executes the *Statement* inside the loop first. After the computer executes the *Statement*, the computer goes on to check the *Condition*. If the *Condition* is true, the computer goes back for another iteration of the *Statement*.

With a do loop, the computer always executes the statements inside the loop at least once:

```
//This code prints something:
int twoPlusTwo = 2 + 2;
do {
    System.out.println("Are you kidding?");
    System.out.println("2+2 doesn't equal 5.");
    System.out.print  ("Everyone knows that");
    System.out.println(" 2+2 equals 3.");
} while (twoPlusTwo == 5);
```

This code displays Are you kidding? 2+2 doesn't equal 5 . . . *and so on*, and then tests the condition twoPlusTwo == 5. Because twoPlusTwo == 5 is false, the computer doesn't go back for another iteration. Instead, the computer jumps to whatever code comes immediately after the loop.

Repeating with Predetermined Values (Java's Enhanced for Statement)

Most people say that they "never win anything." Other people win raffles, drawings, and contests, but they don't win things. Well, I have news for these people — other people don't win things either. Nobody wins things. That's how the laws of probability work. Your chance of winning one of the popular U.S. lottery jackpots is roughly 1 in 135,000,000. If you sell your quarter-million dollar house and use all the money to buy lottery tickets, your chance of winning is still only 1 in 540. If you play every day of the month (selling a house each day), your chance of winning the jackpot is still less than 1 in 15.

Of course, nothing in the previous paragraph applies to me. I don't buy lottery tickets, but I often win things. My winning streak started a few years ago. I won some expensive Java software at the end of an online seminar. Later that month, I won a microchip-enabled pinky ring (a memento from a 1998 Java conference). The following year I won a wireless PDA. Just last week I won a fancy business-class printer.

I never spend money to enter any contests. All these winnings are freebies. When the national computer science educators' conference met in Reno, Nevada, my colleagues convinced me to try the slot machines. I lost $23, and then I won back $18. At that point, I stopped playing. I wanted to quit while I was only $5 behind.

That's why my writing a Java program about slot machines is such a strange occurrence. A typical slot machine has three reels, with each reel having about twenty symbols. But to illustrate this section's ideas, I don't need twenty symbols. Instead I use four symbols — a cherry, a lemon, a kumquat, and a rutabaga.

Creating an enhanced for loop

When you play my simplified slot machine you can spin any one of over 60 combinations — cherry+cherry+kumquat, rutabaga+rutabaga+rutabaga, or whatever. This chapter's goal is to list all possible combinations. But first, I show you another kind of loop. Listing 15-5 defines an enum type for a slot machine's symbols, and Listing 15-6 displays a list of the symbols.

Listing 15-5:   Slot Machine Symbols

```
enum Symbol {cherry, lemon, kumquat, rutabaga}
```

Listing 15-6:   Listing the Symbols

```
import static java.lang.System.out;

class ListSymbols {

    public static void main(String args[]) {
        for (Symbol leftReel : Symbol.values()) {
            out.println(leftReel);
        }
    }
}
```

Listing 15-6 uses Java's *enhanced for loop*. The word "enhanced" means "enhanced compared with the loops in earlier versions of Java." The enhanced for loop is new to Java version 5.0. If you run Java version 1.4.2 (or something like that) then you can't use an enhanced for loop.

Here's the format of the enhanced for loop:

```
for (TypeName variableName : RangeOfValues) {
    Statements
}
```

Here's how the loop in Listing 15-6 follows the format:

✔ **In Listing 15-6, the word** `Symbol` **is the name of a type.**

The `int` type describes values like -1, 0, 1, and 2. The `boolean` type describes the values `true` and `false`. And (because of the code in Listing 15-5) the `Symbol` type describes the values `cherry`, `lemon`, `kumquat`, and `rutabaga`. For more information on enum types like `Symbol`, see Chapter 10.

✔ **In Listing 15-6, the word** `leftReel` **is the name of a variable.**

The loop in Listing 15-1 defines `count` to be an `int` variable. Similarly, the loop in Listing 15-6 defines `leftReel` to be a `Symbol` variable. So in theory, the variable `leftReel` can take on any of the four `Symbol` values.

By the way, I call this variable `leftReel` because the code lists all the symbols that can appear on the leftmost of the slot machine's three reels. Because all three of the slot machine's reels have the same symbols, I may also have named this variable `middleReel` or `rightReel`. But on second thought, I'll save the names `middleReel` and `rightReel` for a later example.

✔ **In Listing 15-6, the expression** `Symbol.values()` **stands for the four values in Listing 15-5.**

To quote myself in the previous bullet, "in theory, the variable `leftReel` can take on any of the four `Symbol` values." Well, the *RangeOfValues* part of the `for` statement turns theory into practice. This third item inside the parentheses says "Have as many loop iterations are there are `Symbol` values, and have the `leftReel` variable take on a different `Symbol` value during each of the loop's iterations."

So the loop in Listing 15-6 undergoes four iterations — an iteration in which `leftReel` has value `cherry`, another iteration in which `leftReel` has value `lemon`, a third iteration in which `leftReel` has value `kumquat`, and a fourth iteration in which `leftReel` has value `rutabaga`. During each iteration, the program prints the `leftReel` variable's value. The result is in Figure 15-8.

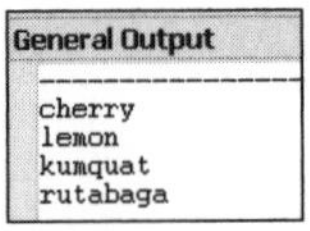

Figure 15-8:
The out-
put of the
code in
Listing 15-6.

General Output

```
cherry
lemon
kumquat
rutabaga
```

In general, a *someEnumTypeName*.values() expression stands for the set of values that a particular enum type's variable can have. For example, in Listings 10-7 and 10-8 you may use the expression WhoWins.values() to refer to the home, visitor, and neither values.

The difference between a type's name (like Symbol) and the type's values (as in Symbol.values()) is really subtle. Fortunately, you don't have to worry about the difference. As a beginning programmer, you can just use the .values() suffix in an enhanced loop's *RangeOfValues* part.

Nesting the enhanced for loops

Listing 15-6 solves a simple problem in a very elegant way. So after reading about Listing 15-6, you ask about more complicated problems. "Can I list all possible three-reel combinations of the slot machine's four symbols?" Yes, you can. Listing 15-7 shows you how to do it.

Listing 15-7:   Listing the Combinations

```
import static java.lang.System.out;

class ListCombinations {

    public static void main(String args[]) {

        for (Symbol leftReel : Symbol.values()) {
            for (Symbol middleReel : Symbol.values()) {
                for (Symbol rightReel : Symbol.values()) {
                    out.print(leftReel);
                    out.print(" ");
                    out.print(middleReel);
                    out.print(" ");
                    out.println(rightReel);
                }
            }
        }
    }
}
```

When you run the program in Listing 15-7, you get 64 lines of output. Some of those lines are shown in Figure 15-9.

```
General Output
-------------------------Configu
cherry cherry cherry
cherry cherry lemon
cherry cherry kumquat
cherry cherry rutabaga
cherry lemon cherry
cherry lemon lemon
cherry lemon kumquat
cherry lemon rutabaga
cherry kumquat cherry
cherry kumquat lemon
cherry kumquat kumquat
cherry kumquat rutabaga
cherry rutabaga cherry
cherry rutabaga lemon
cherry rutabaga kumquat
cherry rutabaga rutabaga
lemon cherry cherry
lemon cherry lemon
lemon cherry kumquat
lemon cherry rutabaga
lemon lemon cherry
lemon lemon lemon
lemon lemon kumquat
```

Figure 15-9:
The first
several lines
of output
from the
code in
Listing 15-7.

Like the code in Listing 15-3, the program in Listing 15-7 contains a loop within a loop. In fact Listing 15-7 has a loop within a loop within a loop. Here's the strategy in Listing 15-7:

```
for (each of the 4 symbols that
    can appear on the left reel),

    for (each of the 4 symbols that
        can appear on the middle reel),

        for (each of the 4 symbols that
            can appear on the right reel),

            display the three reels' symbols.
```

So you start the outer loop with the cherry symbol. Then you march on to the middle loop and begin that loop with the cherry symbol. Then you proceed to the inner loop and pick the cherry (pun intended). At last, with each loop tuned to the cherry setting, you display cherry cherry cherry combination. (See Figure 15-10.)

After displaying cherry cherry cherry, you continue with other values of the innermost loop. That is, you change the right reel's value from cherry to lemon. (See Figure 15-11.) Now the three reels' values are cherry cherry lemon, so you display these values on the screen. (See the second line in Figure 15-9.)

After exhausting the four values of the innermost (right reel) loop, you jump out of that innermost loop. But the jump puts you back to the top of the middle loop, where you change the value of middleReel from cherry to lemon. Now the values of leftReel and middleReel are cherry and lemon respectively. (See Figure 15-12.)

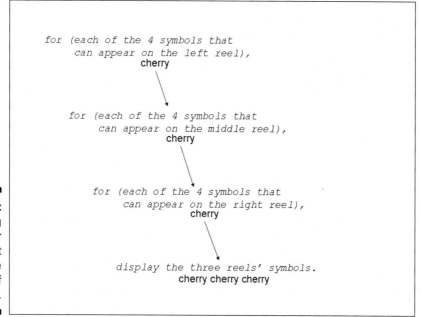

Figure 15-10:
Entering
loops for
the first
time in the
program of
Listing 15-7.

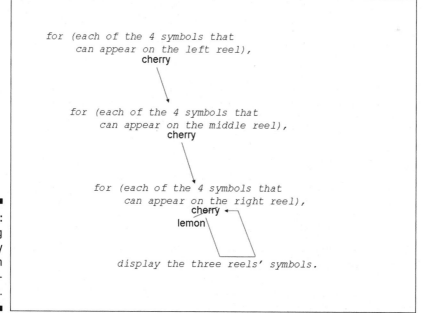

Figure 15-11:
Changing
from cherry
to lemon in
the inner-
most loop.

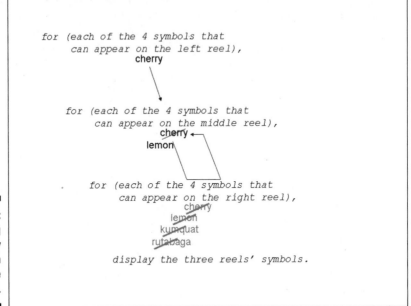

Figure 15-12:
Changing
from cherry
to lemon in
the middle
loop.

Having changed to lemon on the middle loop, you go barreling again into the innermost loop. As if you'd never seen this inner loop before, you set the loop's variable to cherry. (See Figure 15-13.)

```
for (each of the 4 symbols that
     can appear on the left reel),
           cherry



     for (each of the 4 symbols that
          can appear on the middle reel),
                   cherry
                 lemon



          for (each of the 4 symbols that
               can appear on the right reel),
                      cherry



          display the three reels' symbols.
```

Figure 15-13:
Restarting
the inner
loop.

After displaying the tasty `cherry lemon cherry` combination, you start changing the values of the innermost loop. (See Figure 15-14.)

The loop keeps going until it displays all 64 combinations. Whew!

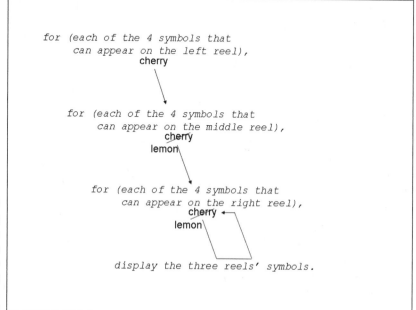

Figure 15-14:
Traveling a
second time
through the
innermost
loop.

Part IV
Using Program Units

The 5th Wave   By Rich Tennant

"Well, this is festive— a miniature intranet amidst a swirl of Java applets."

In this part . . .

*W*ay back in the Elvis Era, people thought that computer programs should be big lists of instructions. Then, during the Groovy Sixties, people decided to modularize their programs. A typical program consisted of several methods (like the `main` methods in this book's examples). Finally, during the Weighty Eighties, programmers grouped methods and other things into units called *objects*.

Far from being the flavor of the month, object-oriented programming has become the backbone of modern computing. This part of the book tells you all about it.

Chapter 16

Using Loops and Arrays

This chapter has seven illustrations. For these illustrations, the people at Wiley Publishing insist on following numbering: Figure 16-1, Figure 16-2, Figure 16-3, Figure 16-4, Figure 16-5, Figure 16-6, and Figure 16-7. But I like a different kind of numbering. I'd like to number the illustrations figure[0], figure[1], figure[2], figure[3], figure[4], figure[5], and figure[6]. Read on in this chapter and you'll find out why.

Some for Loops in Action

The Java Motel, with its ten comfortable rooms, sits in a quiet place off the main highway. Aside from a small, separate office, the motel is just one long row of ground floor rooms. Each room is easily accessible from the spacious front parking lot.

Oddly enough, the motel's rooms are numbered 0 through 9. I could say that the numbering is a fluke — something to do with the builder's original design plan. But the truth is, starting with 0 makes the examples in this chapter easier to write.

You, as the Java Motel's manager, store occupancy data in a file on your computer's hard drive. The file has one entry for each room in the motel. For example, in Figure 16-1, Room 0 has one guest, Room 1 has four guests, Room 2 is empty, and so on.

Figure 16-1:
Occupancy
data for the
Java Motel.

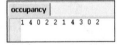

You want a report showing the number of guests in each room. Because you
know how many rooms you have, this problem begs for a `for` loop. The code
to solve this problem is in Listing 16-1, and a run of the code is shown in
Figure 16-2.

Listing 16-1:   A Program to Generate an Occupancy Report

```java
import java.util.Scanner;
import java.io.File;
import java.io.FileNotFoundException;
import static java.lang.System.out;

class ShowOccupancy {

    public static void main(String args[])
        throws FileNotFoundException {

        Scanner diskScanner =
            new Scanner(new File("occupancy"));

        out.println("Room\tGuests");

        for (int roomNum = 0; roomNum < 10; roomNum++) {
            out.print(roomNum);
            out.print("\t");
            out.println(diskScanner.nextInt());
        }
    }
}
```

Figure 16-2:
Running
the code in
Listing 16-1.

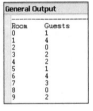

Listing 16-1 uses a `for` loop — a loop of the kind described in Chapter 15. As the `roomNum` variable's value marches from 0 to 9, the program displays one number after another from the `occupancy` file. To read more about getting numbers from a disk file like my `occupancy` file, see Chapter 13.

This example's input file is named `occupancy` — not `occupancy.txt`. If you use JCreator's File Wizard to make an `occupancy` file, you must put a dot in the wizard's Name field. That is, you must type `occupancy.` (occupancy-"dot") in the Name field. If you don't type your own dot anywhere in the Name field, then JCreator adds a default extension to the file's name (turning `occupancy` into `occupancy.java`).

Grabbing input here and there

Listing 16-2 illustrates some pithy issues surrounding the input of data. For one thing, the program gets input from both the keyboard and a disk file. (The program gets a room number from the keyboard. Then the program gets the number of guests in that room from the `occupancy` file.) To make this happen, Listing 16-2 sports two `Scanner` declarations — one to declare `myScanner`, and a second to declare `diskScanner`.

Later in the program, the call `myScanner.nextInt` reads from the keyboard, and `diskScanner.nextInt` reads from the file. Within the program, you can read from the keyboard or the disk as many times as you want. You can even intermingle the calls — reading once from the keyboard, then three times from the disk, then twice from the keyboard, and so on. All you have to do is remember to use `myScanner` whenever you read from the keyboard, and use `diskScanner` whenever you read from the disk.

Another interesting tidbit in Listing 16-2 concerns the `occupancy` file. Many of this chapter's examples read from an `occupancy` file, and I use the same data in each of the examples. (I use the data shown in Figure 16-1.) To run an example, I copy the occupancy file from one project to another. (Before running the code in Listing 16-2, I go to the old Listing 16-1 project in JCreator's File View. I right-click the `occupancy` file in the Listing 16-1 project, and select Copy from the context menu. Then I right-click the new Listing 16-2 branch, and select Paste from the context menu.)

In real life, having several copies of a data file can be dangerous. You can modify one copy, and then accidentally read out-of-date data from a different copy. Sure, you should have backup copies, but you should have only one "master" copy — the copy from which all programs get the same input.

So in a real-life program, you don't copy the occupancy file from one project to another. What do you do instead? You put an `occupancy` file in one place on your hard drive, and then have each program refer to the file using the names of the file's directories. For example, if your `occupancy` file is in the `c:\data\hotel` directory, you write

```
Scanner diskScanner =
    new Scanner(new
    File("c:\\data\\hotel\\occu
    pancy"));
```

A sidebar in Chapter 13 has more details about filenames and double backslashes.

Deciding on a loop's limit at runtime

On occasion, you may want a more succinct report than the one in Figure 16-2. "Don't give me a long list of rooms," you say. "Just give me the number of guests in Room 3." To get such a report, you need a slightly smarter program. The program is in Listing 16-2, with runs of the program shown in Figure 16-3.

Listing 16-2:   Report on One Room Only, Please

```
import java.util.Scanner;
import java.io.File;
import java.io.FileNotFoundException;
import static java.lang.System.out;

public class ShowOneRoomOccupancy {

    public static void main(String args[])
        throws FileNotFoundException {

        Scanner myScanner = new Scanner(System.in);
        Scanner diskScanner =
            new Scanner(new File("occupancy"));
        int whichRoom;

        out.print("Which room? ");
        whichRoom = myScanner.nextInt();

        for(int roomNum = 0; roomNum < whichRoom; roomNum++){
            diskScanner.nextInt();
        }

        out.print("Room ");
        out.print(whichRoom);
        out.print(" has ");
        out.print(diskScanner.nextInt());
        out.println(" guest(s).");
    }
}
```

If Listing 16-2 has a moral, it's that the number of for loop iterations can vary from one run to another. The loop in Listing 16-2 runs on and on as long as the counting variable roomNum is less than a room number specified by the user. When the roomNum is the same as the number specified by the user (that is, when roomNum is the same as whichRoom), the computer jumps out of the loop. Then the computer grabs one more int value from the occupancy file and displays that value on the screen.

```
Which room? 3
Room 3 has 2 guest(s).

Which room? 5
Room 5 has 1 guest(s).

Which room? 8
Room 8 has 0 guest(s).

Which room? 10
Room 10 has Exception in thread "main" java.util.NoSuchElementException
        at java.util.Scanner.throwFor(Scanner.java:817)
        at java.util.Scanner.next(Scanner.java:1431)
        at java.util.Scanner.nextInt(Scanner.java:2040)
        at java.util.Scanner.nextInt(Scanner.java:2000)
        at ShowOneRoomOccupancy.main(ShowOneRoomOccupancy.java:26)
```

Figure 16-3:
A few
one-room
reports.

As you stare at the runs in Figure 16-3, it's important to remember the unusual numbering of rooms. Room 3 has two guests because Room 3 is the *fourth* room in the occupancy file of Figure 16-1. That's because the motel's rooms are numbered 0 through 9.

Using all kinds of conditions in a for loop

Look at the run in Figure 16-3, and notice the program's awful behavior when the user mistakenly asks about a nonexistent room. The motel has no Room 10. If you ask for the number of guests in Room 10, the program tries to read more numbers than the occupancy file contains. This unfortunate attempt causes a NoSuchElementException.

Listing 16-3 fixes the end-of-file problem.

Listing 16-3: A More Refined Version of the One-Room Code

```java
import java.util.Scanner;
import java.io.File;
import java.io.FileNotFoundException;
import static java.lang.System.out;

public class BetterShowOneRoom {

    public static void main(String args[])
        throws FileNotFoundException {

        Scanner myScanner = new Scanner(System.in);
        Scanner diskScanner =
            new Scanner(new File("occupancy"));
        int whichRoom;
```

(continued)

Listing 16-3 *(continued)*

```
        out.print("Which room? ");
        whichRoom = myScanner.nextInt();

        for (int roomNum = 0;
             roomNum < whichRoom && diskScanner.hasNext();
             roomNum++) {

            diskScanner.nextInt();
        }
        if (diskScanner.hasNext()) {
            out.print("Room ");
            out.print(whichRoom);
            out.print(" has ");
            out.print(diskScanner.nextInt());
            out.println(" guest(s).");
        }
    }
}
```

The code in Listing 16-3 isn't earth shattering. To get this code, you take the code in Listing 16-2 and add a few tests for the end of the occupancy file. You perform the diskScanner.hasNext test before each call to nextInt. That way, if the call to nextInt is doomed to failure, you catch the potential failure before it happens. A few test runs of the code in Listing 16-3 are shown in Figure 16-4.

Figure 16-4:
The bad room number 10 gets no response.

```
Which room? 0
Room 0 has 1 guest(s).

Which room? 6
Room 6 has 4 guest(s).

Which room? 2
Room 2 has 0 guest(s).

Which room? 10
```

In Listing 16-3, I want to know if the occupancy file contains any more data (any data that I haven't read yet). So I call the Scanner class's hasNext method. The hasNext method looks ahead to see if I can read any kind of data — an int value, a double value, a word, a boolean, or whatever. That's okay for this section's example, but in some situations, you need to be pickier about your input data. For example, you may want to know if you can call nextInt (as opposed to nextDouble or nextLine). Fortunately, Java has methods for your pickiest input needs. The code if (diskScanner.hasNextInt()) tests to see if you can read an int value from the disk file. Java also has methods like hasNextLine, hasNextDouble, and so on. For more information on the plain old hasNext method, see Chapter 14.

Listing 16-3 has a big fat condition to keep the `for` loop going:

```
for (int roomNum = 0;
    roomNum < whichRoom && diskScanner.hasNext();
    roomNum++) {
```

Many `for` loop conditions are simple "less than" tests, but there's no rule saying that all `for` loop conditions have to be so simple. In fact, any expression can be a `for` loop's condition, as long as the expression has value `true` or `false`. The condition in Listing 16-3 combines a "less than" with a call to the `Scanner` class's `hasNext` method.

Reader, Meet Arrays; Arrays, Meet the Reader

A weary traveler steps up to the Java Motel's front desk. "I'd like a room," says the traveler. So the desk clerk runs a report like the one in Figure 16-2. Noticing the first vacant room in the list, the clerk suggests Room 2. "I'll take it," says the traveler.

It's so hard to get good help these days. How many times have you told the clerk to fill the higher numbered rooms first? The lower numbered rooms are older, and they are badly in need of repair. For example, Room 3 has an indoor pool. (The pipes leak, so the carpet is soaking wet.) Room 2 has no heat (not in wintertime, anyway). Room 1 has serious electrical problems (so, for that room, you always get payment in advance). Besides, Room 8 is vacant, and you charge more for the higher numbered rooms.

Here's where a subtle change in presentation can make a big difference. You need a program that lists vacant rooms in reverse order. That way, Room 8 catches the clerk's eye before Room 2 does.

Think about strategies for a program that displays data in reverse. With the input from Figure 16-1, the program's output should look like the display shown in Figure 16-5.

Figure 16-5:
A list
of vacant
rooms, with
higher num-
bered rooms
shown first.

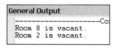

Here's the first (bad) idea for a programming strategy:

```
Get the last value in the occupancy file.
If the value is 0, print the room number.

Get the next-to-last value in the occupancy file.
If the value is 0, print the room number.

...And so on.
```

With some fancy input/output programs, this may be a workable strategy. But no matter what input/output program you use, jumping directly to the end or to the middle of a file is a big pain in the boot. It's especially bad if you plan to jump repeatedly. So go back to the drawing board and think of something better.

Here's an idea! Read all the values in the occupancy file and store each value in a variable of its own. Then you step through the variables in reverse order, displaying a room number when it's appropriate to do so.

This idea works, but the code is so ugly that I refuse to dignify it by calling it a "Listing." No, this is just a "see the following code" kind of thing. So please, see the following ugly code:

```java
/*
 * Ugh! I can't stand this ugly code!
 */
guestsIn0 = diskScanner.nextInt();
guestsIn1 = diskScanner.nextInt();
guestsIn2 = diskScanner.nextInt();
guestsIn3 = diskScanner.nextInt();
guestsIn4 = diskScanner.nextInt();
guestsIn5 = diskScanner.nextInt();
guestsIn6 = diskScanner.nextInt();
guestsIn7 = diskScanner.nextInt();
guestsIn8 = diskScanner.nextInt();
guestsIn9 = diskScanner.nextInt();

if (guestsIn9 == 0) {
    System.out.println(9);
}
if (guestsIn8 == 0) {
    System.out.println(8);
}
if (guestsIn7 == 0) {
    System.out.println(7);
}
if (guestsIn6 == 0) {

// ... And so on.
```

What you're lacking is a uniform way of naming ten variables. That is, it would be nice to write

```
/*
 * Nice idea, but this is not real Java code:
 */
for (int roomNum = 0; roomNum < 10; roomNum++) {
    guestsInroomNum = diskScanner.nextInt(); //Read forwards
}

for (int roomNum = 9; roomNum >= 0; roomNum--) {
    if (guestsInroomNum == 0) {
        System.out.println(roomNum);          //Write backwards
    }
}
```

Well, there is a way to write loops of this kind. All you need is some square brackets. When you add square brackets to the idea shown in the preceding code, you get what's called an array. An *array* is a row of values, like the row of rooms in a one-floor motel. To picture the array, just picture the Java Motel:

✔ First, picture the rooms, lined up next to one another.

✔ Next, picture the same rooms with their front walls missing. Inside each room you can see a certain number of guests.

✔ If you can, forget that the two guests in Room 9 are putting piles of bills into a big briefcase. Ignore the fact that the guest in Room 5 hasn't moved away from the TV set in a day and a half. Instead of all these details, just see numbers. In each room, see a number representing the count of guests in that room. (If freeform visualization isn't your strong point, then take a look at Figure 16-6.)

In the lingo of Java programming, the entire row of rooms is called an *array*. Each room in the array is called a *component* of the array (also known as an array *element*). Each component has two numbers associated with it:

✔ **Index:** In the case of the Java Motel array, the index is the room number (a number from 0 to 9).

✔ **Value:** In the Java Motel array, the value is the number of guests in a given room (a number stored in a component of the array).

Using an array saves you from having to declare ten separate variables: `guestsIn0`, `guestsIn1`, `guestsIn2`, and so on. To declare an array with ten values in it, you can write two fairly short lines of code:

```
int guestsIn[];
guestsIn = new int[10];
```

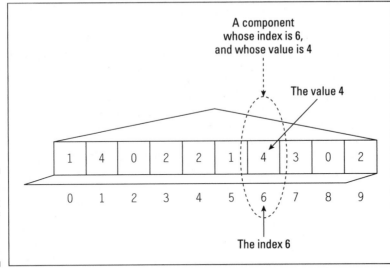

Figure 16-6:
An abstract
snapshot of
rooms in the
Java Motel.

You can even squish these two lines into one longer line:

```
int guestsIn[] = new int[10];
```

In either of these code snippets, notice the use of the number 10. This number tells the computer to make the guestsIn array have ten components. Each component of the array has a name of its own. The starting component is named guestsIn[0], the next is named guestsIn[1], and so on. The last of the ten components is named guestsIn[9].

In creating an array, you always specify the number of components. The array's indices always start with 0 and end with the number that's one less than the total number of components. For example, if your array has ten components (and you declare the array with new int[10]), then the array's indices go from 0 to 9.

Storing values in an array

After you've created an array, you can put values into the array's components. For example, the guests in Room 6 are fed up with all those mint candies that you put on peoples' beds. So they check out and Room 6 becomes vacant. You should put the value 0 into the 6 component. You can do it with this assignment statement:

```
guestsIn[6] = 0;
```

On one weekday, business is awful. No one's staying at the motel. But then you get a lucky break. A big bus pulls up to the motel. The side of the bus has a sign that says "Loners' Convention." Out of the bus come 25 people, each walking to the motel's small office, none paying attention to the others who were on the bus. Each person wants a private room. Only 10 of them can stay at the Java Motel, but that's okay, because you can send the other 15 loners down the road to the old C-Side Resort and Motor Lodge.

Anyway, to register 10 of the loners into the Java Motel, you put one guest in each of your 10 rooms. Having created an array, you can take advantage of the array's indexing and write a `for` loop, like this:

```
for (int roomNum = 0; roomNum < 10; roomNum++) {
    guestsIn[roomNum] = 1;
}
```

This loop takes the place of ten assignment statements, because the computer executes the statement `guestsIn[roomNum] = 1` ten times. The first time around, the value of `roomNum` is 0, so in effect, the computer executes

```
guestsIn[0] = 1;
```

In the next loop iteration, the value of `roomNum` is 1, so the computer executes the equivalent of the following statement:

```
guestsIn[1] = 1;
```

During the next iteration, the computer behaves as if it's executing

```
guestsIn[2] = 1;
```

And so on. When `roomNum` gets to be 9, the computer executes the equivalent of the following statement:

```
guestsIn[9] = 1;
```

Notice how the loop's counter goes from 0 to 9. Compare this with Figure 16-6, and remember that the indices of an array go from 0 to one less than the number of components in the array. Looping with room numbers from 0 to 9 covers all the rooms in the Java Motel.

When you work with an array, and you step through the array's components using a `for` loop, you normally start the loop's counter variable at 0. To form the condition that tests for another iteration, you often write an expression like `roomNum < arraySize`, where *arraySize* is the number of components in the array.

Creating a report

The code to create the report in Figure 16-5 is shown in Listing 16-4. This new program uses the idea in the world's ugliest code (the code from several pages back with variables `guestsIn0`, `guestsIn1`, and so on). But instead of having ten separate variables, Listing 16-4 uses an array.

Listing 16-4:   Traveling through Data Both Forwards and Backwards

```java
import java.util.Scanner;
import java.io.File;
import java.io.FileNotFoundException;

class VacanciesInReverse {

    public static void main(String args[])
        throws FileNotFoundException {

        Scanner diskScanner =
            new Scanner(new File("occupancy"));
        int guestsIn[];
        guestsIn = new int[10];

        for (int roomNum = 0; roomNum < 10; roomNum++) {
            guestsIn[roomNum] = diskScanner.nextInt();
        }

        for (int roomNum = 9; roomNum >= 0; roomNum--) {
            if (guestsIn[roomNum] == 0) {
                System.out.print("Room ");
                System.out.print(roomNum);
                System.out.println(" is vacant.");
            }
        }
    }
}
```

Notice the stuff in parentheses in the `VacanciesInReverse` program's second `for` loop. It's easy to get these things wrong. You're aiming for a loop that checks Room 9, then Room 8, and so on.

```
if (guestsIn[9] == 0) {
    System.out.print(roomNum);
}
if (guestsIn[8] == 0) {
    System.out.print(roomNum);
}
if (guestsIn[7] == 0) {
    System.out.print(roomNum);
}

...And so on, until you get to...

if (guestsIn[0] == 0) {
    System.out.print(roomNum);
}
```

Some observations about the code:

- The loop's counter must start at 9:

  ```
  for (int roomNum = 9; roomNum >= 0; roomNum--)
  ```

- Each time through the loop, the counter goes *down* by one:

  ```
  for (int roomNum = 9; roomNum >= 0; roomNum--)
  ```

- The loop keeps going as long as the counter is *greater than or equal to* 0:

  ```
  for (int roomNum = 9; roomNum >= 0; roomNum--)
  ```

Think through each of these three items, and you'll write a perfect `for` loop.

Working with Arrays

Earlier in this chapter, a busload of loners showed up at your motel. When they finally left, you were glad to get rid them, even if it meant having all your rooms empty for a while. But now, another bus pulls into the parking lot. This bus has a sign that says "Gregarian Club." Out of the bus come 50 people, each more gregarious than the next. Now everybody in your parking lot is clamoring to meet everyone else. While they meet and greet, they're all frolicking toward the front desk, singing the club's theme song. (Oh no! It's the Gregarian Chant!)

The first five Gregarians all want Room 7. It's a tight squeeze, but you were never big on fire codes anyway. Next comes a group of three with a yen for Room 0. (They're computer programmers, and they think the room number is cute.) Then there's a pack of four Gregarians who want Room 3. (The in-room pool sounds attractive to them.)

Looping in style

Listing 15-7 uses an enhanced `for` loop to step through a bunch of values. In that program, the values belong to an enum type. Well, this chapter also deals with a bunch of values; namely, the values in an array. So you're probably not surprised if I show you an enhanced `for` loop that steps through an array's values.

To see such a loop, start with the code in Listing 16-5. The last loop in that program looks something like this:

```
for (int roomNum = 0; roomNum <
    10; roomNum++) {

    out.println(guestsIn[roomNu
m]);

}
```

To turn this into an enhanced `for` loop, you make up a new variable name. (What about the name `howMany`? I like that name.) Whatever name you choose, the new variable ranges over the values in the `guestsIn` array.

```
for (int howMany : guestsIn) {
    out.println(howMany);
}
```

This enhanced loop uses the same format as the loop in Chapter 15.

```
for (TypeName variableName :
    RangeOfValues) {
    Statements
}
```

In Chapter 15, the `RangeOfValues` belongs to an enum type. But in this sidebar's example, the `RangeOfValues` belongs to an array.

Enhanced `for` loops are nice and concise. But don't be too anxious to use enhanced loops with arrays. This feature has some nasty limitations. For example, my new `howMany` loop doesn't display room numbers. I avoid room numbers because the room numbers in my `guestsIn` array are the indices 0 through 9. Unfortunately, an enhanced loop doesn't provide easy access to an array's indices.

And here's another unpleasant surprise. Start with the following loop from Listing 16-4:

```
for (int roomNum = 0; roomNum <
    10; roomNum++) {
    guestsIn[roomNum] =
    diskScanner.nextInt();
}
```

Turn this traditional `for` loop into an enhanced `for` loop, and you get the following misleading code:

```
for (int howMany : guestsIn) {
    howMany =
    diskScanner.nextInt();
    //Don't do this
}
```

The new enhanced loop doesn't do what you want it to do. This loop reads values from an input file and then dumps these values into the garbage can. In the end, the array's values remain unchanged.

It's sad but true. To make full use of an array, you have to fall back on Java's plain old `for` loop.

With all this traffic, you better switch on your computer. You start a program that enables you to enter new occupancy data. The program has five parts:

✔ **Create an array, and then put 0 in each of the array's components.**

When the Loners' Club members left, the motel was suddenly empty. (Heck, even before the Loners' Club members left, the motel seemed empty.) To declare an array and fill the array with zeros, you execute code of the following kind:

```
int guestsIn[];
guestsIn = new int[10];

for (int roomNum = 0; roomNum < 10; roomNum++) {
    guestsIn[roomNum] = 0;
}
```

✔ **Get a room number, and then get the number of guests who will be staying in that room.**

Reading numbers typed by the user is pretty humdrum stuff. Do a little prompting and a little nextInt calling, and you're all set:

```
out.print("Room number: ");
whichRoom = myScanner.nextInt();
out.print("How many guests? ");
numGuests = myScanner.nextInt();
```

✔ **Use the room number and the number of guests to change a value in the array.**

Earlier in this chapter, to put one guest in Room 2, you executed

```
guestsIn[2] = 1;
```

So now, you have two variables — numGuests and whichRoom. Maybe numGuests is 5, and whichRoom is 7. To put numGuests in whichRoom (that is, to put 5 guests in Room 7), you can execute

```
guestsIn[whichRoom] = numGuests;
```

That's the crucial step in the design of your new program.

✔ **Ask the user if the program should keep going.**

Are there more guests to put in rooms? To find out, execute this code:

```
    out.print("Do another? ");
} while (myScanner.findInLine(".").charAt(0) == 'Y');
```

✔ **Display the number of guests in each room.**

No problem! You already did this. You can steal the code (almost verbatim) from Listing 16-1:

```
out.println("Room\tGuests");
for (int roomNum = 0; roomNum < 10; roomNum++) {
    out.print(roomNum);
    out.print("\t");
    out.println(guestsIn[roomNum]);
}
```

The only difference between this latest code snippet and the stuff in
Listing 16-1 is that this new code uses the guestsIn array. The first time
through this loop, the code does

```
out.println(guestsIn[0]);
```

displaying the number of guests in Room 0. The next time through the
loop, the code does

```
out.println(guestsIn[1]);
```

displaying the number of guests in Room 1. The last time through the
loop, the code does

```
out.println(guestsIn[9]);
```

That's perfect.

The complete program (with these five pieces put together) is in Listing 16-5.
A run of the program is shown in Figure 16-7.

Listing 16-5:   Storing Occupancy Data in an Array

```
import java.util.Scanner;
import static java.lang.System.out;

class AddGuests {

    public static void main(String args[]) {
        Scanner myScanner = new Scanner(System.in);
        int whichRoom, numGuests;
        int guestsIn[];
        guestsIn = new int[10];

        for (int roomNum = 0; roomNum < 10; roomNum++) {
            guestsIn[roomNum] = 0;
        }

        do {
            out.print("Room number: ");
            whichRoom = myScanner.nextInt();
            out.print("How many guests? ");
            numGuests = myScanner.nextInt();
            guestsIn[whichRoom] = numGuests;
```

```
                        out.println();
                        out.print("Do another? ");
               } while (myScanner.findInLine(".").charAt(0) == 'Y');

               out.println();
               out.println("Room\tGuests");
               for (int roomNum = 0; roomNum < 10; roomNum++) {
                        out.print(roomNum);
                        out.print("\t");
                        out.println(guestsIn[roomNum]);
               }
          }
}
```

General Output

```
----------------------Co
Room number: 7
How many guests? 5

Do another? Y
Room number: 0
How many guests? 3

Do another? Y
Room number: 3
How many guests? 4

Do another? N

Room     Guests
0        3
1        0
2        0
3        4
4        0
5        0
6        0
7        5
8        0
9        0
```

Figure 16-7:
Running
the code in
Listing 16-5.

Hey! The program in Listing 16-5 is pretty big! It may be the biggest program so far in this book. But *big* doesn't necessarily mean *difficult.* If each piece of the program makes sense, you can create each piece on its own, and then put all the pieces together. Voilà! The code is manageable.

Chapter 17

Programming with Objects and Classes

. . . .

In This Chapter

▶ Creating classes

▶ Making objects from classes

▶ Joining the exclusive "I understand classes and objects" society

. . . .

Chapters 6, 7, and 8 introduce Java's primitive types — things like `int`, `double`, `char`, and `boolean`. That's great, but how often does a real-world problem deal exclusively with such simple values? Consider an exchange between a merchant and a customer. The customer makes a purchase, which can involve item names, model numbers, credit card info, sales tax rates, and lots of other stuff.

In older computer programming languages, you treat an entire purchase like a big pile of unbundled laundry. Imagine a mound of socks, shirts, and other pieces of clothing. You have no basket, so you grab as much as you can handle. As you walk to the washer, you drop a few things — a sock here and a wash-cloth there. This is like the older way of storing the values in a purchase. In older languages, there's no purchase. There are only `double` values, `char` values, and other loose items. You put the purchase amount in one variable, the customer's name in another, and the sales tax data somewhere else. But that's awful. You tend to drop things on your way to the compiler. With small errors in a program, you can easily drop an amount here and a customer's name there.

So with laundry and computer programming, you're better off if you have a basket. The newer programming languages, like Java, allow you to combine values and make new, more useful kinds of values. For example, in Java you can combine `double` values, `boolean` values, and other kinds of values to create something that you call a `Purchase`. Because your purchase info is all in one big bundle, it's easier to keep track of the purchase's pieces. That's the start of an important computer programming concept — the notion of *object-oriented programming*.

Creating a Class

I start with a "traditional" example. The program in Listing 17-1 processes simple purchase data. Two runs of the program are shown in Figure 17-1.

Listing 17-1:   Doing It the Old-Fashioned Way

```java
import java.util.Scanner;

class ProcessData {

    public static void main(String args[]) {
        Scanner myScanner = new Scanner(System.in);
        double amount;
        boolean taxable;
        double total;

        System.out.print("Amount: ");
        amount = myScanner.nextDouble();
        System.out.print("Taxable? (true/false) ");
        taxable = myScanner.nextBoolean();

        if (taxable) {
           total = amount * 1.05;
        } else {
            total = amount;
        }

        System.out.print("Total: ");
        System.out.println(total);
    }
}
```

If the output in Figure 17-1 looks funny, it's because I do nothing in the code to control the number of digits beyond the decimal point. So in the output, the value $20.00 looks like 20.0. That's okay. I show you how to fix the problem in Chapter 18.

Figure 17-1:
Processing
a customer's
purchase.

```
Amount: 20.00
Taxable? (true/false) false
Total: 20.0

Amount: 20.00
Taxable? (true/false) true
Total: 21.0
```

Reference types and Java classes

The code in Listing 17-1 involves a few simple values — amount, taxable, and total. So here's the main point of this chapter: By combining several simple values, you can get a single, more useful value. That's the way it works. You take some of Java's primitive types, whip them together to make a primitive type stew, and what do you get? You get a more useful type called a *reference type*. Listing 17-2 has an example.

Listing 17-2:   What It Means to Be a Purchase

```
class Purchase {
    double amount;
    boolean taxable;
    double total;
}
```

The code in Listing 17-2 has no main method, so you can compile the code, but you can't run it. When you choose Build⇨Compile Project in JCreator's main menu, you get a nice Process completed message. But then choose Build⇨Execute Project, and the computer balks. (You get the message box shown in Figure 17-2.) Because Listing 17-2 has no main method, there's no place to start the executing. (In fact, the code in Listing 17-2 has no statements at all. There's nothing to execute.)

Figure 17-2:
The code in
Listing 17-2
has no main
method.

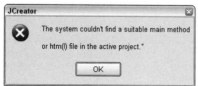

Using a newly defined class

To do something useful with the code in Listing 17-2, you need a main method. You can put the main method in a separate file. Listing 17-3 shows you such a file.

Listing 17-3:   Making Use of Your Purchase Class

```
import java.util.Scanner;

class ProcessPurchase {

    public static void main(String args[]) {
        Scanner myScanner = new Scanner(System.in);
        Purchase onePurchase = new Purchase();

        System.out.print("Amount: ");
        onePurchase.amount = myScanner.nextDouble();
        System.out.print("Taxable? (true/false) ");
        onePurchase.taxable = myScanner.nextBoolean();

        if (onePurchase.taxable) {
            onePurchase.total = onePurchase.amount * 1.05;
        } else {
            onePurchase.total = onePurchase.amount;
        }

        System.out.print("Total: ");
        System.out.println(onePurchase.total);
    }
}
```

The best way to understand the code in Listing 17-3 is to compare it, line by line, with the code in Listing 17-1. In fact, there's a mechanical formula for turning the code in Listing 17-1 into the code in Listing 17-3. Table 17-1 describes the formula.

Table 17-1	Converting Your Code to Use a Class
In Listing 17-1	*In Listing 17-3*
double amount; boolean taxable; double total;	Purchase onePurchase = new Purchase();
amount	onePurchase.amount
taxable	onePurchase.taxable
total	onePurchase.total

The two programs (in Listings 17-1 and 17-3) do essentially the same thing, but one uses primitive variables, and the other leans on the Purchase code from Listing 17-2. Both programs have runs like the ones shown back in Figure 17-1.

Running code that straddles two separate files

From JCreator's point of view, a project that contains two Java source files is no big deal. You create two classes in the same project, and then you choose Build⇨Compile Project. Finally, you choose Build⇨Execute Project. Everything works the way you expect it to work.

The only time things become tricky is when you have two main methods in the one project. This section's example (Listings 17-2 and 17-3) doesn't suffer from that malady. But as you experiment with your code, you can easily add classes with additional main methods. You may also create a large application with several starting points.

When a project has more than one main method, JCreator may prompt you and ask which class's main method you want to run. But sometimes JCreator doesn't prompt you. Instead, JCreator arbitrarily picks one of the main methods and ignores all the others. This can be very confusing. You add a println call to the wrong main method, and nothing appears in the General Output pane. Hey, what gives?

You can fix the problem by following these steps:

1. **Right-click the project's branch in the File View tree.**

2. **In the resulting context menu, select Properties.**

   A Project Properties dialog box appears. The dialog box contains a list box labeled Run. This list box contains the names of all the classes in the project that contain main methods.

3. **In the Run list box, select the class whose main method you want to run.**

4. **Click OK.**

   The Project Properties dialog box disappears.

5. **In JCreator's main menu, choose Build⇨Execute Project.**

You cannot execute a project that has no `main` method. If you try, you get a message box like the one shown earlier in Figure 17-2.

Why bother?

On the surface, the code in Listing 17-3 is longer, more complicated, and harder to read. But think about a big pile of laundry. It may take time to find a basket, and to shovel socks into the basket. But when you have clothes in the basket, the clothes are much easier to carry. It's the same way with the code in Listing 17-3. When you have your data in a `Purchase` basket, it's much easier to do complicated things with purchases.

From Classes Come Objects

The code in Listing 17-2 defines a class. A *class* is a design plan; it describes the way in which you intend to combine and use pieces of data. For example, the code in Listing 17-2 announces your intention to combine `double`, `boolean`, and `double` values to make new `Purchase` values.

Classes are central to all Java programming. But Java is called an object-oriented language. Java isn't called a class-oriented language. In fact, no one uses the term class-oriented language. Why not?

Well, you can't put your arms around a class. A class isn't real. A class without an object is like a day without chocolate. If you're sitting in a room right now, glance at all the chairs in the room. How many chairs are in the room? Two? Five? Twenty? In a room with five chairs, you have five chair objects. Each chair (each object) is something real, something you can use, something you can sit on.

A language like Java has classes and objects. So what's the difference between a class and an object?

 ✔ An object is a thing.

 ✔ A class is a design plan for things of that kind.

For example, how would you describe what a chair is? Well, a chair has a seat, a back, and legs. In Java, you may write the stuff in Listing 17-4.

Listing 17-4:   What It Means to Be a Chair

```
/*
 * This is real Java code, but this code cannot be compiled
 *  on its own:
 */

class Chair {
    FlatHorizonalPanel seat;
    FlatVerticalPanel back;
    LongSkinnyVerticalRods legs;
}
```

The code above is a design plan for chairs. The code tells you that each chair has three things. The code names the things (seat, back, and legs), and tells you a little bit about each thing. (For example, a seat is a FlatHorizontal Panel.) In the same way, the code in Listing 17-2 tells you that each purchase has three things. The code names the things (amount, taxable, and total), and tells you the primitive type of each thing.

So imagine some grand factory at the edge of the universe. While you sleep each night, this factory stamps out tangible objects — objects that you'll encounter during the next waking day. Tomorrow you'll go for an interview at the Sloshy Shoes Company. So tonight, the factory builds chairs for the company's offices. The factory builds chair objects, as shown in Figure 17-3, from the almost-real code in Listing 17-4.

In Listing 17-3, the line

```
Purchase onePurchase = new Purchase();
```

behaves like that grand factory at the edge of the universe. Instead of creating chair objects, that line in Listing 17-3 creates a purchase object, as shown in Figure 17-4. That Listing 17-3 line is a declaration with an initialization. Just as the line

```
int count = 0;
```

declares the count variable and sets count to 0, the line in Listing 17-3 declares the onePurchase variable, and makes onePurchase point to a brand new object. That new object contains three parts: an amount part, a taxable part, and a total part.

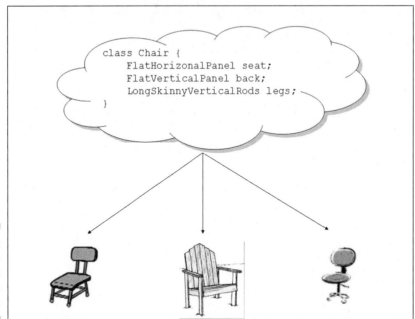

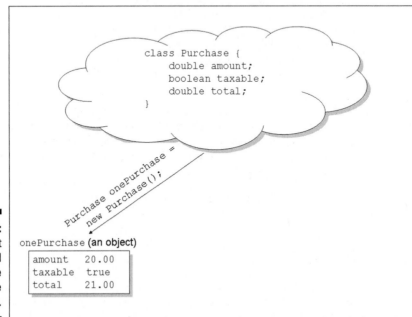

If you want to be picky, there's a difference between the stuff in Figure 17-4 and the action of the big bold statement in Listing 17-3. Figure 17-4 shows an object with the values 20.00, true, and 21.00 stored in it. The statement in Listing 17-3 creates a new object, but it doesn't fill the object with useful values. Getting values comes later in Listing 17-3.

Understanding (or ignoring) the subtleties

Sometimes, when you refer to a particular object, you want to emphasize which class the object came from. Well, subtle differences in emphasis call for big differences in terminology. So here's how Java programmers use the terminology:

- ✔ The bold line in Listing 17-3 creates a new *object*.
- ✔ The bold line in Listing 17-3 creates a new *instance of the* Purchase *class*.

The words *object* and *instance* are almost synonymous, but Java programmers never say "object of the Purchase class" (or if they do, they feel funny).

By the way, if you mess up this terminology and say something like "object of the Purchase class," then no one jumps down your throat. Everyone understands what you mean, and life goes on as usual. In fact, I often use a phrase like "Purchase object" to describe an instance of the Purchase class. The difference between object and instance isn't terribly important. But it's very important to remember that the words object and instance have the same meaning. (Okay! They have *nearly* the same meaning.)

Making reference to an object's parts

After you've created an object, you use dots to refer to the object's parts. For example, in Listing 17-3, I put a value into the onePurchase object's amount part with the following code:

```
onePurchase.amount = myScanner.nextDouble();
```

Later in Listing 17-3, I get the amount part's value with the following code:

```
onePurchase.total = onePurchase.amount * 1.05;
```

This dot business may look cumbersome, but it really helps programmers when they're trying to organize the code. In Listing 17-1, each variable is a separate entity. But in Listing 17-3, each use of the word amount is inextricably linked to the notion of a purchase. That's good.

Creating several objects

After you've created a Purchase class, you can create as many purchase objects as you want. For example, in Listing 17-5, I create three purchase objects.

Listing 17-5:   Processing Purchases

```java
import java.util.Scanner;

class ProcessPurchasesss {

    public static void main(String args[]) {
        Scanner myScanner = new Scanner(System.in);
        Purchase aPurchase;

        for (int count = 0; count < 3; count++) {
            aPurchase = new Purchase();

            System.out.print("Amount: ");
            aPurchase.amount = myScanner.nextDouble();
            System.out.print("Taxable? (true/false) ");
            aPurchase.taxable = myScanner.nextBoolean();

            if (aPurchase.taxable) {
                aPurchase.total = aPurchase.amount * 1.05;
            } else {
                aPurchase.total = aPurchase.amount;
            }

            System.out.print("Total: ");
            System.out.println(aPurchase.total);
            System.out.println();
        }
    }
}
```

Figure 17-5 has a run of the code in Listing 17-5, and Figure 17-6 illustrates the concept.

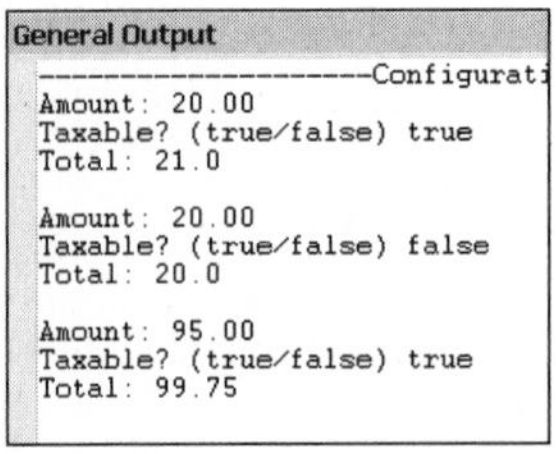

Figure 17-5:
Running the
code in
Listing 17-5.

```
General Output
─────────────────────Configurati
Amount: 20.00
Taxable? (true/false) true
Total: 21.0

Amount: 20.00
Taxable? (true/false) false
Total: 20.0

Amount: 95.00
Taxable? (true/false) true
Total: 99.75
```

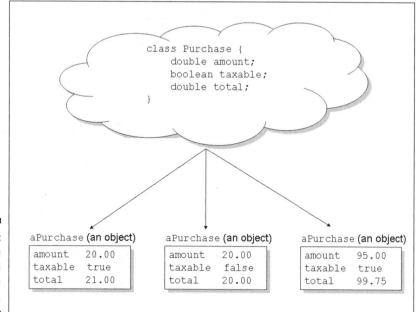

```
class Purchase {
    double amount;
    boolean taxable;
    double total;
}
```

Figure 17-6:
From one
class come
three
objects.

aPurchase **(an object)**

amount	20.00
taxable	true
total	21.00

aPurchase **(an object)**

amount	20.00
taxable	false
total	20.00

aPurchase **(an object)**

amount	95.00
taxable	true
total	99.75

To compile the code in Listing 17-5 you must have a copy of the Purchase class in the same project. (The Purchase class is in Listing 17-2.) To copy a class's code from one project to another, see Chapter 16. (One of that chapter's sidebars describes the copy-and-paste routine.)

Listing 17-5 has only one variable that refers to purchase objects. (The variable's name is aPurchase.) The program has three purchase objects because the assignment statement

```
aPurchase = new Purchase();
```

is executed three times (once for each iteration of the for loop). Just as you can separate an int variable's assignment from the variable's declaration

```
int count;
count = 0;
```

you can also separate a Purchase variable's assignment from the variable's declaration:

```
Purchase aPurchase;

for (int count = 0; count < 3; count++) {
    aPurchase = new Purchase();
```

In fact, after you've created the code in Listing 17-2, the word `Purchase` stands for a brand new type — a reference type. Java has eight built-in primitive types, and has as many reference types as people can define during your lifetime. In Listing 17-2, I define the `Purchase` reference type, and you can define reference types too.

Table 17-2 has a brief comparison of primitive types and reference types.

Table 17-2	Java Types	
	Primitive Type	*Reference Type*
How it's created	Built into the language	Defined as a Java class
How many are there	Eight	Indefinitely many
Sample variable declaration	`int count;`	`Purchase aPurchase;`
Sample assignment	`count = 0;`	`aPurchase = new Purchase();`
Assigning a value to one of its parts	(Not applicable)	`aPurchase.amount = 20.00;`

Another Way to Think About Classes

When you start learning object-oriented programming, you may think this class idea is a big hoax. Some geeks in Silicon Valley had nothing better to do, so they went to a bar and made up some confusing gibberish about classes. They don't know what it means, but they have fun watching people struggle to understand it.

Well, that's not what classes are all about. Classes are serious stuff. What's more, classes are useful. Many reputable studies have shown that classes and object-oriented programming save time and money.

Even so, the notion of a class can be very elusive. Even experienced programmers — the ones who are new to object-oriented programming — have trouble understanding how an object differs from a class.

Classes, objects, and tables

Because classes can be so mysterious, I'll expand your understanding with another analogy. Figure 17-7 has a table of three purchases. The table's title consists of one word (the word "Purchase") and the table has three column headings — the words "amount," "taxable," and "total." Well, the code in Listing 17-2 has the same stuff — Purchase, amount, taxable, and total. So in Figure 17-7, think of the top part of the table (the title and column headings) as a class. Like the code in Listing 17-2, this top part of the table tells us what it means to be a Purchase. (It means having an amount value, a taxable value, and a total value.)

A class is like the top part of a table. And what about an object? Well, an object is like a row of a table. For example, with the code in Listing 17-5 and the input in Figure 17-5, I create three objects (three instances of the Purchase class). The first object has amount value 20.00, taxable value true, and total value 21.00. In the table, the first row has these three values — 20.00, true, and 21.00, as shown in Figure 17-8.

	Purchase	
amount	**taxable**	**total**
20.00	true	21.00
20.00	false	20.00
95.00	true	99.75

```
class Purchase {
    double amount;
    boolean taxable;
    double total;
}
```

Figure 17-7:
A table of
purchases.

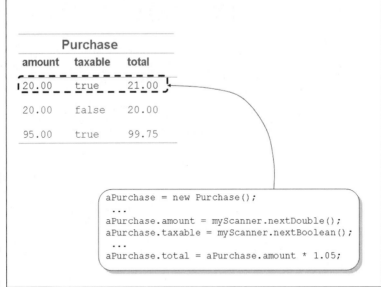

Figure 17-8:
A purchase
corre-
sponds to
a row of
the table.

Some questions and answers

Here's the world's briefest object-oriented programming FAQ:

✔ **Can I have an object without having a class?**

No, you can't. In Java, every object is an instance of a class.

✔ **Can I have a class without having an object?**

Yes, you can. In fact, almost every program in this book creates a class without an object. Take Listing 17-5, for example. The code in Listing 17-5 defines a class named `ProcessPurchasesss`. And nowhere in Listing 17-5 (or anywhere else) do I create an instance of the `ProcessPurchasesss` class. I have a class with no objects. That's just fine. It's business as usual.

✔ **After I've created a class and its instances, can I add more instances to the class?**

Yes, you can. In Listing 17-5, I create one instance, then another, and then a third. If I went one additional time around the `for` loop, I'd have a fourth instance, and I'd put a fourth row in the table of Figure 17-8. With no objects, three objects, four objects, or more objects, I still have the same old `Purchase` class.

✔ **Can an object come from more than one class?**

Bite your tongue! Maybe other object-oriented languages allow this nasty class cross-breeding, but in Java, it's strictly forbidden. That's one of the things that distinguishes Java from some of the languages that preceded it. Java is cleaner, more uniform, and easier to understand.

Chapter 18

Using Methods and Variables from a Java Class

In This Chapter

▶ Using Java's String class

▶ Calling methods

▶ Understanding static and non-static methods and variables

▶ Making numbers look good

1 hope you didn't read Chapter 17, because I tell a big lie in the beginning of the chapter. Actually, it's not a lie. It's an exaggeration.

Actually, it's not an exaggeration. It's a careful choice of wording. In Chapter 17, I write that the gathering of data into a class is the start of object-oriented programming. Well, that's true. Except that many programming languages had data-gathering features before object-oriented programming became popular. Pascal had *records*. C had *structs*.

To be painfully precise, the grouping of data into usable blobs is only a prerequisite to object-oriented programming. You're not really doing object-oriented programming until you combine both data and methods in your classes.

This chapter starts the "data and methods" ball rolling, and Chapter 19 rounds out the picture.

The String Class

The String class is declared in the Java API. This means that, somewhere in the stuff you download from java.sun.com is a file named String.java. If you hunt down this String.java file and peek at the file's code, you find some very familiar-looking stuff:

```
class String {
    ...And so on.
```

In your own code, you can use this String class without ever seeing what's inside the String.java file. That's one of the great things about object-oriented programming.

A simple example

A String is bunch of characters. It's like having several char values in a row. You can declare a variable to be of type String and store several letters in the variable. Listing 18-1 has a tiny example.

Listing 18-1:   I'm Repeating Myself Again (Again)

```
import java.util.Scanner;

class JazzyEchoLine {

    public static void main(String args[]) {
        Scanner myScanner = new Scanner(System.in);
        String lineIn;

        lineIn = myScanner.nextLine();
        System.out.println(lineIn);
    }
}
```

A run of Listing 18-1 is shown in Figure 18-1. This run bears an uncanny resemblance to runs of Listing 5-1 from Chapter 5. That's because Listing 18-1 is a reprise of the effort in Listing 5-1.

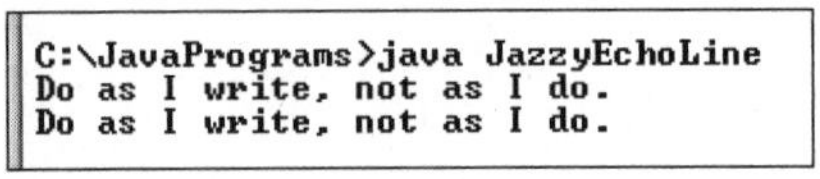

Figure 18-1:
Running
the code in
Listing 18-1.

```
C:\JavaPrograms>java JazzyEchoLine
Do as I write, not as I do.
Do as I write, not as I do.
```

The new idea in Listing 18-1 is the use of a String. In Listing 5-1, I have no variable to store the user's input. But in Listing 18-1, I create the lineIn variable. This variable stores a bunch of letters, like the letters Do as I write, not as I do.

Putting String variables to good use

The program in Listing 18-1 takes the user's input and echoes it back on the screen. This is a wonderful program, but (like many college administrators that I know) it doesn't seem to be particularly useful.

So take a look at a more useful application of Java's String type. A nice one is in Listing 18-2.

Listing 18-2:   Putting a Name in a String Variable

```java
import java.util.Scanner;
import static java.lang.System.out;

class ProcessMoreData {

    public static void main(String args[]) {
        Scanner myScanner = new Scanner(System.in);
        String fullName;
        double amount;
        boolean taxable;
        double total;

        out.print("Customer's full name: ");
        fullName = myScanner.nextLine();
        out.print("Amount: ");
        amount = myScanner.nextDouble();
        out.print("Taxable? (true/false) ");
        taxable = myScanner.nextBoolean();

        if (taxable) {
            total = amount * 1.05;
        } else {
            total = amount;
        }

        out.println();
        out.print("The total for ");
        out.print(fullName);
        out.print(" is ");
        out.print(total);
        out.println(".");
    }
}
```

A run of the code in Listing 18-2 is shown in Figure 18-2. The code stores `Barry A. Burd` in a variable called `fullName`, and displays the `fullName` variable's content as part of the output. To make this program work, you have to store `Barry A. Burd` somewhere. After all, the program follows a certain outline:

```
Get a name.
Get some other stuff.
Compute the total.
Display the name (along with some other stuff).
```

Figure 18-2:
Making a
purchase.

```
C:\JavaPrograms>java ProcessMoreData
Customer's full name: Barry A. Burd
Amount: 20.00
Taxable? (true/false) true

The total for Barry A. Burd is 21.0.
```

If you don't have the program store the name somewhere then, by the time it's done getting other stuff and computing the total, it forgets the name (so the program can't display the name).

Reading and writing strings

To read a `String` value from the keyboard, you can call either `next` or `nextLine`:

✔ **The method `next` reads up to the next blank space.**

For example, with the input `Barry A. Burd`, the statements

```
String firstName = myScanner.next();
String middleInit = myScanner.next();
String lastName = myScanner.next();
```

assign `Barry` to `firstName`, `A.` to `middleInit`, and `Burd` to `lastName`.

✔ **The method `nextLine` reads up to the end of the current line.**

For example, with input `Barry A. Burd`, the statement

```
String fullName = myScanner.nextLine();
```

assigns `Barry A. Burd` to the variable `fullName`. (Hey, being an author has some hidden perks.)

To display a `String` value, you can call one of your old friends, `System.out.print` or `System.out.println`. In fact, most of the programs in this book display `String` values. In Listing 18-2, a statement like

```
out.print("Customer's full name: ");
```

displays the `String` value `"Customer's full name: "`.

You can use `print` and `println` to write `String` values to a disk file. For details, see Chapter 13.

Chapter 4 introduces a bunch of characters, enclosed in double quote marks:

```
"Chocolate, royalties, sleep"
```

In Chapter 4, I call this a *literal* of some kind. (It's a literal because, unlike a variable, it looks just like the stuff that it represents.) Well, in this chapter, I can continue the story about Java's literals:

- ✔ In Listing 18-2, `amount` and `total` are `double` variables, and `1.05` is a `double` literal.
- ✔ In Listing 18-2, `fullName` is a `String` variable, and things like `"Customer's full name: "` are `String` literals.

In a Java program, you surround the letters in a `String` literal with double quote marks.

Using an Object's Methods

If you're not too concerned about classes and reference types, then the use of the type `String` in Listing 18-2 is no big deal. Almost everything you can do with a primitive type seems to work with the `String` type as well. But there's danger around the next curve. Take a look at the code in Listing 18-3, and the run of the code shown in Figure 18-3.

Figure 18-3:
But I typed
the correct
password!

```
C:\JavaPrograms>java TryToCheckPassword
What's the password? swordfish
You're a menace.
```

Listing 18-3:   A Faulty Password Checker

```
/*
 * This code does not work:
 */
import java.util.Scanner;
import static java.lang.System.out;

class TryToCheckPassword {

    public static void main(String args[]) {
        Scanner myScanner = new Scanner(System.in);
        String password = "swordfish";
        String userInput;

        out.print("What's the password? ");
        userInput = myScanner.next();

        if (password == userInput) {
            out.println("You're okay!");
        } else {
            out.println("You're a menace.");
        }
    }
}
```

Here are the facts as they appear in this example:

✔ According to the code in Listing 18-3, the value of `password` is `"swordfish"`.

✔ In Figure 18-3, in response to the program's prompt, the user types `swordfish`. So in the code, the value of `userInput` is `"swordfish"`.

✔ The `if` statement checks the condition `password == userInput`. Because both variables have the value `"swordfish"`, the condition *should* be true, but. . . .

✔ The condition is *not* true, because the program's output is `You're a menace.`

What's going on here? I try beefing up the code to see if I can find any clues. An enhanced version of the password-checking program is in Listing 18-4, with a run of the new version shown in Figure 18-4.

Listing 18-4:   An Attempt to Debug the Code in Listing 18-3

```
import java.util.Scanner;
import static java.lang.System.out;

class DebugCheckPassword {
```

```
public static void main(String args[]) {
    Scanner myScanner = new Scanner(System.in);
    String password = "swordfish";
    String userInput;

    out.print("What's the password? ");
    userInput = myScanner.next();

    out.println();
    out.print("You typed              ");
    out.println(userInput);
    out.print("But the password is ");
    out.println(password);
    out.println();

    if (password == userInput) {
        out.println("You're okay!");
    } else {
        out.println("You're a menace.");
    }
}
}
```

Figure 18-4:
This looks
even worse.

```
C:\JavaPrograms>java DebugCheckPassword
What's the password? swordfish

You typed              swordfish
But the password is swordfish

You're a menace.
```

Ouch! I'm stumped this time. The run in Figure 18-4 shows that both the userInput and password variables have value swordfish. So why doesn't the program accept the user's input?

When you compare two things with a double equal sign, reference types and primitive types don't behave the same way. Consider, for example, int versus String:

✔ You can compare two int values with a double equal sign. When you do, things work exactly as you would expect. For example, the condition in the following code is true:

```
int apples = 7;
int oranges = 7;

if (apples == oranges)
    System.out.println("They're equal.");
```

✔ When you compare two String values with the double equal sign, things don't work the way you expect. The computer doesn't check to see if the two String values contain the same letters. Instead, the computer checks some esoteric property of the way variables are stored in memory.

For your purposes, the term *reference type* is just a fancy name for a class. Because String is defined to be a class in the Java API, I call String a reference type. This terminology highlights the parallel between primitive types (such as int) and classes (that is, reference types, such as String).

Comparing strings

In the preceding bullets, the difference between int and String is mighty interesting. But if the double equal sign doesn't work for String values, how do you check to see if Joe User enters the correct password? You do it with the code in Listing 18-5.

Listing 18-5:   Calling an Object's Method

```
/*
 * This program works!
 */
import java.util.Scanner;
import static java.lang.System.out;

class CheckPassword {

    public static void main(String args[]) {
        Scanner myScanner = new Scanner(System.in);
        String password = "swordfish";
        String userInput;

        out.print("What's the password? ");
        userInput = myScanner.next();

        if (password.equals(userInput)) {
            out.println("You're okay!");
        } else {
            out.println("You're a menace.");
        }
    }
}
```

A run of the new password-checking code is shown in Figure 18-5 and, let me tell you, it's a big relief! The code in Listing 18-5 actually works! When the user types swordfish, the if statement's condition is true.

Figure 18-5:
At last,
Joe User
can log in.

```
C:\JavaPrograms>java CheckPassword
What's the password? swordfish
You're okay!
```

The truth about classes and methods

The magic in Listing 18-5 is the use of a method named `equals`. I have two ways to explain the `equals` method — a simple way, and a more detailed way. First, here's the simple way: The `equals` method compares the characters in one string with the characters in another. If the characters are the same, then the condition inside the `if` statement is true. That's all there is to it.

Don't use a double equal sign to compare two `String` objects. Instead, use one of the objects' `equals` methods.

For a more detailed understanding of the `equals` method, flip back to Chapter 17 and take a look at Figures 17-7 and 17-8. Those figures illustrate the similarities between classes, objects, and the parts of a table. In the figures, each row represents a purchase, and each column represents a feature that purchases possess.

You can observe the same similarities for any class, including Java's `String` class. In fact, what Figure 17-7 does for purchases, Figure 18-6 does for strings.

Figure 18-6:
Viewing the String class and String objects as parts of a table.

String		
value	count	equals
swordfish	9	(A method to compare swordfish with any string)
catfish	7	(A method to compare catfish with any string)

The stuff shown in Figure 18-6 is much simpler than the real `String` class story. But Figure 18-6 makes a good point. Like the purchases in Figure 17-7, each string has its own features. For example, each string has a `value` (the actual characters stored in the string) and each string has a `count` (the number of characters stored in the string). You can't really write the following line of code:

```
//This code does NOT work:
System.out.println(password.count);
```

but that's because the stuff in Figure 18-6 omits a few subtle details.

Anyway, each row in Figure 18-6 has three items — a `value`, a `count`, and an `equals` method. So each row of the table contains more than just data. Each row contains an `equals` method, a way of doing something useful with the data. It's as if each object (each instance of the `String` class) has three things:

- ✔ A bunch of characters (the object's `value`)
- ✔ A number (the object's `count`)
- ✔ A way of being compared with other strings (the object's `equals` method)

That's the essence of object-oriented programming. Each string has its own personal copy of the `equals` method. For example, in Listing 18-5, the `password` string has its own `equals` method. When you call the `password` string's `equals` method and put the `userInput` string in the method's parentheses, the method compares the two strings to see if those strings contain the same characters.

The `userInput` string in Listing 18-5 has an `equals` method too. I could use the `userInput` string's `equals` method to compare this string with the `password` string. But I don't. In fact, in Listing 18-5, I don't use the `userInput` string's `equals` method at all. (To compare the `userInput` with the `password`, I had to use either the `password` string's `equals` method or the `userInput` string's `equals` method. So I made an arbitrary choice: I chose the `password` string's method.)

Calling an object's methods

Calling a string's `equals` method is like getting a purchase's `total`. With both `equals` and `total`, you use your old friend, the dot. For example, in Listing 17-3, you write

```
System.out.println(onePurchase.total);
```

and in Listing 18-5, you write

```
if (password.equals(userInput))
```

A dot works the same way for an object's variables and its methods. In either case, a dot takes the object and picks out one of the object's parts. It works whether that part is a piece of data (as in `onePurchase.total`) or a method (as in `password.equals`).

Combining and using data

At this point in the chapter, I can finally say, "I told you so." Here's a quotation from Chapter 17:

> A class is a design plan. The class describes the way in which you intend to *combine* and *use* pieces of data.

A class can define the way you *use* data. How do you use a password and a user's input? You check to see if they're the same. That's why Java's String class defines an equals method.

An object can be more than just a bunch of data. With object-oriented programming, each object possesses copies of methods for using that object.

Static Methods

You have a fistful of checks. Each check has a number, an amount, and a payee. You print checks like these with your very own laser printer. To print the checks, you use a Java class. Each object made from the Check class has three variables (number, amount, and payee). And each object has one method (a print method). You can see all this in Figure 18-7.

You'd like to print the checks in numerical order. So you need a method to *sort* the checks. If the checks in Figure 18-7 were sorted, the check with number 1699 would come first, and the check with number 1705 would come last.

Figure 18-7: The Check class and some check objects.

Check			
number	amount	payee	print
1705	$25.09	**The Butcher**	(method to cut the check)
1699	$31.27	**The Baker**	(method to cut the check)
1702	$12.35	**The Candlestick Maker**	(method to cut the check)

sort

The big question is, should each check have its own `sort` method? Does the check with number 1699 need to sort itself? And the answer is no. Some methods just shouldn't belong to the objects in a class.

So where do such methods belong? How can you have a `sort` method without creating a separate `sort` for each check?

Here's the answer. You make the `sort` method be *static*. Anything that's static belongs to a whole class, not to any particular instance of the class. If the `sort` method is static, then the entire `Check` class has just one copy of the `sort` method. This copy stays with the entire `Check` class. No matter how many instances of the `Check` class you create — three, ten, or none — you have just one `sort` method.

For an illustration of this concept, look back at Figure 18-7. The whole class has just one `sort` method. So the `sort` method is static. No matter how you call the `sort` method, that method uses the same values to do its work.

Of course, each individual check (each object, each row of the table in Figure 18-7) still has its own `number`, its own `amount`, its own `payee`, and it's own `print` method. When you `print` the first check, you get one amount, and when you `print` the second check get another. Because there's a `number`, an `amount`, a `payee`, and a `print` method for each object, I call these things *non-static*. I call them non-static, because . . . well . . . because they're not static.

Calling static and non-static methods

In this book, my first use of the word `static` is way back in Listing 3-1. I use `static` as part of every `main` method (and this book's listings have lots of `main` methods). In Java, your `main` method has to be static. That's just the way it goes.

To call a static method, you use a class's name along with a dot. This is just slightly different from the way you call a non-static method:

  ✔ **To call an ordinary (non-static) method, you follow an object with a dot.**

  For example, a program to process the checks in Figure 18-7 may contain code of the following kind:

```
Check firstCheck;
firstCheck.number = 1705;
firstCheck.amount = 25.09;
firstCheck.payee = "The Butcher";
firstCheck.print();
```

  ✔ **To call a class's static method, you follow the class name with a dot.**

  For example, to sort the checks in Figure 18-7, you may call

```
Check.sort();
```

Turning strings into numbers

The code in Listing 18-5 introduces a non-static method named `equals`. To compare the `password` string with the `userInput` string, you preface `.equals` with either of the two string objects. In Listing 18-5, I preface `.equals` with the `password` object:

```
if (password.equals(userInput))
```

Each string object has an `equals` method of its own, so I can achieve the same effect by writing

```
if (userInput.equals(password))
```

But Java has another class named `Integer`, and the whole `Integer` class has a static method named `parseInt`. If someone hands you a string of characters, and you want to turn that string into an `int` value, you can call the `Integer` class's `parseInt` method. Listing 18-6 has a small example.

Listing 18-6:   More Chips, Please

```
import java.util.Scanner;
import static java.lang.System.out;

class AddChips {

    public static void main(String args[]) {
        Scanner myScanner = new Scanner(System.in);
        String reply;
        int numberOfChips;

        out.print("How many chips do you have?");
        out.print(" (Type a number,");
        out.print(" or type 'Not playing') ");
        reply = myScanner.nextLine();

        if (!reply.equals("Not playing")) {
            numberOfChips = Integer.parseInt(reply);
            numberOfChips += 10;

            out.print("You now have ");
            out.print(numberOfChips);
            out.println(" chips.");
        }
    }
}
```

Some runs of the code in Listing 18-6 are shown in Figure 18-8. You want to give each player ten chips. But some party poopers in the room aren't playing. So two people, each with no chips, may not get the same treatment. An empty-handed player gets ten chips, but an empty-handed party pooper gets none.

```
C:\JavaPrograms>java AddChips
How many chips do you have? (Type a number, or type 'Not playing') 30
You now have 40 chips.

C:\JavaPrograms>java AddChips
How many chips do you have? (Type a number, or type 'Not playing') 0
You now have 10 chips.

C:\JavaPrograms>java AddChips
How many chips do you have? (Type a number, or type 'Not playing') Not playing

C:\JavaPrograms>_
```

Figure 18-8:
Running
the code in
Listing 18-6.

So in Listing 18-6, you call the Scanner class's `nextLine` method, allowing a user to enter any characters at all — not just digits. If the user types `Not playing`, then you don't give the killjoy any chips.

If the user types some digits, then you're stuck holding these digits in the string variable named `reply`. You can't add ten to a string like `reply`. So you call the `Integer` class's `parseInt` method, which takes your string, and hands you back a nice `int` value. From there, you can add ten to the `int` value.

Java has a loophole that allows you to add a number to a string. The problem is, you don't get real addition. Adding the number 10 to the string `"30"` gives you `"3010"`, not 40.

Don't confuse `Integer` with `int`. In Java, `int` is the name of a primitive type (a type that I use throughout this book). But `Integer` is the name of a class. Java's `Integer` class contains handy methods for dealing with `int` values. For example, in Listing 18-6, the `Integer` class's `parseInt` method makes an `int` value from a string.

Turning numbers into strings

In Chapter 17, Listing 17-1 adds tax to the amount of a purchase. But a run of the code in Listing 17-1 has an anomaly. Look back at Figure 17-1. With five percent tax on 20 dollars, the program displays a total of 21.0. That's peculiar. Where I come from, currency amounts aren't normally displayed with just one digit beyond the decimal point.

If you don't choose your purchase amount carefully, the situation is even worse. For example, in Figure 18-9, I run the same program (the code in Listing 17-1) with purchase amount 19.37. The resulting display looks very nasty.

With its internal zeros and ones, the computer doesn't do arithmetic quite the way you and I are used to doing it. So how do you fix this problem?

Figure 18-9:
Do you have
change for
20.33850000
0000003?

```
C:\JavaPrograms>java ProcessData
Amount: 19.37
Taxable? (true/false) true
Total: 20.338500000000003
```

The Java API has a class named `NumberFormat`, and the `NumberFormat` class has a static method named `getCurrencyInstance`. When you call `Number Format.getCurrencyInstance()` with nothing inside the parentheses, you get an object that can mold numbers into U.S. currency amounts. Listing 18-7 has an example.

Listing 18-7:   The Right Way to Display a Dollar Amount

```java
import java.text.NumberFormat;
import java.util.Scanner;

class BetterProcessData {

    public static void main(String args[]) {
        Scanner myScanner = new Scanner(System.in);
        double amount;
        boolean taxable;
        double total;
        NumberFormat currency =
            NumberFormat.getCurrencyInstance();
        String niceTotal;

        System.out.print("Amount: ");
        amount = myScanner.nextDouble();
        System.out.print("Taxable? (true/false) ");
        taxable = myScanner.nextBoolean();

        if (taxable) {
            total = amount * 1.05;
        } else {
            total = amount;
        }

        niceTotal = currency.format(total);
        System.out.print("Total: ");
        System.out.println(niceTotal);
    }
}
```

For some beautiful runs of the code in Listing 18-7, see Figure 18-10. Now at last, you see a total like $20.34, not 20.338500000000003. Ah! That's much better.

Figure 18-10:
See the
pretty
numbers.

```
Amount: 20.00
Taxable? (true/false) false
Total: $20.00

Amount: 20.00
Taxable? (true/false) true
Total: $21.00

Amount: 19.37
Taxable? (true/false) true
Total: $20.34
```

How the NumberFormat works

For my current purposes, the code in Listing 18-7 contains three interesting variables:

- ✔ The variable `total` stores a number, such as 21.0.
- ✔ The variable `currency` stores an object that can mold numbers into U.S. currency amounts.
- ✔ The variable `niceTotal` is set up to store a bunch of characters.

The `currency` object has a `format` method. So to get the appropriate bunch of characters into the `niceTotal` variable, you call the `currency` object's `format` method. You apply this format method to the variable `total`.

Understanding the Big Picture

In this section, I answer some of the burning questions that I raise throughout the book. "What does `java.util` stand for?" "Why do I need the word `static` at certain points in the code?" "How can a degree in Horticultural Studies help you sort cancelled checks?"

I also explain "static" in some unique and interesting ways. After all, static methods and variables aren't easy to understand. It helps to read about Java's static feature from several points of view.

Packages and import declarations

In Java, you can group a bunch of classes into something called a *package*. In fact, the classes in Java's standard API are divided into about 170 packages. This book's examples make heavy use of three packages — the packages named java.util, java.lang, and java.io.

The class java.util.Scanner

The package java.util contains about 50 classes, including the very useful Scanner class. Like most other classes, this Scanner class has two names — a *fully qualified name* and an abbreviated *simple name*. The class's fully qualified name is java.util.Scanner, and the class's simple name is Scanner. You get the fully qualified name by adding the package name to the class's simple name. (That is, you add the package name java.util to the simple name Scanner. You get java.util.Scanner.)

An import declaration lets you abbreviate a class's name. With the declaration

```
import java.util.Scanner;
```

the Java compiler figures out where to look for the Scanner class. So instead of writing java.util.Scanner throughout your code, you can just write Scanner.

The class java.lang.System

The package java.lang contains about 35 classes, including the ever popular System class. (The class's fully qualified name is java.lang.System, and the class's simple name is System.) Instead of writing java.lang.System throughout your code, you can just write System. You don't even need an import declaration.

All ye need to know

I can summarize much of Java's complexity in only a few sentences:

✔ The Java API contains many packages.

✔ A package contains classes.

✔ From a class, you can create objects.

✔ An object can have its own methods. An object can also have its own variables.

✔ A class can have its own static methods. A class can also have its own static variables.

Among all of Java's packages, the `java.lang` package is special. With or without an import declaration, the compiler imports everything in the `java.lang` package. You can start your program with `import java.lang.System`. But if you don't, the compiler adds this declaration automatically.

The static System.out variable

What kind of importing must you do in order to abbreviate `System.out.println`? How can you shorten it to `out.println`? An import declaration lets you abbreviate a *class's* name. But in the expression `System.out`, the word `out` isn't a class. The word `out` is a static variable. (The `out` variable refers to the place where a Java program sends text output.) So you can't write

```
//This code is bogus. Don't use it:
import java.lang.System.out;
```

What do you do instead? You write

```
import static java.lang.System.out;
```

To find out more about the `out` variable's being a static variable, read the next section.

Shedding light on the static darkness

I love to quote myself. When I quote my own words, I don't need written permission. I don't have to think about copyright infringement and I never hear from lawyers. Best of all, I can change and distort anything I say. When I paraphrase my own ideas, I can't be misquoted.

With that in mind, here's a quote from the previous section:

> *"Anything that's static belongs to a whole class, not to any particular instance of the class. . . . To call a static method, you use a class's name along with a dot."*

How profound! In Listing 18-6, I introduce a static method named `parseInt`. Here's the same quotation applied to the static `parseInt` method:

> *The static `parseInt` method belongs to the whole `Integer` class, not to any particular instance of the `Integer` class. . . . To call the static `parseInt` method, you use the `Integer` class's name along with a dot. You write something like `Integer.parseInt(reply)`.*

That's very nice! How about the `System.out` business that I introduce in Chapter 3? I can apply my quotation to that too.

> *The static `out` variable belongs to the whole `System` class, not to any particular instance of the `System` class. . . . To refer to the static `out` variable, you use the `System` class's name along with a dot. You write something like `System.out.println()`.*

If you think about what `System.out` means, this static business makes sense. After all, the name `System.out` refers to the place where a Java program sends text output. (When you use JCreator, the name `System.out` refers to JCreator's General Output pane.) A typical program has only one place to send its text output. So a Java program has only one `out` variable. No matter how many objects you create — three, ten, or none — you have just one `out` variable. And when you make something static, you insure that the program has only one of those things.

Alright, then! The `out` variable is static.

To abbreviate the name of a static variable (or a static method), you don't use an ordinary import declaration. Instead, you use a static import declaration. That's why, in Chapter 9 and beyond, I use the word `static` to import the `out` variable:

```
import static java.lang.System.out;
```

Barry makes good on an age-old promise

In Chapter 6, I pull a variable declaration outside of a `main` method. I go from code of the kind in Listing 18-8, to code of the kind that's in Listing 18-9.

Listing 18-8:   Declaring a Variable Inside the main Method

```
class SnitSoft {

    public static void main(String args[]) {
        double amount = 5.95;

        amount = amount + 25.00;
        System.out.println(amount);
    }
}
```

Listing 18-9: Pulling a Variable Outside of the main Method

```
class SnitSoft {
    static double amount = 5.95;

    public static void main(String args[]) {
        amount = amount + 25.00;
        System.out.println(amount);
    }
}
```

In Chapter 6, I promise to explain why Listing 18-9 needs the extra word static (in static double amount = 5.95). Well, with all the fuss about static methods in this chapter, I can finally explain everything.

Look back to Figure 18-7. In that figure, you have checks and you have a sort method. Each individual check has its own number, its own amount, and its own payee. But the entire Check class has just one sort method.

I don't know about you, but to sort my cancelled checks, I hang them on my exotic Yucca Elephantipes tree. I fasten the higher numbered checks to the upper leaves, and put the lower numbered checks on the lower leaves. When I find a check whose number comes between two other checks, I select a free leaf (one that's between the upper and lower leaves).

A program to mimic my sorting method looks something like this:

```
class Check {
    int number;
    double amount;
    String payee;

    static void sort() {
        Yucca tree;

        if (myCheck.number > 1700) {
            tree.attachHigh(myCheck);
        }
        // ... etc.
    }
}
```

Because of the word static, the Check class has only one sort method. And because I declare the tree variable inside the static sort method, this program has only one tree variable. (Indeed, I hang all my cancelled checks on just one Yucca tree.) I can move the tree variable's declaration outside of the sort method. But if I do, I may have too many Yucca trees.

```
class Check {
    int number;
    double amount;
    String payee;
    Yucca tree;    //This is bad! Each check has its own tree.

    static void sort() {
        if (myCheck.number > 5000) {
            tree.attachHigh(myCheck);
        }
        // ... etc.
    }
}
```

In the nasty code above, each check has its own number, its own amount, its own payee, and its own tree. But that's ridiculous! I don't want to fasten each check to its own Yucca tree. Everybody knows you're supposed to sort checks with just one Yucca tree. (That's the way the big banks do it.)

When I move the `tree` variable's declaration outside of the `sort` method, I want to preserve the fact that I have only one tree. (To be more precise, I have only one tree for the entire `Check` class.) To make sure that I have only one tree, I declare the `tree` variable to be static.

```
class Check {
    int number;
    double amount;
    String payee;
    static Yucca tree;    //That's better!

    static void sort() {
        if (myCheck.number > 5000) {
            tree.attachHigh(myCheck);
        }
        // ... etc.
    }
}
```

For exactly the same reason, I write `static double amount` when I move from Listing 18-8 to 18-9.

 To find out more about sorting, read *UNIX For Dummies Quick Reference*, 4th Edition, by Margaret Levine Young and John R. Levine. To learn more about bank checks, read *Managing Your Money Online For Dummies* by Kathleen Sindell. To learn more about trees, read *Landscaping For Dummies* by Phillip Giroux, Bob Beckstrom, and Lance Walheim.

Chapter 19

Creating New Java Methods

. . . .

In This Chapter

▶ Creating methods that work with existing values

▶ Creating methods that modify existing values

▶ Creating methods that return new values

. . . .

*I*n Chapters 3 and 4, I introduce Java methods. I show you how to create a `main` method and how to call the `System.out.println` method. Between that chapter and this one, I make very little noise about methods. In Chapter 18, I introduce a bunch of new methods for you to call, but that's only half of the story.

This chapter completes the circle. In this chapter, you create your own Java methods — not the tired old `main` method that you've been using all along, but some new, powerful Java methods.

Defining a Method within a Class

In Chapter 18, Figure 18-6 introduces an interesting notion — a notion that's at the core of object-oriented programming. Each Java string has its own `equals` method. That is, each string has, built within it, the functionality to compare itself with other strings. That's an important point. When you do object-oriented programming, you bundle data and functionality into a lump called a class. Just remember Barry's immortal words from Chapter 17:

> A class describes the way in which you intend to combine *and use* pieces of data.

And why are these words so important? They're important because, in object-oriented programming, chunks of data take responsibility for themselves. With object-oriented programming, everything you have to know about a string is located in the file `String.java`. So if anybody has problems with the strings, they know just where to look for all the code. That's great!

So this is the deal — objects contain methods. Chapter 18 shows you how to use an object's methods, and this chapter shows you how to create an object's methods.

Making a method

Imagine a table containing the information about three accounts. (If you have trouble imagining such a thing, just look at Figure 19-1.) In the figure, each account has a last name, an identification number, and a balance. In addition (and here's the important part), each account knows how to display itself on the screen. Each row of the table has its own copy of a `display` method.

		Account	
lastName	**id**	**balance**	**display**
Aju	9936	$8,734.00	(method to display account info)
Iap	3492	$6,718.00	(method to display account info)
Ngp	2151	$1,008.00	(method to display account info)

Figure 19-1:
A table of accounts.

The last names in Figure 19-1 may seem strange to you. That's because I generated the table's data randomly. Each last name is a haphazard combination of three letters — one uppercase letter followed by two lowercase letters.

Though it may seem strange, generating account values at random is common practice. When you write new code, you want to test the code to find out if it runs correctly. You can make up your own data (with values like "Smith", 0000, and 1000.00). But to give your code a challenging workout, you should use some unexpected values. If you have values from some real-life case studies, you should use them. But if you have don't have real data, randomly generated values are easy to create.

I need some code to implement the ideas in Figure 19-1. Fortunately, I have some code in Listing 19-1.

Listing 19-1:   An Account Class

```
import java.text.NumberFormat;
import static java.lang.System.out;

class Account {
    String lastName;
    int id;
    double balance;

    void display() {
        NumberFormat currency =
            NumberFormat.getCurrencyInstance();

        out.print("The account with last name ");
        out.print(lastName);
        out.print(" and ID number ");
        out.print(id);
        out.print(" has balance ");
        out.println(currency.format(balance));
    }
}
```

The Account class in Listing 19-1 defines four things — a lastName, an id, a balance, and a display. So each instance of Account class has its own lastName variable, its own id variable, its own balance variable, and its own display method. These things match up with the four columns in Figure 19-1.

Examining the method's header

Listing 19-1 contains the display method's declaration. Like a main method's declaration, the display declaration has a header and a body. (See Chapter 4.) The header has two words and some parentheses:

✔ **The word** void **tells the computer that, when the** display **method is called, the** display **method doesn't return anything to the place that called it.**

Later in this chapter, a method does return something. For now, the display method returns nothing.

✔ **The word** display **is the method's name.**

Every method must have a name. Otherwise, you don't have a way to call the method.

✔ **The parentheses contain all the things you're going to pass to the method when you call it.**

When you call a method, you can pass information to that method on the fly. This display example, with its empty parentheses, looks strange. That's because no information is passed to the display method when you call it. That's okay. I give a meatier example later in this chapter.

Examining the method's body

The display method's body contains some print and println calls. The interesting thing here is that the body makes reference to the variables lastName, id, and balance. A method's body can do that. But with each object having its own lastName, id, and balance variables, what does a variable in the display method's body mean?

Well, when I use the Account class, I create little account objects. Maybe I create an object for each row of the table in Figure 19-1. Each object has its own values for the lastName, id, and balance variables, and each object has its own copy of the display method.

So take the first display method in Figure 19-1 — the method for Aju's account. The display method for that object behaves as if it had the code in Listing 19-2.

Listing 19-2: How the display Method Behaves When No One's Looking

```
/*
 * This is not real code:
 */
void display() {
    NumberFormat currency =
        NumberFormat.getCurrencyInstance();

    out.print("The account with last name ");
    out.print("Aju");
    out.print(" and ID number ");
    out.print(9936);
    out.print(" has balance ");
    out.println(currency.format(8734.00));
}
```

In fact, each of the three display methods behaves as if its body has a slightly different code. Figure 19-2 illustrates this idea for two instances of the Account class.

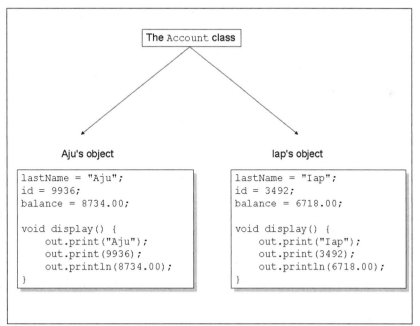

Figure 19-2:
Two objects, each with its own display method.

Calling the method

To put the previous section's ideas into action, you need more code. So the next listing (see Listing 19-3) creates instances of the Account class.

Listing 19-3: Making Use of the Code in Listing 19-1

```
import java.util.Random;

class ProcessAccounts {

    public static void main(String args[]) {

        Random myRandom = new Random();
        Account anAccount;

        for (int i = 0; i < 3; i++) {
            anAccount = new Account();

            anAccount.lastName = "" +
                (char) (myRandom.nextInt(26) + 'A') +
                (char) (myRandom.nextInt(26) + 'a') +
                (char) (myRandom.nextInt(26) + 'a');

            anAccount.id = myRandom.nextInt(10000);
            anAccount.balance = myRandom.nextInt(10000);
            anAccount.display();
        }
    }
}
```

Here's a summary of the action in Listing 19-3:

```
Do the following three times:
    Create a new object (an instance of the Account class).
    Randomly generate values for the object's lastName,
        id and balance.
    Call the object's display method.
```

The first of the three display calls prints the first object's lastName, id, and balance values. The second display call prints the second object's lastName, id, and balance values. And so on.

A run of the code from Listing 19-3 is shown in Figure 19-3.

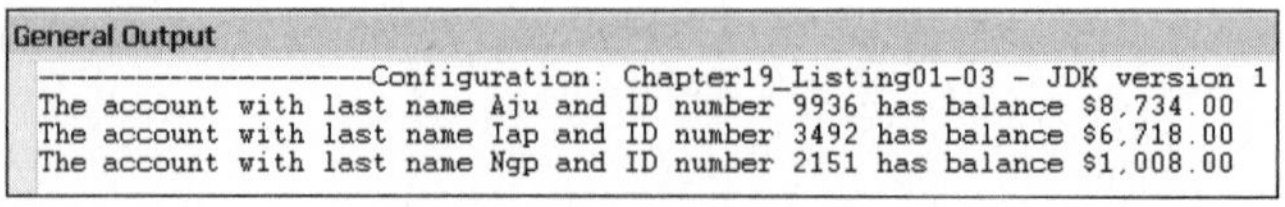

Figure 19-3:
Running
the code in
Listing 19-3.

```
General Output
-------------------Configuration: Chapter19_Listing01-03 - JDK version 1
The account with last name Aju and ID number 9936 has balance $8,734.00
The account with last name Iap and ID number 3492 has balance $6,718.00
The account with last name Ngp and ID number 2151 has balance $1,008.00
```

Generating words randomly

Most programs don't work correctly the first time you run them, and some programs don't work without extensive trial and error. This section's code is a case in point.

To write this section's code, I needed a way to generate three-letter words randomly. After about a dozen attempts, I got the code to work. But I didn't stop there. I kept working for a few hours looking for a *simple* way to generate three-letter words randomly. In the end, I settled on the following code (in Listing 19-3):

```
anAccount.lastName = "" +
    (char)
    (myRandom.nextInt(26) +
    'A') +
    (char)
    (myRandom.nextInt(26) +
    'a') +
    (char)
    (myRandom.nextInt(26) +
    'a');
```

This code isn't simple, but it's not nearly as bad as my original working version. Anyway, here's how the code works:

✔ **Each call to** myRandom.nextInt(26) **generates a number from 0 to 25.**

✔ **Adding** 'A' **gives you a number from 65 to 90.**

To store a letter 'A', the computer puts the number 65 in its memory. That's why adding 'A' to 0 gives you 65, and why adding 'A' to 25 gives you 90. For more information on letters being stored as numbers, see the discussion of Unicode characters at the end of Chapter 8.

✔ **Applying** (char) **to a number turns the number into a** char **value.**

To store the letters 'A' through 'Z', the computer puts the numbers 65 through 90 in its memory. So applying (char) to a number from 65 to 90 turns the number into an uppercase letter. For more information about applying things like (char), see the discussion of casting in Chapter 7.

Let's pause for a brief summary. The expression (char) (myRandom.nextInt(26) + 'A') represents a randomly generated uppercase letter. In a similar way, (char) (myRandom. nextInt(26) + 'a') represents a randomly generated lowercase letter.

Watch out! The next couple of steps can be tricky.

✔ **Java doesn't allow you to assign a** char **value to a string variable.**

So in Listing 19-3, the following statement would lead to a compiler error:

```
//Bad statement:
anAccount.lastName = (char)
    (myRandom.nextInt(26) +
    'A');
```

✔ **In Java, you can use a plus sign to add a** char **value to a string. When you do, the result is a string.**

So "" + (char) (myRandom.nextInt (26) + 'A') is string containing one randomly generated uppercase character. And when you add (char) (myRandom.next Int(26) + 'a') onto the end of that string, you get another string — a string containing two randomly generated characters. Finally, when you add another (char) (myRandom.nextInt(26) + 'a') onto the end of that string, you get a string containing three randomly generated characters. So you can assign that big string to anAccount.lastName. That's how the statement in Listing 19-3 works.

When you write a program like the one in Listing 19-3, you have to be very careful with numbers, char values and strings. I don't do this kind of programming every day of the week. So before I got this section's example to work, I had many false starts. That's okay. I'm very persistent.

The flow of control

Suppose that you're running the code in Listing 19-3. The computer reaches the display method call:

```
anAccount.display();
```

At that point, the computer starts running the code inside the display method. In other words, the computer jumps to the middle of the Account class's code (the code in Listing 19-1).

After executing the display method's code (that forest of print and println calls), the computer returns to the point where it departed from Listing 19-3. That is, the computer goes back to the display method call and continues on from there.

So when you run the code in Listing 19-3, the flow of action in each loop iteration isn't exactly from the top to the bottom. Instead, the action goes from the for loop to the display method, and then back to the for loop. The whole business is pictured in Figure 19-4.

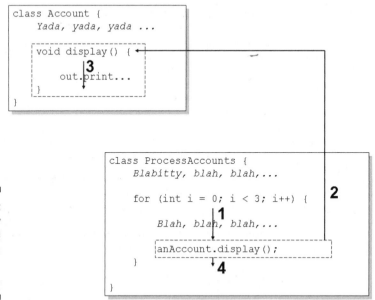

Figure 19-4:
The flow
of control
between
Listings 19-1
and 19-3.

Using punctuation

In Listing 19-3, notice the use of dots. To refer to the `lastName` stored in the `anAccount` object, you write

```
anAccount.lastName
```

To get the `anAccount` object to `display` itself, you write

```
anAccount.display();
```

That's great! When you refer to an object's variable, or call an object's method, the only difference is parentheses:

- ✔ To refer to an object's variable, you don't use parentheses.
- ✔ To call an object's method, you use parentheses.

When you call a method, you put parentheses after the method's name. You do this even if you have nothing to put inside the parentheses.

The versatile plus sign

The program in Listing 19-3 uses some cute tricks. In Java, you can do two different things with a plus sign:

- ✔ **You can add numbers with a plus sign.**

  For example, you can write
  ```
  numberOfSheep = 2 + 5;
  ```
- ✔ **You can *concatenate* strings with a plus sign.**

  When you concatenate strings, you scrunch them together, one right after another. For example, the expression
  ```
  "Barry" + " " + "Burd"
  ```
  scrunches together `Barry`, a blank space, and `Burd`. The new scrunched-up string is (you guessed it) `Barry Burd`.

In Listing 19-3, the statement

```
anAccount.lastName = "" +
    (char) (myRandom.nextInt(26) + 'A') +
    (char) (myRandom.nextInt(26) + 'a') +
    (char) (myRandom.nextInt(26) + 'a');
```

has many plus signs, and some of the plus signs concatenate things together. The first thing is a mysterious empty string (" "). This empty string is invisible, so it never gets in the way of your seeing the second, third, and fourth things.

Onto the empty string, the program concatenates a second thing. This second thing is the value of the expression (char) (myRandom.nextInt(26) + 'A'). The expression may look complicated, but it's really no big deal. This expression represents an uppercase letter (any uppercase letter, generated randomly).

Onto the empty string and the uppercase letter, the program concatenates a third thing. This third thing is the value of the expression (char) (myRandom. nextInt(26) + 'a'). This expression represents a lowercase letter (any lowercase letter, generated randomly).

Onto all this stuff, the program concatenates another lowercase letter. So altogether, you have a randomly generated three-letter name. For more details, see the sidebar.

In Listing 19-3, the statement anAccount.balance = myRandom.nextInt (10000) assigns an int value to balance. But balance is a double variable, not an int variable. That's okay. In a rare case of permissiveness, Java allows you to assign an int value to a double variable. The result of the assignment is no big surprise. If you assign the int value 8734 to the double variable balance, then the value of balance becomes 8734.00. The result is shown on the first line of Figure 19-3.

Let the Objects Do the Work

When I was a young object, I wasn't as smart as the objects you have nowadays. Consider, for example, the object in Listing 19-4. Not only does this object display itself, the object can also fill itself with values.

Listing 19-4:   A Class with Two Methods

```
import java.util.Random;
import java.text.NumberFormat;
import static java.lang.System.out;

class BetterAccount {
    String lastName;
    int id;
    double balance;
```

```
void fillWithData() {
    Random myRandom = new Random();

    lastName = "" +
        (char) (myRandom.nextInt(26) + 'A') +
        (char) (myRandom.nextInt(26) + 'a') +
        (char) (myRandom.nextInt(26) + 'a');

    id = myRandom.nextInt(10000);
    balance = myRandom.nextInt(10000);
}


void display() {
    NumberFormat currency =
        NumberFormat.getCurrencyInstance();

    out.print("The account with last name ");
    out.print(lastName);
    out.print(" and ID number ");
    out.print(id);
    out.print(" has balance ");
    out.println(currency.format(balance));
}
}
```

I wrote some code to use the class in Listing 19-4. This new code is in Listing 19-5.

Listing 19-5:   This Is So Cool!

```
class ProcessBetterAccounts {

    public static void main(String args[]) {

        BetterAccount anAccount;

        for (int i = 0; i < 3; i++) {
            anAccount = new BetterAccount();
            anAccount.fillWithData();
            anAccount.display();
        }
    }
}
```

Listing 19-5 is pretty slick. Because the code in Listing 19-4 is so darn smart, the new code in Listing 19-5 has very little work to do. This new code just creates a BetterAccount object, and then calls the methods in Listing 19-4. When you run all this stuff, you get results like the ones in Figure 19-3.

Passing Values to Methods

Think about sending someone to the supermarket to buy bread. When you do this, you say, "Go to the supermarket and buy some bread." (Try it at home. You'll have a fresh loaf of bread in no time at all!) Of course, some other time, you send that same person to the supermarket to buy bananas. You say, "Go to the supermarket and buy some bananas." And what's the point of all this? Well, you have a method, and you have some on-the-fly information that you pass to the method when you call it. The method is named "Go to the super-market and buy some. . . ." The on-the-fly information is either "bread" or "bananas," depending on your culinary needs. In Java, the method calls would look like this:

```
goToTheSupermarketAndBuySome(bread);
goToTheSupermarketAndBuySome(bananas);
```

The things in parentheses are called *parameters* or *parameter lists*. With para-meters, your methods become much more versatile. Instead of getting the same thing each time, you can send somebody to the supermarket to buy bread one time, bananas another time, and birdseed the third time. When you call your goToTheSupermarketAndBuySome method, you decide right there and then what you're going to ask your pal to buy.

These concepts are made more concrete in Listings 19-6 and 19-7.

Listing 19-6:   Adding Interest

```
import java.text.NumberFormat;
import static java.lang.System.out;

class NiceAccount {
    String lastName;
    int id;
    double balance;

    void addInterest(double rate) {
        out.print("Adding ");
        out.print(rate);
        out.println(" percent...");

        balance += balance * (rate / 100.0);
    }
```

```
    void display() {
        NumberFormat currency =
            NumberFormat.getCurrencyInstance();

        out.print("The account with last name ");
        out.print(lastName);
        out.print(" and ID number ");
        out.print(id);
        out.print(" has balance ");
        out.println(currency.format(balance));
    }
}
```

Listing 19-7: Calling the addInterest Method

```
import java.util.Random;

class ProcessNiceAccounts {

    public static void main(String args[]) {
        Random myRandom = new Random();
        NiceAccount anAccount;
        double interestRate;

        for (int i = 0; i < 3; i++) {
            anAccount = new NiceAccount();

            anAccount.lastName = "" +
                (char) (myRandom.nextInt(26) + 'A') +
                (char) (myRandom.nextInt(26) + 'a') +
                (char) (myRandom.nextInt(26) + 'a');
            anAccount.id = myRandom.nextInt(10000);
            anAccount.balance = myRandom.nextInt(10000);

            anAccount.display();

            interestRate = myRandom.nextInt(5);
            anAccount.addInterest(interestRate);

            anAccount.display();
            System.out.println();
        }
    }
}
```

In Listing 19-7, the line

```
anAccount.addInterest(interestRate);
```

plays the same role as the line goToTheSupermarketAndBuySome(bread) in my little supermarket example. The word addInterest is a method name, and the word interestRate in parentheses is a parameter. Taken as a whole, this statement tells the code in Listing 19-6 to execute its addInterest method. This statement also tells Listing 19-6 to use a certain number (whatever value is stored in the interestRate variable) in the method's calculations. The value of interestRate can be 1.0, 2.0, or whatever other value you get by calling myRandom.nextInt(5). In the same way, the goToTheSupermarket AndBuySome method works for bread, bananas, or whatever else you need from the market.

The next section has a detailed description of addInterest and its action. In the meantime, a run of the code in Listings 19-6 and 19-7 is shown in Figure 19-5.

General Output
```
--------------------Configuration: Chapter19_Listing06-07 - JDK version 1.
The account with last name Cbj and ID number 6151 has balance $8,983.00
Adding 2.0 percent...
The account with last name Cbj and ID number 6151 has balance $9,162.66

The account with last name Bry and ID number 529 has balance $3,756.00
Adding 0.0 percent...
The account with last name Bry and ID number 529 has balance $3,756.00

The account with last name Dco and ID number 2162 has balance $8,474.00
Adding 3.0 percent...
The account with last name Dco and ID number 2162 has balance $8,728.22
```

Figure 19-5:
Running
the code in
Listing 19-7.

Java has very strict rules about the use of types. For example, you can't assign a double value (like 3.14) to an int variable. (The compiler simply refuses to chop off the .14 part. You get an error message. So what else is new?) But Java isn't completely unreasonable about the use of types. Java allows you to assign an int value (like myRandom.nextInt(5)) to a double variable (like interestRate). If you assign the int value 2 to the double variable interestRate, then the value of interestRate becomes 2.0. The result is shown on the second line of Figure 19-5.

Handing off a value

When you call a method, you can pass information to that method on the fly. This information is in the method's parameter list. Listing 19-7 has a call to the addInterest method:

```
anAccount.addInterest(interestRate);
```

The first time through the loop, the value of interestRate is 2.0. (Remember, I'm using the data in Figure 19-5.) So at that point in the program's run, the method call behaves as if it's the following statement:

```
anAccount.addInterest(2.0);
```

The computer is about to run the code inside the addInterest method (a method in Listing 19-6). But first, the computer *passes* the value 2.0 to the parameter in the addInterest method's header. So inside the addInterest method, the value of rate becomes 2.0. For an illustration of this idea, see Figure 19-6.

Here's something interesting. The parameter in the addInterest method's header is rate. But, inside the ProcessNiceAccounts class, the parameter in the method call is interestRate. That's okay. In fact, it's standard practice.

In Listings 19-6 and 19-7, the names of the parameters don't have to be the same. The only thing that matters is that both parameters (rate and interestRate) have the same type. In Listings 19-6 and 19-7, both of these parameters are of type double. So everything is fine.

Inside the addInterest method, the += assignment operator adds balance * (rate / 100.0) to the existing balance value. For some info about the += assignment operator, see Chapter 7.

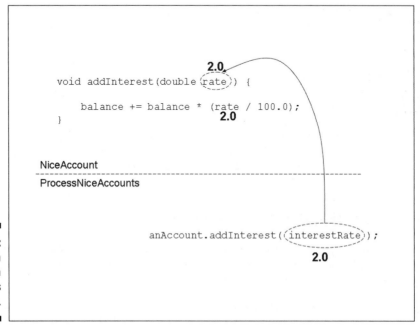

Figure 19-6:
Passing a
value to a
method's
parameter.

Working with a method header

In the next few bullets, I make some observations about the addInterest method header (in Listing 19-6):

- ✔ **The word** void **tells the computer that, when the** addInterest **method is called, the** addInterest **method doesn't send a value back to the place that called it.**

  The next section has an example in which a method sends a value back.

- ✔ **The word** addInterest **is the method's name.**

  That's the name you use to call the method when you're writing the code for the ProcessNiceAccounts class. (See Listing 19-7.)

- ✔ **The parentheses in the header contain placeholders for all the things you're going to pass to the method when you call it.**

  When you call a method, you can pass information to that method on the fly. This information is the method's parameter list. The addInterest method's header says that the addInterest method takes one piece of information and that piece of information must be of type double:

  ```
  void addInterest(double rate)
  ```

  Sure enough, if you look at the call to addInterest (down in the ProcessNiceAccounts class's main method), that call has the variable interestRate in it. And interestRate is of type double. When I call getInterest, I'm giving the method a value of type double.

How the method uses the object's values

The addInterest method in Listing 19-6 is called three times from the main method in Listing 19-7. The actual account balances and interest rates are different each time:

- ✔ **In the first call of Figure 19-5, the** balance **is 8983.00 and the interest rate is 2.0.**

  When this call is made, the expression balance * (rate / 100.0) stands for 8983.00 * (2.0 / 100.00). See Figure 19-7.

- ✔ **In the second call of Figure 19-5, the balance is 3756.00 and the interest rate is 0.0.**

  When the call is made, the expression balance * (rate / 100.0) stands for 3756.00 * (0.0 / 100.00). Again, see Figure 19-7.

✔ **In the third call of Figure 19-5, the balance is 8474.00 and the interest rate is 3.0.**

When the `addInterest` call is made, the expression `balance * (rate / 100.0)` stands for 8474.00 * (3.0 / 100.00).

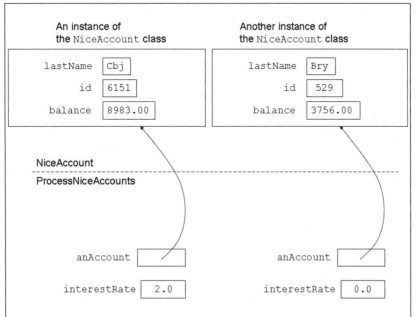

Figure 19-7:
Cbj's
account
and Bry's
account.

Getting a Value from a Method

The last section had a story about sending a friend to buy groceries. I revisit that scenario in this section to see what treasures it holds.

You make requests for groceries in the form of method calls. You issue calls such as

```
goToTheSupermarketAndBuySome(bread);
goToTheSupermarketAndBuySome(bananas);
```

The things in parentheses are parameters. Each time you call your `goToThe SupermarketAndBuySome` method, you put a different value in the method's parameter list.

Now what happens when your friend returns from the supermarket? "Here's the bread you asked me to buy," says your friend. As a result of carrying out your wishes, your friend returns something to you. You made a method call, and the method returns information (or better yet, the method returns some food).

The thing returned to you is called the method's *return value,* and the type of thing returned to you is called the method's *return type*.

An example

To see how return values and a return types work in a real Java program, check out the code in Listings 19-8 and 19-9.

Listing 19-8:   A Method That Returns a Value

```java
import java.text.NumberFormat;
import static java.lang.System.out;

class GoodAccount {
    String lastName;
    int id;
    double balance;

    double getInterest(double rate) {
        double interest;

        out.print("Adding ");
        out.print(rate);
        out.println(" percent...");

        interest = balance * (rate / 100.0);
        return interest;
    }


    void display() {
        NumberFormat currency =
            NumberFormat.getCurrencyInstance();

        out.print("The account with last name ");
        out.print(lastName);
        out.print(" and ID number ");
        out.print(id);
        out.print(" has balance ");
        out.println(currency.format(balance));
    }
}
```

Listing 19-9:   Calling the Method in Listing 19-8

```java
import java.util.Random;
import java.text.NumberFormat;

class ProcessGoodAccounts {

    public static void main(String args[]) {
        Random myRandom = new Random();
        NumberFormat currency =
            NumberFormat.getCurrencyInstance();
        GoodAccount anAccount;
        double interestRate;
        double yearlyInterest;

        for (int i = 0; i < 3; i++) {
            anAccount = new GoodAccount();

            anAccount.lastName = "" +
                (char) (myRandom.nextInt(26) + 'A') +
                (char) (myRandom.nextInt(26) + 'a') +
                (char) (myRandom.nextInt(26) + 'a');
            anAccount.id = myRandom.nextInt(10000);
            anAccount.balance = myRandom.nextInt(10000);

            anAccount.display();

            interestRate = myRandom.nextInt(5);
            yearlyInterest =
                anAccount.getInterest(interestRate);

            System.out.print("This year's interest is ");
            System.out.println
                (currency.format(yearlyInterest));
            System.out.println();
        }
    }
}
```

To see a run of code from Listings 19-8 and 19-9, take a look at Figure 19-8.

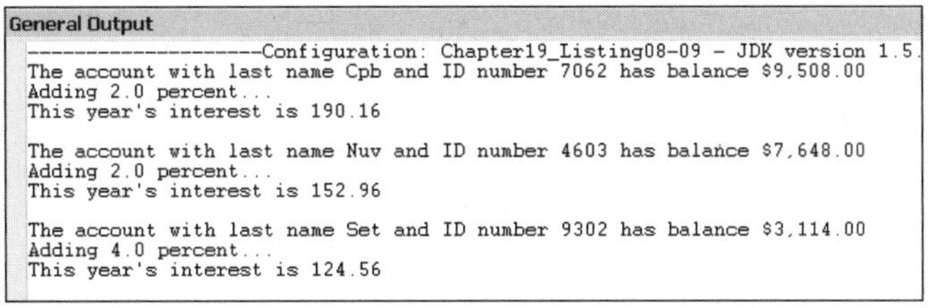

Figure 19-8:
Running
the code in
Listing 19-9.

```
General Output
-------------------Configuration: Chapter19_Listing08-09 - JDK version 1.5
The account with last name Cpb and ID number 7062 has balance $9,508.00
Adding 2.0 percent...
This year's interest is 190.16

The account with last name Nuv and ID number 4603 has balance $7,648.00
Adding 2.0 percent...
This year's interest is 152.96

The account with last name Set and ID number 9302 has balance $3,114.00
Adding 4.0 percent...
This year's interest is 124.56
```

How return types and return values work

I want to trace a piece of the action in Listings 19-8 and 19-9. For input data, I use the first set of values in Figure 19-8.

Here's what happens when `getInterest` is called (you can follow along in Figure 19-9):

- ✔ The value of `balance` is 9508.00, and the value of `rate` is 2.0. So the value of `balance * (rate / 100.0)` is 190.16 — one-hundred-ninety dollars and sixteen cents.

- ✔ The value 190.16 gets assigned to the `interest` variable, so the statement

  ```
  return interest;
  ```

  has the same effect as

  ```
  return 190.16;
  ```

- ✔ The `return` statement sends this value 190.16 back to the code that called the method. *At that point in the process, the entire method call in Listing 19-9 —* `anAccount.getInterest(interestRate)` *— takes on the value 190.16.*

- ✔ Finally, the value 190.16 gets assigned to the variable `yearlyInterest`.

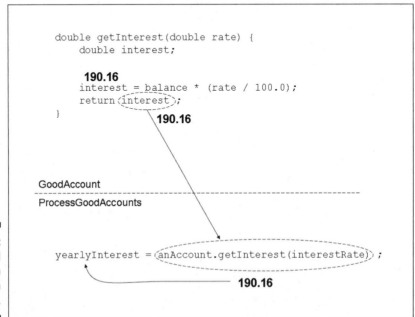

Figure 19-9:
A method
call is an
expression
with a value.

If a method returns anything, then a call to the method is an expression with a value. That value can be printed, assigned to a variable, added to something else, or whatever. Anything you can do with any other kind of value, you can do with a method call.

Working with the method header (again)

When you create a method or a method call, you have to be careful to use Java's types consistently. So make sure you check for the following:

✔ In Listing 19-8, the getInterest method's header starts with the word double. So when the method is executed, it should send a double value back to the place that called it.

✔ Again in Listing 19-8, the last statement in the getInterest method is return interest. So the method returns whatever value is stored in the interest variable, and the interest variable has type double. So far, so good.

✔ In Listing 19-9, the value returned by the call to getInterest is assigned to a variable named yearlyInterest. Sure enough, yearlyInterest is of type double.

That settles it! The use of types in the handling of method getInterest is consistent in Listings 19-8 and 19-9. I'm thrilled!

Chapter 20

Oooey GUI Was a Worm

....

In This Chapter

▶ Swinging into action

▶ Displaying an image

▶ Using buttons and textboxes

....

*T*here's a wonderful old joke about a circus acrobat jumping over mice. Unfortunately, I'd get sued for copyright infringement if I included the joke in this book.

Anyway, the joke is about starting small and working your way up to bigger things. That's what you do when you read *Beginning Programming with Java For Dummies,* 2nd Edition.

Most of the programs in this book are text-based. A *text-based* program has no windows, no dialog boxes, nothing of that kind. With a text-based program, the user types characters in the command prompt window, and the program displays output in the same command prompt window.

These days, very few publicly available programs are text-based. Almost all programs use a *GUI* — a *Graphical User Interface.* So if you've read every word of this book up to now, you're probably saying to yourself, "When am I going to find out how to create a GUI?"

I'm sorry, Skipper. A Java program with a GUI takes some muscle to write. The code itself isn't long or ponderous. What's difficult is understanding how the code works.

So with these inspiring words of discouragement, please march ahead anyway. This chapter gives you a glimpse of the world of GUI programming in Java.

The Java Swing Classes

Java's *Swing* classes create graphical objects on a computer screen. The objects can include buttons, icons, text fields, check boxes, and other good things that make windows so useful.

The name "Swing" isn't an acronym. When the people at Sun Microsystems were first creating the code for these classes, one of the developers named it "Swing" because swing music was enjoying a nostalgic revival. And yes, in addition to `String` and `Swing`, the standard Java API has a `Spring` class. But that's another story.

Actually, Java's API has several sets of windowing components. An older set is called *AWT* — the *Abstract Windowing Toolkit*. But to use some of the Swing classes, you have to call on some of the old AWT classes. Go figure!

Showing an image on the screen

The program in Listing 20-1 displays a window on your computer screen. To see the window, look at Figure 20-1.

Listing 20-1:   Creating a Window with an Image in It

```java
import javax.swing.JFrame;
import javax.swing.ImageIcon;
import javax.swing.JLabel;
import java.awt.Container;

class ShowPicture {

    public static void main(String args[]) {
        JFrame frame = new JFrame();
        ImageIcon icon = new ImageIcon("j2fd.jpg");
        JLabel label = new JLabel(icon);
        Container contentPane = frame.getContentPane();

        contentPane.add(label);
        frame.setDefaultCloseOperation(JFrame.EXIT_ON_CLOSE);
        frame.pack();
        frame.setVisible(true);
    }
}
```

The code in Listing 20-1 has very little logic of its own. Instead, this code pulls together a bunch of classes from the Java API.

Back in Listing 17-3, I create an instance of the Purchase class with the line

```
Purchase onePurchase = new Purchase();
```

So in Listing 20-1, I do the same kind of thing. I create instances of the JFrame, ImageIcon, and JLabel classes with the following lines:

```
JFrame frame = new JFrame();
ImageIcon icon = new ImageIcon("j2fd.jpg");
JLabel label = new JLabel(icon);
```

Here's some gossip about each of these lines:

✔ A JFrame is like a window (except that it's called a JFrame, not a "window"). In Listing 20-1, the line

```
JFrame frame = new JFrame();
```

creates a JFrame object, but this line doesn't display the JFrame object anywhere. (The displaying comes later in the code.)

✔ An ImageIcon object is a picture. In the directory that contains the Java code, I have a file named j2fd.jpg. That file contains the picture shown in Figure 20-1. So in Listing 20-1, the line

```
ImageIcon icon = new ImageIcon("j2fd.jpg");
```

creates an ImageIcon object — an icon containing the j2fd.jpg picture.

✔ I need a place to put the icon. I can put it on something called a JLabel. So in Listing 20-1, the line

```
JLabel label = new JLabel(icon);
```

creates a JLabel object and puts the j2fd.jpg icon on the new label's face.

If you read the previous bullets, you may get a false impression. The wording may suggest that the use of each component (JFrame, ImageIcon, JLabel, and so on) is a logical extension of what you already know. "Where do you put an ImageIcon? Well of course, you put it on a JLabel." When you've worked long and hard with Java's Swing components, all these things become natural to you. But until then, writing GUI code takes hours of trial and error (along with many hours of reading the API documentation).

You never need to memorize the names or features of Java's API classes. Instead, you keep Java's API documentation handy. When you need to know about a class, you look it up in the documentation. If you need a certain class often enough, you'll remember its features. For classes that you don't use often, you always have the docs.

For tips on using Java's API documentation, see the Appendix on this book's web site. To find gobs of sample Java code, visit some of the Web sites listed in Chapter 21.

Just another class

What is a JFrame? Like any other class, a JFrame has several parts. For a simplified view of some of these parts, see Figure 20-2.

Like the String in Figure 18-6 in Chapter 18, each object formed from the JFrame class has both data parts and method parts. The data parts include the frame's height and width. The method parts include getContentPane, setDefaultCloseOperation, pack, and setVisible. (I can't squeeze into setDefaultCloseOperation into Figure 20-2, but I don't feel guilty about this. All told, the JFrame class has about 320 methods. So with or without the setDefaultCloseOperation method in Figure 20-2, you have to use your imagination.)

JFrame				
height	**width**	**getContentPane**	**pack**	**setVisible**
153	116	(method for getting a content pane; that is, for getting a container)	(method to shrink wrap the frame)	(method to make the frame visible or invisible)

Container	
components	**add**
label	(method to put stuff into the container)

Figure 20-2: A simplified depiction of the JFrame and Container classes.

For technical reasons too burdensome for this book, you can't use dots to refer to a frame's height or width. But you can call many `JFrame` methods with those infamous dots. In Listing 20-1, I call the frame's methods by writing `frame.getContentPane()`, `frame.setDefaultCloseOperation (JFrame.EXIT_ON_CLOSE)`, `frame.pack()`, and `frame.setVisible(true)`.

Here's the scoop on the `JFrame` methods in Listing 20-1:

✔ You can't put an icon directly onto a `JFrame` object. In fact, you can't put a button, a text field, or anything else like that onto a `JFrame` object. Instead, you have to grab something called a *content pane,* and then put these widgets onto the content pane.

In Listing 20-1, the call to `frame.getContentPane` grabs a content pane. Then the call `contentPane.add(label)` plops the label onto the pane. It seems tedious but, when you work with the Java Swing classes, you have to call all these methods.

✔ A call to `frame.setDefaultCloseOperation` tells Java what to do when you try to close the frame. (In Windows, you click the 'x' in the upper-right-hand corner by the title bar.) For a frame that's part of a larger application, you may want the frame to disappear when you click the 'x', but you probably don't want the application to stop running.

But in Listing 20-1, the frame is the entire application — the whole enchilada. So when you click the 'x', you want the Java virtual machine to shut itself down. To make this happen, you call the `setDefaultClose Operation` method with parameter `JFrame.EXIT_ON_CLOSE`. The other alternatives are as follows:

- `JFrame.HIDE_ON_CLOSE`: The frame disappears, but it still exists in the computer's memory.

- `JFrame.DISPOSE_ON_CLOSE`: The frame disappears and no longer exists in the computer's memory.

- `JFrame.DO_NOTHING_ON_CLOSE`: The frame still appears, still exists, and still does everything it did before you clicked the 'x.' Nothing happens when you click 'x.' So with this `DO_NOTHING_ ON_CLOSE` option, you can become very confused.

If you don't call `setDefaultCloseOperation`, then Java automatically chooses the `HIDE_ON_CLOSE` option. When you click the 'x', the frame disappears but the Java program keeps running. Of course, with no visible frame, the running of Listing 20-1 doesn't do much. The only noticeable effect of the run is your development environment's behavior. With JCreator, you don't see the familiar `Process completed` message. In addition, many JCreator menu items (items like Compile Project and Execute Project) are unavailable. To end the Java program's run and get back your precious menu items, choose Tools⇨Stop Tool on JCreator's main menu.

✔ A frame's `pack` method shrink-wraps the frame around whatever has been added to the frame's content pane. Without calling `pack`, the frame can be much bigger or much smaller than is necessary.

Unfortunately, the default is to make a frame much smaller than necessary. If, in Listing 20-1, you forget to call `frame.pack`, you get the tiny frame shown in Figure 20-3. Sure, you can enlarge the frame by dragging the frame's edges with your mouse. But why should you have to do that? Just call `frame.pack` instead.

✔ Calling `setVisible(true)` makes the frame appear on your screen. If you forget to call `setVisible(true)` (and I often do), when you run the code in Listing 20-1, you'll see nothing on your screen. It's always so disconcerting until you figure out what you did wrong.

Figure 20-3:
A frame that
hasn't been
packed.

What I call a "content pane" is really an instance of Java's `Container` class, and each `Container` instance has its own `add` method. (Refer to Figure 20-2.) That's why the call to `contentPane.add(label)` in Listing 20-1 puts the thing that holds the `j2fd.jpg` picture into the content pane.

Keeping the User Busy (Working with Buttons and Text Fields)

It takes some muscle to create a high-powered GUI program. First, you create a frame with buttons and other widgets. Then you write extra methods to respond to keystrokes, button clicks, and other such things.

The next section contains some "take-my-word-for-it" code to respond to a user's button clicks. But in this section, the example simply displays a button and a text field. The code is in Listing 20-2, and two views of the code's frame are shown in Figures 20-4 and 20-5.

Listing 20-2:   Adding Components to a Frame

```java
import javax.swing.JFrame;
import javax.swing.JTextField;
import javax.swing.JButton;
import java.awt.Container;
import java.awt.FlowLayout;

class MyLittleGUI {

    public static void main(String args[]) {
        JFrame frame;
        Container contentPane;
        JTextField textfield;
        JButton button;
        FlowLayout layout;
        String sorry;

        frame = new JFrame();
        frame.setTitle("Interact");

        contentPane = frame.getContentPane();

        textfield = new JTextField("Type your text here.");

        sorry = "This button is temporarily out of order.";
        button = new JButton(sorry);

        contentPane.add(textfield);
        contentPane.add(button);
        layout = new FlowLayout();
        contentPane.setLayout(layout);

        frame.setDefaultCloseOperation(JFrame.EXIT_ON_CLOSE);
        frame.pack();
        frame.setVisible(true);
    }
}
```

Figure 20-4:
The frame in
Listing 20-2.

Figure 20-5:
The frame in
Listing 20-2
with the but-
ton pressed.

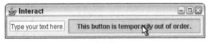

As with other programs that use classes from Java's API, Listing 20-2 comes with my litany of descriptions and explanations of the classes' features. One way or another, it's all the same story. Each object has its own data and its own methods. To refer to an object's data or methods, use a dot. And to find out more about an object's data or methods, use Java's API documentation.

- Each frame (that is, each instance of the JFrame class) has a setTitle method. If you want, get a pencil and add a setTitle column to the JFrame table in Figure 20-2.

  In Listing 20-2, I make the frame's title be the word Interact (as if interacting with this frame makes anything useful happen). You can see Interact in the frame's title bar in Figures 20-4 and 20-5.

- The JTextField class describes those long white boxes, like the box containing the words Type your text here in Figures 20-4 and 20-5. In Listing 20-2, I create a new text field (an instance of the JTextField class), and I add this new text field to the frame's content pane.

  When you run the code in Listing 20-2, you can type stuff into the text field. But, because I haven't written any code to respond to the typing of text, nothing happens when you type. *C'est la vie.*

- The JButton class describes those clickable things, like the thing containing the words This button is temporarily out of order in Figures 20-4 and 20-5. In Listing 20-2, I create a new button (an instance of the JButton class), and I add this new button to the frame's content pane.

  When you run the code in Listing 20-2, you can click the button all you want. Because I haven't written any code to respond to the clicking, nothing happens when you click the button. For a program that responds to button clicks, see the next section.

- Each Java container has a setLayout method. A call to this method ensures that the doohickeys on the frame are arranged in a certain way.

  In Listing 20-2, I feed a FlowLayout object to the setLayout method. This FlowLayout business arranges the text field and the button one right after another (as in Figures 20-4 and 20-5).

For descriptions of some other things that are going on in Listing 20-2, see the "Showing an image on the screen" section, earlier in this chapter.

Taking Action

The previous section's code leaves me feeling a little empty. When you click the button, nothing happens. When you type in the text field, nothing happens. What a waste!

To make me feel better, I include one more program in this chapter. The program (in Listings 20-3 and 20-4) responds to a button click. When you click the frame's button, any text in the text field becomes all uppercase. That's very nice, but the code is quite complicated. In fact, the code has so many advanced features that I can't fully describe them in the space that I'm allotted. So you may have to trust me.

Listing 20-3:   Capitalism in Action

```
import javax.swing.JFrame;
import javax.swing.JTextField;
import javax.swing.JButton;
import java.awt.Container;
import java.awt.FlowLayout;

class CapitalizeMe {

    public static void main(String args[]) {
        JFrame frame;
        Container contentPane;
        JTextField textfield;
        JButton button;
        FlowLayout layout;

        frame = new JFrame();
        frame.setTitle("Handy Capitalization Service");

        contentPane = frame.getContentPane();

        textfield =
            new JTextField("Type your text here.", 20);

        button = new JButton("Capitalize");
        button.addActionListener
            (new MyActionListener(textfield));

        contentPane.add(textfield);
        contentPane.add(button);
        layout = new FlowLayout();
        contentPane.setLayout(layout);

        frame.setDefaultCloseOperation(JFrame.EXIT_ON_CLOSE);
        frame.pack();
        frame.setVisible(true);
    }
}
```

Listing 20-4:   Responding to Button Clicks

```java
import javax.swing.JTextField;
import java.awt.event.ActionListener;
import java.awt.event.ActionEvent;

class MyActionListener implements ActionListener {

    JTextField textfield;

    MyActionListener(JTextField textfield) {
        this.textfield = textfield;
    }

    public void actionPerformed(ActionEvent e) {
        textfield.setText
            (textfield.getText().toUpperCase());
    }
}
```

You can run the code in Listings 20-3 and 20-4. If you do, you see something like the screen shots in Figures 20-6, 20-7, and 20-8. To get you started reading the code, I include a few hints about the code's features:

- Calling new JTextField("Type your text here.", 20) creates a text field containing the words Type your text here. To allow more space for the user's typing, the new text field is 20 characters wide.

- Java's API has a package named java.awt.event, which includes things like ActionEvent and ActionListener.

  - The clicking of a button is an ActionEvent. Other ActionEvent examples include the user's pressing Enter in a text field or the user's double-clicking an item in a scrolling list.

  - An ActionListener is a piece of code that waits for an Action Event to take place. (In other words, the ActionListener "listens" for an ActionEvent.)

  In Listing 20-3, the call to button.addActionListener tells the Java virtual machine to make an announcement whenever the user clicks the button. The JVM announces the action to the ActionListener code in Listing 20-4. The ActionListener in Listing 20-4 is supposed to do something useful in response to the ActionEvent.

- The JVM's "announcement" fires up the actionPerformed method in Listing 20-4, which in turn makes a call to the toUpperCase method. That's how the letters in the text field become uppercase letters.

Figure 20-6:
A brand-
new frame.

Figure 20-7:
The user
types in the
text box.

Figure 20-8:
Clicking
the button
capitalizes
the text in
the text box.

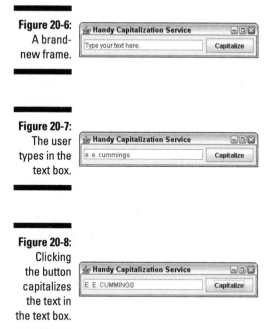

Want to read more? I have a whole chapter about it in *Java 2 For Dummies,*
2nd Edition (written by yours truly and published by Wiley Publishing, Inc.).

Part V
The Part of Tens

The 5th Wave   By Rich Tennant

"They were selling contraband online. We broke through the door just as they were trying to flush the hard drive down the toilet."

In this part . . .

You're near the end of the book, and it's time to sum it all up. This part of the book is your slam-bam two-thousand-words-or-less resource for Java. What? You didn't read every word in the chapters before this one? That's okay. You'll pick up a lot of useful information in this Part of Tens.

Chapter 21

Ten Sets of Web Links

*N*o wonder the Web is so popular: It's both useful and fun. This chapter has ten bundles of resources. Each bundle has Web sites for you to visit. Each Web site has resources to help you write programs more effectively.

The Horse's Mouth

Sun's official Web site for Java is `java.sun.com`. This site has all the latest development kits, and many of them are free. The site also has a great section with online tutorials and mini-courses. The tutorial/mini-course section's Web address is `java.sun.com/developer/onlineTraining`.

In addition, Sun has two special-purpose Java Web sites. Consumers of Java technology should visit `www.java.com`. Programmers and developers interested in sharing Java technology can go to `www.java.net`.

Finding News, Reviews, and Sample Code

The Web has plenty of sites devoted exclusively to Java. Many of these sites feature reviews, links to other sites, and best of all, gobs of sample Java code. They may also offer free mailing lists that keep you informed of the latest Java developments. Here's a brief list of such sites:

- **The JavaRanch:** www.javaranch.com
- **Developer.com/Gamelan:** www.developer.com/java
- **The Giant Java Tree:** www.gjt.org
- **The Java Boutique:** javaboutique.internet.com
- **FreewareJava.com:** www.freewarejava.com
- **Java Shareware:** www.javashareware.com

Improving Your Code with Tutorials

To find out more about Java, you can visit Sun's online training pages. Some other nice sets of tutorials are available at the following Web sites:

- **Richard Baldwin's Web site:** www.dickbaldwin.com
- **IBM developerWorks:** www-106.ibm.com/developerworks/training
- **ProgrammingTutorials.com:** www.programmingtutorials.com

Finding Help on Newsgroups

Have a roadblock you just can't get past? Try posting your question on an Internet newsgroup. Almost always, some friendly expert will post just the right reply.

With or without Java, you should definitely start exploring newsgroups. You can find thousands of newsgroups — groups on just about every conceivable topic. (Yes, there are more newsgroups than *For Dummies* titles!) To get started with newsgroups, visit groups.google.com. For postings specific to Java, look for the groups whose names begin with comp.lang.java. As a novice, you'll probably find the following three groups to be the most useful:

- comp.lang.java.programmer
- comp.lang.java.help
- comp.lang.java.api

Reading Documentation with Additional Commentary

When programmers write documentation, they ask themselves questions and then answer those questions as best they can. But sometimes, they don't ask themselves all the important questions. And often, they assume that the reader already knows certain things. If you're a reader who doesn't already know these things, you may be plain out of luck.

One way or another, all documentation omits some details. That's why other peoples' comments about the documentation can be so helpful. At www.jdocs.com experienced Java programmers annotate existing Java documentation with their own comments. The comments include tips and tricks, but they also add useful pieces of information — pieces that the documentation's original authors omitted. If you need help with an aspect of the Java API, this is a great Web site to visit.

Checking the FAQs for Useful Info

Has the acronym FAQ made it to Oxford English Dictionary yet? Everybody seems to be using FAQ as an ordinary English word. In case you don't already know, FAQ stands for *Frequently Asked Questions*. In reality, a FAQ should be called ATQTWTOA. This acronym stands for *Answers to Questions That We're Tired of Answering*.

You can find several FAQs at the official Sun Web site. You can also check www.javafaq.com — a Web site devoted to questions commonly posed by Java programmers.

Opinions and Advocacy

Java isn't just techie stuff. The field has issues and opinions of all shapes and sizes. To find out more about them, visit any of these sites:

- blogs.sun.com
- www.javablogs.com
- www.javalobby.org

In case you don't know, a *blog* is a Web *log* — an online diary for a person's thoughts and opinions. Someone who writes a blog is called a *blogger*.

Blogs are hot stuff these days. Business people, politicians, and others write blogs to draw attention to their ideas. And many people write blogs just for fun.

When it comes to reading about Java, I have a few favorite blogs. I list them here in alphabetical order:

- **Simon Phipps's blog:** www.webmink.net/minkblog.htm

  Simon is Chief Technology Evangelist at Sun Microsystems. No matter what subject he chooses, Simon always speaks his mind.

- **Jonathan Schwartz's blog:** blogs.sun.com/jonathan

  Jonathan is Chief Operating Officer at Sun Microsystems. When Jonathan speaks, people listen. And when Jonathan writes, people read.

- **Mary Smaragdis's blog:** blogs.sun.com/mary

  Mary is Marketing Manager at Sun Microsystems. When you read Mary's blog, her enthusiasm gushes from the computer screen. And I've met her at several conferences. She's even more lively in person.

Looking for Java Jobs

Are you looking for work? Would you like to have an exciting, lucrative career as a computer programmer? If so, check the SkillMarket at mshiltonj.com/sm. This site has statistics on the demand for various technology areas. The site compares languages, databases, certifications, and more. Best of all, the site is updated every day.

After you've checked all the SkillMarket numbers, try visiting a Web site designed specially for computer job seekers. Point your Web browser to java.computerwork.com and to www.javajobs.com.

Finding Out More about Other Programming Languages

It's always good to widen your view. So to find out more about some languages other than Java, visit the Éric Lévénez site: www.levenez.com/lang. This site includes a cool chart that traces the genealogy of the world's most popular programming languages. For other language lists, visit the following Web sites:

  ✔ **HyperNews:** `www.hypernews.org/HyperNews/get/computing/`
  `lang-list.html`

  ✔ **Open Here!:** `www.openhere.com/tech1/programming/languages`

  ✔ **Steinar Knutsen's Language list page:** `home.nvg.org/~sk/`
  `lang/lang.html`

Finally, for quick information about anything related to computing, visit the `foldoc.doc.ic.ac.uk/foldoc` — the Free On-Line Dictionary of Computing.

Everyone's Favorite Sites

It's true — these two sites aren't devoted exclusively to Java. However, no geek-worthy list of resources would be complete without Slashdot and SourceForge.

Slashdot's slogan, "News for nerds, stuff that matters," says it all. At `slashdot.org` you find news, reviews, and commentary on almost anything related to computing. There's even a new word to describe a Web site that's reviewed or discussed on the Slashdot site. When a site becomes overwhelmed with hits from Slashdot referrals, one says that the site has been *slashdotted*.

Although it's not quite as high-profile, `sourceforge.net` is the place to look for open source software of any kind. The SourceForge repository contains over 80,000 projects. At the SourceForge site, you can download software, read about works in process, contribute to existing projects, and even start a project of your own. SourceForge is a great site for programmers and developers at all levels of experience.

Chapter 22

Ten Useful Classes in the Java API

In This Chapter

▶ Finding out more about some classes that are introduced earlier in this book

▶ Discovering some other helpful classes

I'm proud of myself. I've written around 400 pages about Java using less than thirty classes from the Java API. The standard API has about 3,000 classes, with at least 700 more in the very popular Enterprise Edition API. So I think I'm doing very well.

Anyway, to help acquaint you with some of my favorite Java API classes, this chapter contains a brief list. Some of the classes in this list appear in examples throughout this book. Others are so darn useful that I can't finish the book without including them.

For more information on the classes in this chapter, check Java's API documentation.

Applet

What Java book is complete without some mention of applets? An *applet* is a piece of code that runs inside a Web browser window. For example, a small currency calculator running in a little rectangle on your Web page can be a piece of code written in Java.

At one time, Java applets were really hot stuff, but nowadays, people are much more interested in using Java for business processing. Anyway, if applets are your thing, then don't be shy. Check the `Applet` page of Java's API documentation.

ArrayList

Chapter 16 introduces arrays. This is good stuff but, in any programming language, arrays have their limitations. For example, take an array of size 100. If you suddenly need to store a 101st value, then you're plain out of luck. You can't change an array's size without rewriting some code. Inserting a value into an array is another problem. To squeeze "Tim" alphabetically between "Thom" and "Tom", you may have to make room by moving thousands of "Tyler", "Uriah", and "Victor" names.

But Java has an ArrayList class. An ArrayList is like an array, except that ArrayList objects grow and shrink as needed. You can also insert new values without pain using the ArrayList class's add method. ArrayList objects are very useful, because they do all kinds of nice things that arrays can't do.

File

Talk about your useful Java classes! The File class does a bunch of things that aren't included in this book's examples. Method canRead tells you whether you can read from a file or not. Method canWrite tells you if you can write to a file. Calling method setReadOnly ensures that you can't accidentally write to a file. Method deleteOnExit erases a file, but not until your program stops running. Method exists checks to see if you have a particular file. Methods isHidden, lastModified, and length give you even more information about a file. You can even create a new directory by calling the mkdir method. Face it, this File class is powerful stuff!

Integer

Chapter 18 describes the Integer class and its parseInt method. The Integer class has lots of other features that come in handy when you work with int values. For example, Integer.MAX_VALUE stands for the number 2147483647. That's the largest value that an int variable can store. (Refer to Table 7-1 in Chapter 7.) The expression Integer.MIN_VALUE stands for the number -2147483648 (the smallest value that an int variable can store). A call to Integer.toBinaryString takes an int and returns its base-2 (binary) representation. And what Integer.toBinaryString does for base 2, Integer.toHexString does for base 16 (hexadecimal).

Math

Do you have any numbers to crunch? Do you use your computer to do exotic calculations? If so, try Java's Math class. (It's a piece of code, not a place to sit down and listen to lectures about algebra.) The Math class deals with π, *e*, logarithms, trig functions, square roots, and all those other mathematical things that give most people the creeps.

NumberFormat

Chapter 18 has a section about the NumberFormat.getCurrencyInstance method. With this method, you can turn 20.338500000000003 into $20.34. If the United States isn't your home, or if your company sells products worldwide, you can enhance your currency instance with a Java Locale. For example, with euro = NumberFormat.getCurrencyInstance(Locale.FRANCE), a call to euro.format(3) returns 3,00 € instead of $3.00.

The NumberFormat class also has methods for displaying things that aren't currency amounts. For example, you can display a number with or without commas, with or without leading zeros, and with as many digits beyond the decimal point as you care to include.

Scanner

Java's Scanner class can do more than what it does in this book's examples. Like the NumberFormat class, the Scanner can handle numbers from various locales. For example, to input 3,5 and have it mean "three and half," you can type myScanner.useLocale(Locale.FRANCE). You can also tell a Scanner to skip certain input strings or use numeric bases other than 10. All in all, the Scanner class is very versatile.

String

Chapter 18 examines Java's String class. The chapter describes (in gory detail) a method named equals. The String class has many other useful methods. For example, with the length method, you find the number of characters in a string. With replaceAll, you can easily change the phrase "my fault" to "your fault" wherever "my fault" appears inside a string. And with compareTo, you can sort strings alphabetically.

StringTokenizer

I often need to chop strings into pieces. For example, I have a `fullName` variable that stores my narcissistic `"Barry A. Burd"` string. From this `fullName` value, I need to create `firstName`, `middleInitial`, and `lastName` values. I have one big string (`"Barry A. Burd"`), and I need three little strings — `"Barry"`, `"A."`, and `"Burd"`.

Fortunately, the `StringTokenizer` class does this kind of grunt work. Using this class, you can separate `"Barry A. Burd"` or `"Barry,A.,Burd"` or even `"Barry<tab>A.<tab>Burd"` into pieces. You can also treat each separator as valuable data, or you can ignore each separator as if it were trash. To do lots of interesting processing using strings, check out Java's `StringTokenizer` class.

System

You're probably familiar with `System.in` and `System.out`. But what about `System.getProperty`? The `getProperty` method reveals all kinds of information about your computer. Some of the information you can find includes your operating system name, you processor's architecture, your Java Virtual Machine version, your classpath, your username, and whether your system uses a backslash or a forward slash to separate folder names from one another. Sure, you may already know all this stuff. But does your Java code need to discover it on the fly?

Index

• *C* •

BUSINESS, CAREERS & PERSONAL FINANCE

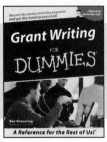

0-7645-5307-0

0-7645-5331-3 *†

Also available:
- Accounting For Dummies †
  0-7645-5314-3
- Business Plans Kit For Dummies †
  0-7645-5365-8
- Cover Letters For Dummies
  0-7645-5224-4
- Frugal Living For Dummies
  0-7645-5403-4
- Leadership For Dummies
  0-7645-5176-0
- Managing For Dummies
  0-7645-1771-6

- Marketing For Dummies
  0-7645-5600-2
- Personal Finance For Dummies *
  0-7645-2590-5
- Project Management For Dummies
  0-7645-5283-X
- Resumes For Dummies †
  0-7645-5471-9
- Selling For Dummies
  0-7645-5363-1
- Small Business Kit For Dummies *†
  0-7645-5093-4

HOME & BUSINESS COMPUTER BASICS

0-7645-4074-2

0-7645-3758-X

Also available:
- ACT! 6 For Dummies
  0-7645-2645-6
- iLife '04 All-in-One Desk Reference
  For Dummies
  0-7645-7347-0
- iPAQ For Dummies
  0-7645-6769-1
- Mac OS X Panther Timesaving
  Techniques For Dummies
  0-7645-5812-9
- Macs For Dummies
  0-7645-5656-8

- Microsoft Money 2004 For Dummies
  0-7645-4195-1
- Office 2003 All-in-One Desk Reference
  For Dummies
  0-7645-3883-7
- Outlook 2003 For Dummies
  0-7645-3759-8
- PCs For Dummies
  0-7645-4074-2
- TiVo For Dummies
  0-7645-6923-6
- Upgrading and Fixing PCs For Dummies
  0-7645-1665-5
- Windows XP Timesaving Techniques
  For Dummies
  0-7645-3748-2

FOOD, HOME, GARDEN, HOBBIES, MUSIC & PETS

0-7645-5295-3

0-7645-5232-5

Also available:
- Bass Guitar For Dummies
  0-7645-2487-9
- Diabetes Cookbook For Dummies
  0-7645-5230-9
- Gardening For Dummies *
  0-7645-5130-2
- Guitar For Dummies
  0-7645-5106-X
- Holiday Decorating For Dummies
  0-7645-2570-0
- Home Improvement All-in-One
  For Dummies
  0-7645-5680-0

- Knitting For Dummies
  0-7645-5395-X
- Piano For Dummies
  0-7645-5105-1
- Puppies For Dummies
  0-7645-5255-4
- Scrapbooking For Dummies
  0-7645-7208-3
- Senior Dogs For Dummies
  0-7645-5818-8
- Singing For Dummies
  0-7645-2475-5
- 30-Minute Meals For Dummies
  0-7645-2589-1

INTERNET & DIGITAL MEDIA

0-7645-1664-7

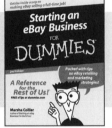

0-7645-6924-4

Also available:
- 2005 Online Shopping Directory
  For Dummies
  0-7645-7495-7
- CD & DVD Recording For Dummies
  0-7645-5956-7
- eBay For Dummies
  0-7645-5654-1
- Fighting Spam For Dummies
  0-7645-5965-6
- Genealogy Online For Dummies
  0-7645-5964-8
- Google For Dummies
  0-7645-4420-9

- Home Recording For Musicians
  For Dummies
  0-7645-1634-5
- The Internet For Dummies
  0-7645-4173-0
- iPod & iTunes For Dummies
  0-7645-7772-7
- Preventing Identity Theft For Dummies
  0-7645-7336-5
- Pro Tools All-in-One Desk Reference
  For Dummies
  0-7645-5714-9
- Roxio Easy Media Creator For Dummies
  0-7645-7131-1

* Separate Canadian edition also available
† Separate U.K. edition also available

Available wherever books are sold. For more information or to order direct: U.S. customers visit www.dummies.com or call 1-877-762-2974.
U.K. customers visit www.wileyeurope.com or call 0800 243407. Canadian customers visit www.wiley.ca or call 1-800-567-4797.

SPORTS, FITNESS, PARENTING, RELIGION & SPIRITUALITY

0-7645-5146-9

0-7645-5418-2

Also available:
- Adoption For Dummies
  0-7645-5488-3
- Basketball For Dummies
  0-7645-5248-1
- The Bible For Dummies
  0-7645-5296-1
- Buddhism For Dummies
  0-7645-5359-3
- Catholicism For Dummies
  0-7645-5391-7
- Hockey For Dummies
  0-7645-5228-7

- Judaism For Dummies
  0-7645-5299-6
- Martial Arts For Dummies
  0-7645-5358-5
- Pilates For Dummies
  0-7645-5397-6
- Religion For Dummies
  0-7645-5264-3
- Teaching Kids to Read For Dummies
  0-7645-4043-2
- Weight Training For Dummies
  0-7645-5168-X
- Yoga For Dummies
  0-7645-5117-5

TRAVEL

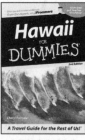

0-7645-5438-7

0-7645-5453-0

Also available:
- Alaska For Dummies
  0-7645-1761-9
- Arizona For Dummies
  0-7645-6938-4
- Cancún and the Yucatán For Dummies
  0-7645-2437-2
- Cruise Vacations For Dummies
  0-7645-6941-4
- Europe For Dummies
  0-7645-5456-5
- Ireland For Dummies
  0-7645-5455-7

- Las Vegas For Dummies
  0-7645-5448-4
- London For Dummies
  0-7645-4277-X
- New York City For Dummies
  0-7645-6945-7
- Paris For Dummies
  0-7645-5494-8
- RV Vacations For Dummies
  0-7645-5443-3
- Walt Disney World & Orlando For Dummies
  0-7645-6943-0

GRAPHICS, DESIGN & WEB DEVELOPMENT

0-7645-4345-8

0-7645-5589-8

Also available:
- Adobe Acrobat 6 PDF For Dummies
  0-7645-3760-1
- Building a Web Site For Dummies
  0-7645-7144-3
- Dreamweaver MX 2004 For Dummies
  0-7645-4342-3
- FrontPage 2003 For Dummies
  0-7645-3882-9
- HTML 4 For Dummies
  0-7645-1995-6
- Illustrator cs For Dummies
  0-7645-4084-X

- Macromedia Flash MX 2004 For Dummies
  0-7645-4358-X
- Photoshop 7 All-in-One Desk
  Reference For Dummies
  0-7645-1667-1
- Photoshop cs Timesaving Techniques
  For Dummies
  0-7645-6782-9
- PHP 5 For Dummies
  0-7645-4166-8
- PowerPoint 2003 For Dummies
  0-7645-3908-6
- QuarkXPress 6 For Dummies
  0-7645-2593-X

NETWORKING, SECURITY, PROGRAMMING & DATABASES

0-7645-6852-3

0-7645-5784-X

Also available:
- A+ Certification For Dummies
  0-7645-4187-0
- Access 2003 All-in-One Desk
  Reference For Dummies
  0-7645-3988-4
- Beginning Programming For Dummies
  0-7645-4997-9
- C For Dummies
  0-7645-7068-4
- Firewalls For Dummies
  0-7645-4048-3
- Home Networking For Dummies
  0-7645-42796

- Network Security For Dummies
  0-7645-1679-5
- Networking For Dummies
  0-7645-1677-9
- TCP/IP For Dummies
  0-7645-1760-0
- VBA For Dummies
  0-7645-3989-2
- Wireless All In-One Desk Reference
  For Dummies
  0-7645-7496-5
- Wireless Home Networking For Dummies
  0-7645-3910-8